THE ARTS

VERMEER IN HIS STUDIO

The elaborately patterned curtain to the left of this, the most celebrated of Vermeer's pictures, is caught back and reveals, like a scene in a play, the artist at work. The model, posed behind a table piled with drapery, and holding a musical instrument is the subject of a picture within a picture.

THE ARTS

PAINTING, THE GRAPHIC ARTS

SCULPTURE AND ARCHITECTURE

CONTRIBUTORS

Mary Chamot   Malcolm Osborne, R.A., P.R.E.

Olive Cook, M.A.   Sir Charles Reilly, M.A., F.R.I.B.A.

W. C. H. King   R. R. Tomlinson, A.R.C.A., R.B.A.

Charles Wheeler, C.B.E., R.A.

President of the Royal Society of British Sculptors

WITH AN INTRODUCTION BY

Professor Thomas Bodkin

Director of the Barber Institute of Fine Arts, Birmingham

ODHAMS PRESS LTD · LONG ACRE · LONDON

CONTENTS

SCULPTURE

Charles Wheeler, C.B.E., R.A. CHAPTER XV
Olive Cook, M.A. CHAPTER XVI
W. C. H. King. CHAPTER XVII

ARCHITECTURE : Sir Charles Reilly, M.A., F.R.I.B.A.

PLATES IN COLOUR

FIFTEENTH-CENTURY SCENE BY AN ITALIAN MASTER

Little is known of the life of Vittore Carpaccio, even the date of his birth being uncertain. First mention of him is in 1472 in the will of his uncle. His series of nine pictures for the School of St. Ursula in Venice are his best known as well as his earliest dated works. They were painted between the years 1490 and 1495 and are now housed in a single room in the Venice Gallery. The Dream of St. Ursula (above), most celebrated painting of the series, affords a delightful glimpse into a Venetian bedroom of the fifteenth century. The picture is painted with thick, rich colour on a rather rough canvas, a method which was to become one of the outstanding features of the works of the later Venetian school of painters.

INTRODUCTION

BY PROFESSOR THOMAS BODKIN

THE British are often supposed by others to be a race peculiarly indifferent to the appeal of the Fine Arts. They themselves incline to admit the justice of the charge. A few of them will even boast about it. Rudyard Kipling once lightly declared: "It is entirely right that the English should distrust and disregard all the Arts: for on that indifference rests their moral grandeur." Tudor and Puritan periods of iconoclasm and the grim materialism of the Industrial Age undoubtedly tended to render them reluctant to look towards æsthetic beauty for possibilities of pleasure.

In the years before the Second World War, the steady diminution in the number of attendances at the greater museums and art galleries caused perturbation to those who felt concern for the maintenance of a decent standard of civilization. The average daily number of visitors to the National Gallery fell to less than two thousand. On the August Bank Holiday it would rise to about five thousand who caused no congestion as they meandered through the twenty-nine great rooms hung with masterpieces of all schools and periods. It is certain that a large proportion of them came from abroad or from the provinces. They paid nothing for admission. On the same day, twenty-five thousand people could be found paying one and sixpence a head to enjoy the exhibits in the Chamber of Horrors at Madame Tussaud's, or to gaze on, and be gazed at by, the Giant Panda in the Zoo. When we think of the millions who find their chief delights in frequenting the films, following football or going to the dogs, it is impossible not to be disturbed by the incontestable evidence of apathy, verging on hostility, which they display towards painting, sculpture and architecture.

Since the Second World War some signs of a better spirit are discernible. We have seen, in 1947, crowds besieging the Victoria and Albert Museum to inspect the work of Picasso and Matisse. The British Council have coyly admitted that it would not be unfair to describe that particular exhibition as "a *succès de scandale*." But the more serious exhibition, in the following year, of the works of van Gogh at the Tate Gallery proved to be even more popular. The long queues composed of all sorts and conditions of men, women and children, stretched in cold, wet weather along the Embankment from Millbank back towards Westminster, as they waited patiently to make a hurried, harassed pilgrimage before a series of pictures that neither moved nor talked, demonstrated that a new generation had arisen who were eager to enlarge their experience and enhance their emotions with the help of whatever artists might have to offer to their anxious gaze.

It is too commonly supposed that British governments are less generous than the governments of other countries towards the Fine Arts. In fact, they spend a prodigious amount of public money annually on all kinds of artistic activities. The chart of State expenditures contained in a publication of the American Works Progress Association, entitled *Art as a Function of Government*, shows that in pre-war times Britain came second, closely

PAINTING THE SUPERNATURAL
The great altar-piece of the Adoration of the Lamb, at Ghent, was painted by the brothers van Eyck probably between the years 1415 and 1432. One of the eleven paintings, that on the central panel shown here, depicts the minutely detailed landscape with the Gothic towers of Ghent in the background which are as precise as a photograph and there is realism in the individual portraits of the ecclesiastics and citizens who, with saints and angels, reverently worship the Lamb. The van Eycks painted the supernatural with conviction and feeling.

behind France, among the European nations making such provision. We have since seen the establishment of several highly expensive new organizations such as the British Council, the Arts Council and U.N.E.S.C.O., which aim at devoting large proportions of their huge grants to foster the Fine Arts, each in its own peculiar way, with the aid of hordes of officials acting under the orders of various "Directors General" and the like. The provincial municipal councils supplement such activities, being usually well aware of the desirability of providing opportunities of culture for the citizens they are elected to serve. They spend over £400,000 annually from the rates on local art galleries. The number of private societies that concern themselves busily with some aspect of the Fine Arts is also surprising.

It may be fairly questioned whether all the outlay and energy involved is directed to best advantage. There is a futile amount of overlapping in the aims of these innumerable organizations and in the personnel that directs their efforts. There are far too many well-meaning but muddled amateurs at work within them, too many careerists, too many members of cliques and coteries who have found congenial, comfortable

niches in which to pose as champions, priests, prophets and patrons of the Fine Arts.

Current art criticism is often ill-informed. The universities are partly to blame for this sad state of affairs. Most of them incline, lamentably, to ignore the Fine Arts. But the public will be served. It has begun to show an eager interest in the subject. It demands lecturers and books for its enlightenment and will soon develop discrimination in assessing the quality of the supply of either offered in satisfaction of its requirements.

Its first need is for more free and frequent access to the best works of art that it already possesses. The great national collections should have been made completely available to their owners long ago. Loan exhibitions should not be encouraged in buildings that were erected to house the nation's own artistic treasure, much of which is now shut away in cellars and storerooms. The bomb damage done to such places as the National Gallery and the Tate should be repaired at the earliest possible moment.

When repaired, these buildings should be kept open longer and, particularly, at night. The present hours of opening make

9

it difficult for the working man or woman to visit them except on Sunday afternoons. Plans should be laid for the frequent circulation of large parts of their contents throughout the whole country. There is something absurd in the fact that not one of the ten pictures by Titian that are national property has ever been seen in Birmingham, Manchester, Liverpool or Leeds. National collections have grown so vast that it is impracticable to display any of them anywhere in its entirety. No sensible person would suggest that such superlative masterpieces as Jan van Eyck's Arnolfini and his Wife, or Titian's Bacchus and Ariadne, should be subjected to the risks of frequent travel, so that all and sundry might have an opportunity of seeing them often. But some risks should be taken with many lesser things, so that people to whom London is not easily accessible may be put in touch with the best of their own artistic possessions, towards whose acquisition they have contributed taxes in equal measure with the Londoner.

It has been truly said that the way to acquire good taste in anything is to make yourself familiar with the best. Sir Joshua Reynolds rightly insisted that "a relish for

RUBENS AND CLASSICAL MYTHOLOGY

In the seventeenth century it was customary for the subject of a large composition to be taken either from the Bible or from classical mythology. Rubens liked to paint mythological subjects; this and his passion for painting flesh can be discerned in The Judgment of Paris which is in the National Gallery. Like many other works of Rubens, this picture, which was painted in the years 1635-36 is on wood.

TITIAN AND CLASSICAL MYTHOLOGY

Classical mythology was of more vital interest to the Renaissance painters than to Rubens for it had all the glamour of a new discovery, moreover Titian was painting in Venice. Bacchus and Ariadne was painted about 1520 for Alfonso I of Ferrara and is now in the National Gallery.

the higher excellencies of art is an acquired taste which no man ever possessed without long cultivation and attention." No one can hope to derive much benefit from works of art who does not frequently contemplate, compare, and appraise them. He must have guidance in such efforts. Books are likely to prove his best source of help. It is important that they should be factually correct. If they express sincere opinions it does not seem necessary for them to be invariably orthodox in judg-

ment. Their main aims should be to provide accurate historical statements and to excite enthusiasm.

John Ruskin was a creature of prejudice, obsessed with the notion that art was intimately concerned with morality. His interests were too diffuse, his sympathies too narrow. He could say of Rembrandt that "his aim was to paint the foulest things he could see—by rushlight." He could find grounds for comparing Kate Greenaway with Raphael. But, despite

PAGEANTRY OF VERONESE

The art of decoration and pageantry which had been practised in Venice from the time of Gentile Bellini and Carpaccio, reached a culminating point in the magnificent compositions of Paulo Veronese, the greatest of all pageant painters. He has treated the Marriage at Cana (Louvre), the scene of the miracle performed by Christ of turning water into wine, not as a religious theme, but like a sumptuous Venetian festival with all the display of brocades, silks and satins customary on such occasion. The picture painted for the refectory of San Giorgio was begun in 1562 and Veronese asked for one year in which to complete the work; he was paid 972 ducats, furnished with canvas and colours and was provided with food and a cask of wine. Most of the figures in the design are portraits. On the left are Suleiman the Sultan; Charles V; Francis I; Vittoria Colonna and Eleanor of Austria. Grouped round the table in the foreground are Veronese himself playing the viol, Tintoretto accompanying him, and Bassano seated by them. It was on account of this picture, where the figure of Christ is relegated to a minor position in the middle distance, that Veronese was summoned before the Inquisition. He made out a good case and was permitted to resume his work.

the flaming nonsense of such views he managed to give inestimable service to the cause of the Fine Arts, because of the range of his experience and the richness of his language, and because he was sensitive to an extraordinary degree and intensely sincere.

This book contains no nonsense. In that respect it is better than any book that Ruskin ever wrote. It is carefully arranged and competently written. It is singularly comprehensive. Every effort has been made to ensure that it is accurate in statement of fact. I did not plan it; nor did I advise on the selection of the team of authors who have collaborated in its production; nor do I agree with all the views that they express; nor would I, if left to myself, have made the same choice of illustrations. But I have read it with

much interest and profit: and I am sure that it should prove very useful. It will make many an ardent student well aware of the Fine Arts: it will excite some of them to explore more fully the source of the choicest pleasures with which we can ennoble and fortify our human nature. The publication of a book of this sort is a real public service. Men and women who find delight in great pictures, statues or buildings must necessarily live more intensely and work more effectively than those who, through ignorance or apathy, have failed to seek the aid such things afford and so to realize that beauty has a functional quality. To spread love and knowledge of the Fine Arts is to teach, through the only universal language, the only kind of history that inevitably does honour to our human nature.

LAUGHING CAVALIER

Frans Hals observed the smile and laugh in all phases. Despite its robust joviality this familiar portrait from the Wallace Collection is a penetrating and realistic study of character treated in a bold and broad manner. Frans Hals, the elder, is regarded as the founder of the Dutch school of genre-painting, that is of paintings from everyday life. Both his brother, Dirk and his sons, of whom Frans Hals, the younger, became best known, were painters of considerable ability.

DOGE LEONARDO LOREDANO

Nothing could be farther removed from the high spirits of the Laughing Cavalier than the gravity and sobriety of this portrait by Giovanni Bellini in the National Gallery. Gravity is as much a keynote of Bellini's art as jollity is of Hals. Gentile and Giovanni were the sons of Jacopo Bellini: all three were noted painters, Giovanni being the most celebrated. Leonardo Loredano became Doge of Venice in 1502 and died in 1521.

MONA LISA GIOCONDA
Leonardo da Vinci worked for four years from 1502 on this inimitable portrait, now in the Louvre. Boldness of drawing is combined with the most subtle modelling and variation of light and shade.

LA BELLE JARDINIÈRE

Raphael's picture in the Louvre of the Virgin and Child with St. John was painted, like most of his Madonnas, between the years 1504 and 1508 which the artist spent in Florence where he gained much valuable experience.

It was an inheritance from his wife's father that, by making him financially independent, enabled Constable (1776-1837) to devote himself exclusively to the unremunerative painting of landscapes. His avowed intent was faithful representation of nature. His work had considerable influence not in England only but also, when exhibited in the Paris Salon, on landscape painting in France. The design of the Cornfield depends on a vista seen through groups of trees. The picture is now in the National Gallery.

VENETIAN LANDSCAPE PAINTING

Giorgione (c. 1478-1511) was one of the greatest of the Venetian school of painters: he exerted considerable influence on his contemporaries, including Titian. Like Constable's Cornfield the design of The Tempest depends on a vista seen through trees. The subject of this picture, now in the Venice Gallery, has not been identified. Despite the storm raging in the background, the figures suggest ease and peace which somehow is lacking from Constable's beautiful presentation of the English countryside.

INFLUENCE OF ENVIRONMENT ON PAINTING

In the fifteenth century the Christian religion played a vital part in everyday life for every individual in the Western world. Most of the employment open to artists came directly from the Church. In such environment Fra Angelico (1387-1455) painted the Annunciation (opposite above), now in the National Gallery. The angel dominates the scene, scarcely allowing the eye to stray to the vista beyond the arches. The Angelus (opposite, below) by Millet (1814-75), now in the Louvre, was more popular with our grandfathers than it is today; the mood and moment it expresses may seem to us to verge on the sentimental. Yet it is a dignified composition, owing much to the contrast of the angles of the bowed heads with the horizontal and vertical lines of the rest of the picture. In 1639, three years before the Company of Crossbowmen in Amsterdam commissioned Rembrandt to paint the Night Watch (above), now in the Rijks Museum, the Dutch under van Tromp had won a great naval victory over the Spanish fleet in the Downs. It was a period of sturdy independence. The members of the Company of Crossbowmen each subscribed to the picture and each expected equal prominence in it. Rembrandt in his painting was concerned with the problem of light and dark in the composition and the portraits were for him of secondary importance. He refused to sacrifice his integrity as an artist to satisfy the demands of his patrons and the picture, painted in the year 1642, was indignantly rejected.

21

MEASURED BEAUTY

Cool, remote and impersonal, the beauty of Piero della Francesca's Nativity
in the National Gallery is such as we usually associate with classical
antiquity. The way in which each figure takes its inevitable place in the
stillness and luminosity of the surrounding space recalls the slow and
measured deliberation of Hellenic architecture. The simplified forms
are like marble columns. The effect of suspended motion and timelessness
is gained by Piero's skilful rendering of the silvery atmosphere and the
precision with which he has related shapes and colour masses.

CHAPTER I

THE SEARCH FOR BEAUTY

ONE of the most primitive instincts in man is the urge to make patterns; in other words, to create works of art. As soon as the basic requirements of food and shelter have been satisfied, we find the human being setting about to adorn his person and his surroundings. In a hot climate, where he does not need clothes for warmth, he uses flowers and shells and feathers for personal adornment. In colder regions he wears the skins of the animals he has slain, and carves their bones into objects for his use. Utility and ornament develop along parallel lines. When man is sufficiently advanced to make vessels of clay he learns to decorate them with incised or painted patterns.

ORIGIN OF THE ARTS

The most primitive decoration is usually produced by simple and appropriate technical methods, but the next step is the desire to imitate one material in another. For example, we often find string handles imitated in clay on early pottery, the pattern of basket work reproduced in metal, or building in stone which imitates the forms of earlier building in wood. This desire for imitation is no doubt responsible for the birth of painting and sculpture.

According to an ancient legend, the first drawing was done by tracing the shadow cast by a figure. Another possible origin is that some natural stain was found to have a vague resemblance to a figure, and was touched up to enhance the likeness. Similarly, a stone or a piece of wood may have been found to suggest a human or animal form and, later, other stones or pieces of wood were deliberately carved into similar forms.

The fact that the cave-men's paintings of animals (pages 24 and 25) are several thousand years earlier than any surviving examples of decorative art does not necessarily mean that imitative art belongs to an earlier stage than pure ornamental art. The remains of the cave-men's art may possibly represent the final stages of a civilization, the beginnings of which have not survived or have not yet been discovered, while the development from neolithic times onwards can be traced step by step. However, the question of whether pattern precedes or follows the imitation of nature in art is far from being solved and it may well be that the two processes of development, from one to the other, alternate in the various stages of civilization.

When once the resemblance to a living creature has been achieved and recognized, we may say that the art of imitation has developed into representation. The artist endeavours to make his image as lifelike as possible. He feels the joy of creation. The creature represented seems to be imbued with the spirit of life. It is feared or worshipped and thus art is harnessed to magic or to religion.

A further stage is reached when the image is represented in action or when a number of figures and animals are combined to record an incident. This leads to the growth of illustration. The Victorian saying that every picture tells a story has been scoffed at by the purist, but it cannot be denied that illustration, or what is now known as literary content, has always played an important part in the representational arts and it is perfectly legitimate that it should do so, provided the story is told in artistic language, in other words, that the subject is expressed in beautiful form.

EMOTION IN ART

This brings us to another important element, the expression of emotion. According to some writers the desire for this expression is the very fount of all artistic creation. Feelings may be communicated through poetry, music and dancing more directly, perhaps, than through the visual arts, but no one can fail to realize the emotional effect of a Gothic cathedral or

SOUTH AFRICAN BUSHMAN ART

Primitive drawing often resembles that of children; it is dominated by the concepts of language and bears little relation to actual appearances. The most striking characteristic of this drawing executed by a South African Bushman is its realism; a momentary action has been treated with photographic verisimilitude, and an extremely complicated pose rendered with extraordinary ease and precision. In primitive art it is usual for such features as the eyes and ears to be drawn disproportionately large. Here the eye is only suggested and all detail is subordinated to the general character of the form of the subject dealt with.

of an Italian palace of the sixteenth century. This effect is not produced by architecture alone. It is equally true that the slightest drawing by Rembrandt is charged with emotion.

In addition to all the motives for artistic creation already cited, there is a more practical one—the need for construction. Whatever man builds or makes can be pleasing to the eye, provided it is adapted to its function and in this sense "well designed." It loses this quality when overladen with unsuitable ornament. Bad taste consists in the failure to see what is appropriate. It is seldom found in primitive objects. It abounds in decadent periods, that is to say, in periods of transition when

art has lost meaning and purpose. When styles are mixed in a pretentious desire to show off, the result is bad, as may well be seen in Victorian architecture. An early motor car, built on the lines of a horse-drawn carriage, now looks an odd compromise, although a streamlined car can be beautiful. It is not unnatural that there should be a desire for beauty in every-day things and efforts are now being made to give beauty of design to houses, furniture (and even such articles of domestic use as saucepans). This beauty has already been achieved in 'planes, ships and bridges. We are living in an age of machinery, but it is a tragic fact that the machines built by our engineers sometimes appear more beautiful,

24

because they are purely functional, than the goods produced.

This century has witnessed the growth of what is called abstract art, which attempts to separate form from the imitation of nature. Here, no doubt, we can see partly the effect of this machine age and partly an extreme reaction against the elaborate imitative detail and sentimentality of Victorian art. By attempting to create simple forms of geometric beauty, some modern artists have suggested a possible improvement in the design of everyday objects of use. At the same time they assert that the beauty of art has a separate existence in form and colour quite apart from its utility or its value as a representation.

The field covered by the visual arts is so vast and it can be approached from so many different angles that it is almost impossible to give a definition of a work of art beyond saying that it is a thing of beauty made by man as opposed to an object of natural beauty. This immediately calls for the further question: "what is beauty?" Writers on aesthetics agree that absolute beauty exists as an ideal to be striven for, although no single achievement in actuality attains this absolute standard or can be regarded as a final test of other efforts to arrive at it.

Plato's theory of beauty, truth and good-

NATURALISM IN STONE AGE DRAWING

This bison from the cave of Altamira in Spain, was drawn by Stone Age man about 10,000 B.C. As far as naturalism goes it surpasses anything created by our own primitive peoples or even the best animal draughtsmen, and shows a still higher level of accomplishment than the drawing by the Bushman reproduced on the opposite page. It reveals the same astonishing power in drawing of capturing with the utmost sobriety and precision a momentary effect.

ness was developed into the moral theory
that beauty disposes man to right conduct
and true thinking. This was elaborated by
Plotinus. "For the absolute good is the
cause and source of all beauty, just as the
sun is the source of all daylight, and it
cannot therefore be spoken or written; yet
we speak and write of it, in order to start
and escort ourselves on the way, and arouse
our minds to the vision, as it were a pilgrim

shown on his way to some shrine that he
would visit: for the teaching is only of
whither and how to go, the vision itself is
the work of him who hath willed to see."

In the eighteenth century, when artistic
appreciation was confined largely to the
art of ancient Greece and Rome and to its
revival in Italy during the Renaissance,
it was possible to speak of the classical standard. But since our acquaintance

ARCHITECTURAL DESIGN

At the early age of twenty-five, Raphael was commissioned in 1508 by Pope Julius II to decorate three huge rooms in the Vatican. The School of Athens shown here, is one of the companion frescoes in the Camera della Segnatura to La Disputa, Parnassus and Justice. Pater said of a more youthful work of Raphael, the Ansidei Madonna (National Gallery), that it gave him something of the pleasure one has in a proposition of Euclid. The qualities implied in that remark are still more evident in the School of Athens. The architectural character of the composition is at once apparent. The science of perspective, so much studied by Renaissance artists, is developed here to the fullest possible extent to represent an interior which in scale and dignity is in entire harmony with sixteenth-century architectural ideals. The magnificent groups of philosophers with the two dominating figures of Plato and Aristotle are not the subject of the picture; they serve but to emphasize the remarkable effect of space created by the vanishing arches, the inward movement of which is further reinforced by the receding lines of the inlaid floor, the steps and the two seated figures.

with artistic achievement has been expanded to include other styles, the old formula no longer suffices to cover all that we feel to be worthy of our admiration. Besides, taste is continually changing and there is no universal agreement as to what is beautiful. The modern critic, Roger Fry, wrote in his *Reflections on British Painting*: "Each generation has to recreate the meaning of our Old Masters by critical appre-ciation; it is only by that means that they are kept alive. Indiscriminate worship would kill them."

Not only has every age its own taste, but different types of beauty appeal to different temperaments. The eighteenth-century philosopher, Hume, wrote: "Beauty is no quality in things themselves, it merely exists in the mind, which contemplates them and each mind perceives a different beauty.

The head of the Egyptian Queen (*top left*), the bronze from Benin (*opposite, bottom left*), the Indian carving from Mathura (*opposite, bottom right*), Praxiteles' Hermes, (*bottom left*), Leonardo's Virgin of the Rocks (*opposite, top right*), and Cézanne's head of his wife (*opposite, top left*), are all the products of widely diverse civilizations and cultures, but they have one quality in common: none of them is primarily concerned with the accidents of an individual human face. The heads of Nefertiti and Cézanne's wife are, indeed, associated with actual persons, but in both cases the features are so formalized and there is so slight an interest in the character of the sitter that they cannot be called portraits in the ordinary sense of the word. To our eyes one head may seem more beautiful than another: the Greek ideal, as shown in the head of Hermes and followed to some extent by Leonardo, has been generally admired in Europe, whereas Mme Cézanne and the African girl may not be sympathetic to everyone. Each head represents an idealized conception of beauty which must vary with different artists and peoples. There can, therefore, be no standard of physical beauty and if there were it would be useless as the criterion of a work of art. The value of all these works resides in qualities of form and sensibility which have no connexion with the type of beauty favoured by the artist, and it is upon these that judgment must be based.

28

FORMAL DESIGN IN ART

The Rout of San Romano, by Paolo Uccello, showing a cavalry victory of the Florentines over the Sienese in 1432, and Sunday at the Grande Jatte painted by Georges Seurat in 1884, have much in common, though they belong to different countries and epochs. Both Uccello and Seurat were men of scientific intellect: Uccello was devoted to the study of perspective, Seurat to the science of related colours. Their pictures are attempts to solve the problems which interested them, and demand in each case that natural fact should be organized into a system of forms. Thus the horses in the battle scene and the French bourgeois are conventionalized.

One person may even perceive deformity where another is sensible of beauty, and every individual ought to acquiesce in his own sentiments without pretending to regulate those of others."

The idea of beauty in works of art varies as much from land to land and from age to age as the idea of beauty in the human form. Although Europeans generally have been brought up to admire the Greek idealization of the healthy, athletic human figure, there have been periods when a more slender or a fuller form was the criterion. Bearing in mind the variations in European taste, we must admit that other races may admire quite different proportions and that these peculiarities may be emphasized and even exaggerated by their artists. To the unaccustomed European eye such forms may appear incorrect, distorted and even ugly, but we are not justified for that reason in claiming that ours is the only standard of beauty.

To assist in a more detailed study of art, the reader will find it advantageous to bear in mind four principal aspects and avenues of approach, listed below.

1. *Art and History*. Art may be enjoyed for its value in explaining history, in illustrating the customs, fashions and types of different countries and epochs.

2. *Art and the Exercise of Taste*. Works of art can be appreciated without any knowledge of their history, place of origin or date. The approach in this case is directed solely to the appreciation of beauty and artistic quality. On the other hand, a person may have a good knowledge of history without having developed taste or the power of differentiating the good from the bad. The latter is important, but a thorough understanding of art should be based on a combination of knowledge and of taste.

3. *Art and Technique*. The technical processes of art are many and some are complex. An understanding of technique is primarily of value to the practising craftsman. Nevertheless, some knowledge of the medium used by the artist is a help to the appreciation of his work (*see* Chapters XI, XII and XIII).

4. *Art and Philosophy*. The branch of study called Aesthetics—the theory of the perception of the beautiful—belongs more to philosophy than to the study of art. Yet some acquaintance with it will enhance our understanding and enjoyment of art. However, the student of art will note that every writer on aesthetics, besides propounding a general theory, makes use of examples, and here his arguments very often break down.

The principal aesthetic theories may be summed up as follows: Many philosophers have held the view that art is the expression of personal emotion; others that the function of art is to imitate, idealize or interpret nature. Matthew Arnold once described it as: "Nature seen through a temperament." Tolstoy's theory was that art is a means of communication, a universal language, which should be understood by all and used for ethical purposes. It had some similarity to the teaching of Ruskin and Morris, who claimed that it is the business of art to further social improvement.

That a work of art is primarily the result of man's creative instinct, and a search for arrangement, selection, order and equilibrium is generally admitted. Such equilibrium or harmony invariably produces pleasure, whether it is found in nature or in a work of art.

Test Yourself

1. Are there standards of beauty?
2. How far is art concerned with the imitation of nature?
3. What is the difference between a child's drawing and the work of a South African Bushman?
4. What points in common have Uccello's Rout of San Romano and Seurat's Sunday at the Grande Jatte?
5. Give a brief analysis of Raphael's School of Athens.

Answers will be found at the end of the book

FIGURE AND WINGED HUMAN HEADED
PALACE OF SARGON, KING OF ASSYRIA, B

DECORATIVE AND PLASTIC ART

The winged attendant of this massive Assyrian Bull moves like a robot and is treated decoratively, the head facing the spectator, the body in profile. The human-headed bull is almost free-standing and is shown with five legs because it is designed to be viewed from either the side or the front, a characteristic feature of Assyrian sculpture.

CHAPTER II

ART AS A RECORD
OF ANCIENT CIVILIZATIONS

WORKS of art were created many thousands of years before the invention of writing and they are our chief source of information concerning prehistoric and ancient man. Cave paintings of the earlier Stone Age, and pottery of the later Stone Age, have already been referred to. Monuments of much more recent date, produced by people who have left no written records or whose writing has not yet been interpreted, belong to the same category. Thus pre-Columbian art in America, the art of the African Negroes, and of various other primitive peoples are of value in the study of race and history. It is only in recent years that they have been considered also as works of art.

METHODS OF APPROACH

When we come to the period of written records, it will be found that the monuments of ancient Egypt, Mesopotamia, India, China, Greece and Rome are at least as important as any literature that has been handed down to us concerning these countries. The historian must sift the material brought to light by the archæologist according to his own requirements. Those of the student of art are quite different.

For the purpose of history, every scrap of information which can throw any light on the life of the people, their government, religion, social and economic systems, has to be examined, and the result is that our museums are filled with objects of great interest, though not all of them are necessarily fine works of art. Taste and experience are needed to select the salient artistic products of each civilization. Art historians have hitherto been too often inclined to base their studies on the whole of the material provided by archæological research instead of making a judicious selection of the most beautiful things. Nevertheless,

the very fact of enjoying a masterpiece arouses interest in the circumstances in which it was produced, so that the historical approach and the artistic approach are bound to be closely related, although they remain distinct in their nature.

ART AND GEOGRAPHY

In looking at the art of ancient Egypt one is tempted to think only of its historical and religious associations, such as the echoes of Egyptian history found in the Old Testament or the Egyptian beliefs concerning the need of embalming the body or making an image of it, in order that the soul might preserve its immortality.

It is also possible to see Egyptian art in terms of geography. This great artistic development can be seen in relation to the geology of the Nile Valley, surrounded by desert and fertilized by periodic floods. The simple geometric forms of the pyramids, sphinxes and temples fit admirably into the landscape of the desert and superb use was made by the Egyptian architects and sculptors of the various hard and soft stones found in the region (page 36).

Over and above these considerations is the purely æsthetic realization of the perfect fitness of Egyptian monuments for their purpose.

EGYPTIAN SCULPTURE

For centuries the Egyptians lived in happy isolation from the rest of the world, attaining a high degree of civilization under the rule of the Pharaohs, whose power was looked upon as divine and absolute, and whose resources in wealth and manpower were almost unlimited. There is a finality in Egyptian forms which could hardly have arisen in any other circumstances, and little change in this traditional style took place during a period lasting some three thousand years.

The prehistoric and archaic sculpture of Egypt is most naturalistic. Figures were usually carved in wood and covered with plaster which was originally painted, the eyes being often inlaid with crystal. The later stone images of the Pharaohs were less realistic. They were often designed to impress and overawe. The figures were represented seated or standing in an impressive and motionless attitude. Sometimes they were carved on a colossal scale in order to attain their most awe-inspiring effect.

Discoveries at Tel-el-Amarna have revealed a brilliant revival of more naturalistic work. It coincides with the unconventional reign of Ikhnaten, the portrait of whose queen, Nefertiti (page 28), is one of the best known of Egyptian sculptures. This period, however, was of brief duration, and after Ikhnaten there was a return to the formal style with a re-establishment of the

METHOD OF CONTINUOUS REPRESENTATION

Trajan set up this column in his Forum, in A.D. 113, to celebrate the success of the Roman campaigns against the Dacians, which are the subjects of the reliefs arranged successively in spiral strips round the monument. Only the base of the column has been reproduced, for, despite the vigour of the style, the figures are so crowded and on so small a scale that after the first few spirals they become difficult to see from ground level, failing in their effect, and so do not satisfy the demands of pictorial unity.

FORM AND CONVENTION

The great statue of black diorite now in the Louvre, bears the name of Gudea, Prince of Sirpoula (Lagash), and is one of the chief monuments of Chaldean art. Features such as the eyebrows are stylized, but the sturdy, muscular figure is full of personality and shows a real sense of form.

ART AND GEOGRAPHY

Egypt is a landscape of lines, vertical, horizontal or diagonal, of immense distances and violent contrasts, flat plains and sheer cliffs, brilliant sunshine and dark shadows. The sloping lines of the pyramids harmonize completely with their surroundings. The great size of the pyramids as well as of much Egyptian sculpture is also explained by the nature of the landscape. The scale of the colossi from the façade of the famous temple of Abu Simbel is determined by the fact that they are meant to be seen from a distance. The size of these vast forms can be gauged from one of the ears which measures 3 feet 5 inches. The colossi represent Rameses II and his queen Nefertiti-mery-Mut, beside him.

CONVENTION AND NATURALISM IN EGYPTIAN PAINTING

This fowling scene of 1500 B.C. (British Museum), portrays Amenemheb of Thebes accompanied by his wife and daughter. In the representation of the figures the artist uses the conventional Egyptian style, features such as the eyes being shown full face, while the heads are in profile. The drawing of the fish, birds and the hunting cat, however, reveals a very delightful and accurate observation of nature.

ancient religion he had formerly discarded. On the whole, sculpture in the Middle Kingdom (i.e. 2000 B.C.) is inferior to the earlier work. During the reign of the Hyksos, the nomadic race of Asia Minor which invaded Egypt in the eighteenth century B.C., there was a break in the continuity. Then, in the period of the war-like Rameses II, whose victories were profusely recorded, there was again an enormous production of colossal statues and reliefs. An example is to be found in the rock-hewn temples and colossal figures at Abu Simbel (page 36) on the bank of the Nile in Upper Egypt. The restoration of the ancient religion after Ikhnaten may be marked by the famous tomb of Tutankhamen (*c.* 1350 B.C.). Discovered at Thebes in 1922, it revealed great riches of Egyptian art and decoration.

PRIMITIVE IMAGES

Reliefs were made to decorate tombs and palaces, the primitive intention being to supply the needs of the dead in images, shown above. They often represent the preparation of food, and hunting scenes, and are carved in low relief, sometimes in sunk relief, with rigidly maintained conventions of style. The figure is always in profile, but the eyes and shoulders are drawn full face. The law of frontality is strictly observed— that is to say, the figure is perfectly erect, with no movement from side to side, and both feet are planted firmly on the ground. In large reliefs, figures are superimposed in tiers to suggest distance, but are generally on the same scale.

It is difficult to draw the line between Egyptian painting and sculpture. The reliefs, designed for interior decoration, were often covered with fine plaster and coloured, while the paintings consist of little more than sharp outlines and flat colours, using the same conventions as the reliefs. In both, we can enjoy delightful pattern and rhythmic movement. Although there is no great depth of expression, we can find in them a vast amount of information about the life and customs of the ancient Egyptians.

The Saite period of the seventh century B.C. was a brief renaissance in the course of the long decline of Egyptian art which reached its end and its lowest level in the Roman period. Charming and elegant works were produced by the Saite sculptors, the slender, elongated figures showing all the Egyptian sense of linear beauty.

Egypt was long considered the cradle of civilization, the first country to produce a great tradition in art. But discoveries in Mesopotamia go to prove that civilization began there quite as early as in Egypt and objects showing great skill in the use of gold, ivory and other rich materials have been brought to light in Ur, the ancient capital of the Sumerian Kingdom in South Babylonia.

Mesopotamia, an alluvial plain fertilized by the Rivers Tigris and Euphrates, has no wood or stone. Buildings were mostly of sun-dried brick, sometimes covered with glazed tiles or with metal ornamentation. Stone for sculpture had to be imported, except in the upper valley of the Tigris (Assyria) which could produce supplies of limestone and alabaster.

A number of heads and figures of Prince Gudea of Chaldea (c. 2450 B.C.), found at Tello and now in the Louvre, are carved of imported diorite rock (page 35). They are

RECORD OF ASSYRIAN PASTIME

Like the reliefs on Trajan's column, the hunting scenes from Ashurbanipal's palace, Nineveh, of which this is one, are illustrations. Their value lies in the fact that they are vivid records of one of the chief pastimes of the Assyrians. The poses of both lions and horses show close observation of nature and a subsequent true-to-life interpretation of it.

ART AND RELIGION

The impulse behind this judgment scene from the papyrus Book of the Dead found in the tomb of Ani, an Egyptian official who lived about 1400 B.C., is a purely religious one. Ani, lead by Anubis, sees his soul weighed against a feather and is finally presented to Osiris. Above sit the gods whose help Ani invokes in the prayer inscribed in the background, that he may enter the Abode of the Blessed.

squat, thick-set, massive and very realistic. On the other hand, a bronze figure of a queen (*c.* 1500 B.C.), to be seen in the Louvre, is almost cylindrical and highly stylized. Other Babylonian works are almost all reliefs, such as the stele of Naram Sin (*c.* 2600 B.C., Louvre).

Assyrian art reaches its highest point in the eighth and seventh centuries B.C. The works are all secular, made for the glorification of rulers without the religious significance of Egyptian sculpture. Reliefs from the palaces of Nineveh, now in the British Museum, represent fighting and hunting scenes, royal processions and the building of palaces (page 38). The style is heavy and conventional but, nevertheless, expressive and decorative. The wounded lioness from the hunting scene of Ashurbanipal is a masterpiece of dramatic expression. These reliefs were probably originally coloured. The doors of the palaces were flanked by winged lions or monsters with human heads and the bodies of bulls, and these are carved in relief so that they can be seen from the front and side, with two legs in the frontal view and four in the side view, making altogether five.

The Persian palaces at Susa were decorated with processions of figures and animals in glazed brick. Persian sculpture is somewhat more delicate, colourful and sensitive than the earlier Assyrian style, and had a wide influence over the Near East, stretching across from India to the Mediterranean.

Test Yourself

1. Describe some of the chief characteristics of Assyrian art.
2. Can the conventional style of much Egyptian art be attributed, in your opinion, to an inability to represent nature?
3. Account for the vast scale of much Egyptian architecture and sculpture.

Answers will be found at the end of the book

RHYTHM IN GREEK SCULPTURE

> *The Victory of Samothrace (306 B.C.) is informed with an intense feeling*
> *for rhythm, movement and the value of shadows, which is new in Greek*
> *art and foreshadows the baroque sculpture of the seventeenth century.*

40

CHAPTER III

THE CLASSICAL IDEAL IN GREEK AND ROMAN ART

THE word classical, meaning first class or of high excellence, is usually applied indiscriminately to all antiquity. This dates from the time when the study of Greek and Roman writers, "the classics," was considered superior in educational value to the knowledge of any other literature.

When it is applied to art, the term often covers not only Greek and Roman work but any subsequent style based on a study of antiquity. Thus, the Renaissance in Italy implied a rebirth or rediscovery of both the learning and the art of the ancients. The French architects and painters of the seventeenth century reveal a later stage of this influence. The neo-classical revival of the late eighteenth century in France and Germany coincided with excavations and discoveries at Pompeii and was affected by them. Strictly speaking, the word classic should be applied only to the finest Greek work of the fifth century B.C. After that, the art of Greece continued to inspire neighbouring countries. The later phases might be described as post-classic, Hellenistic (of the type produced in Alexandria) or Greco-Roman.

EVIDENCE IN LITERATURE

In the previous chapter it was noted that artistic monuments could provide the basis of historical study when no other records were available. With regard to ancient Greece the process was reversed. Traditions, handed down through literature, led archæologists to search definite sites, and as a result the walls of ancient Troy, the so-called Treasury of Atreus at Mycenæ and the Palace of Knossos at Crete were discovered.

The Cretans, who prospered through growing maritime trade in the Mediterranean, must have attained a high degree of refinement in their life, to judge from the architectural remains and the decorative objects that have been discovered. Vases, superbly painted with plant forms and sea creatures, ivory statuettes and frescoes provide evidence of Minoan culture between 3000 and 1500 B.C.

The figures represented in the Cretan wall paintings are slim-waisted, elaborately made-up and adorned with jewels. A form of bull-fighting appears to have been the national sport. Fragments of frescoes, depicting bulls and female athletes are painted in flat, bright colours with vigorous

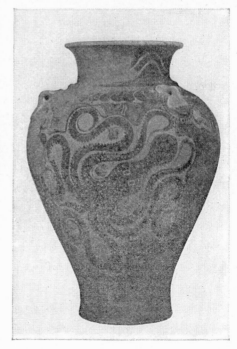

PLASTIC VALUE OF DECORATION

The Octopus emphasizes the volume of the Cretan vase, whilst retaining the reality of nature.

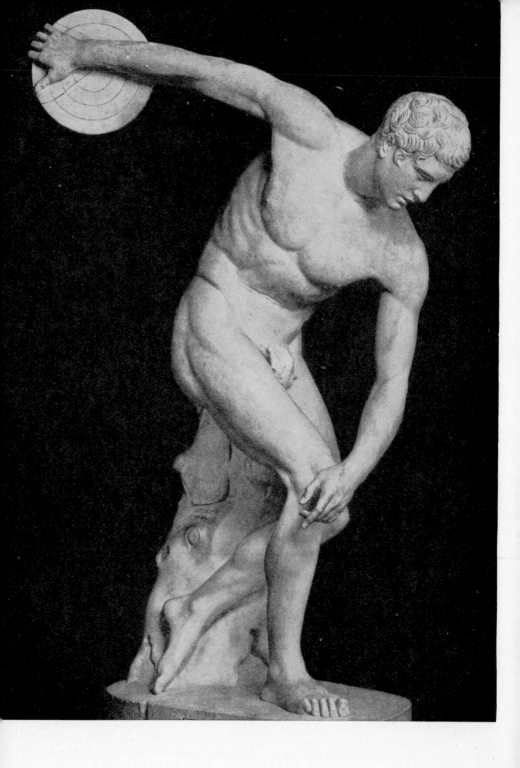

The Discobolus on the opposite page *is* an idealized figure. The boxer, a Hellenistic bronze in the Terme Museum, Rome, forms a contrast to this generalized type. His swollen face, naturalistic pose, and the realistic detail in the thongs binding his hands make him an actual character.

outlines and bear some resemblance to the wall paintings of Egypt (page 45).

A later offshoot of this civilization developed on the mainland of Greece and is probably contemporary with the Trojan War. Richly embossed gold cups and finely wrought daggers, such as that shown on the left, have been discovered at Mycenæ, although no monumental sculpture appears to have been produced either there or in Crete. A number of extremely simplified images in stone and clay have been found in islands of the Ægean and have been much admired by some modern sculptors for their simplicity of form.

GREEK ART

These early civilizations were swept away by the Dorian Greeks who drove out the Achæans. When Greek art proper began to develop it had a very different character from the hitherto vivid but still conventional art of the Mediterranean. Repose and simplicity in architecture, perfect mastery in the rendering of the human form in sculpture, and extraordinary beauty of line in vase painting are some of the principal features of Greek art at its best.

The Greeks were satisfied with a traditional form of architecture, which was based on earlier wooden construction, and instead of inventing new styles they concentrated on the refinement of proportion and detail, until they arrived at such perfection that their buildings have been looked upon as models ever since.

It may be questioned whether Greek ornament is a legitimate adjunct to a modern building in ferro-concrete, but in the past, whenever the Greek style has been revived, it has exercised a healthy influence against extravagance in design.

Greek art of the sixth century B.C. produced chiefly images of gods, votive offerings and reliefs for the decoration of buildings. The standing or seated figures, based probably on Egyptian models, retained the conventional symmetry and rigidity till the early fifth century B.C. They are naked male figures with the left leg advancing, or draped female figures. The slightly curved and set expression of

DECORATION ADAPTED TO SHAPE

The scene of a lion hunt decorating this Cretan dagger blade is admirably adapted to the tapering shape.

44

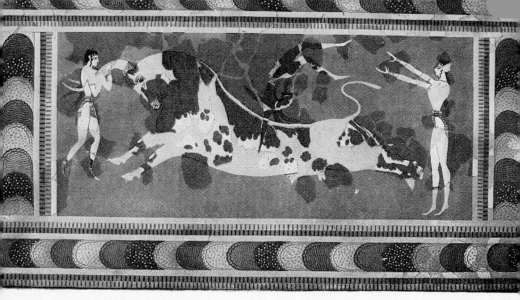

DECORATION AND MOVEMENT

Decorative and dramatic qualities are combined in this wall painting of bull grappling, a popular sport of the Cretans. The sense of instantaneous movement is achieved by the elongation of the forms, which at the same time gives a decorative effect heightened by the S-curves in the horns and tail of the animal and in the figure of the vaulting youth.

the lips so commonly found has come to be known as the archaic smile. The sculptors reveal the dignity of the human figure. Gradually, their rendering of anatomical details became more realistic and the statues therefore more life-like.

CORRECT PROPORTIONS

About 460 B.C. the sculptor Polykleitos marks the definite departure from rigid, archaic tradition. He gave the appearance of natural movement to his Doryphoros, with the weight thrown on one leg, the other flexed, the body curved, the shoulders sloped and the head turned. The proportions may still seem heavy in the surviving copies, but this statue of an ideal athletic type became known as the Canon, because it embodied the correct proportions of the human form. The cult of athletics and their familiarity with the human form in the various postures of athletic sports enabled the Greek sculptors to attain a remarkable perfection in their single figure sculptures. At the same time, however, temples were being adorned with groups

in the pediments and reliefs in the spaces (metope and frieze) above the beam or architrave which rested on the columns.

The principal works of the Greek sculptors, whose names are recorded, have perished. They were the ivory and gold images of gods in the temples. Of their bronze figures only a few survive. Pheidias, the most famous of the Greek sculptors, a contemporary of Polykleitos, was in charge of the decoration of the Parthenon at Athens (c. 447-33 B.C.). Among the works traditionally attributed to him were the statue of Zeus at Olympia and that of Athena in the Parthenon. The beauty of the Parthenon frieze can be appreciated at the British Museum, though it is not certain whether Pheidias did any of the work on these surviving sculptures himself or not. They have long been considered as a highwater mark of Greek art.

REPRESENTATION OF MOVEMENT

Probably all the sculptures were originally painted, not naturalistically, but conventionally to harmonize with the

POUSSIN AND CLASSICAL ART

Poussin made a copy of one of the few surviving Greek paintings, the Aldobrandini Wedding, and comparison of his Bacchanalian Dance (National Gallery) with the fresco from Pompeii reproduced left, shows how much he derived from the ancients. Both pictures are characterized by figures turning outward away from the centre of design. Poussin balances the composition by the movement of the dance and the introduction of the two infant bacchanals (below left), the classical painter attempts less successfully to do so by the inward bending figure and the arcs of the draperies.

HUMAN FIGURE IN POTTERY DECORATION

Probably no other people have used the human figure so frequently or so skilfully as did the Greeks. The vigour and animation of the group on this black-figured vase of about 600 B.C. are enhanced by the clever distortion of the forms to suit the shape of the pot. The decorative element is maintained by precision and economy of line and by the schematic treatment of details such as the eyes.

architecture. Certain traces of colour have survived on some of the earlier figures found at the foot of the Acropolis in Athens. A few washes of colour on parts of the figures would no doubt have enchanced their effect against the buildings, taking into consideration the strong sunlight and the beautiful quality of the marble.

During the fifth century B.C. the Greek sculptors attained full mastery in the representation of movement, but it was always combined with reserve and balance. The fourth-century sculptor Praxiteles made the figure of his Hermes at Olympia more human, softer, subtler in modelling— the classic dignity and aloofness had begun to wane. More dramatic expression

appeared from the third century B.C. onward. Terra-cotta statuettes which were found at Tanagra have an intimate and domestic character.

Hellenistic is the term applied to Greek art, or to art produced under Greek influence in Alexandria and Asia Minor. The centre of activity shifted from Greece to the cities of Pergamon, Antioch, Alexandria and to Rhodes. Violence of movement and expression characterize the altar of Pergamon, lately removed from Berlin to Russia, and the Laocoon of the second century, now in the Vatican. A new taste for everyday subjects corresponds to the favourite poetic form of the period, the pastoral idyll. Great technical dexterity

PICASSO AND GREEK DRAWING

The drawing of a bather (above) which Picasso made in 1923 is astonishingly like the drawing (opposite) of a Greek youth, from a vase of the fifth century B.C. The Greek drawing, from the National Museum, Athens, was not photographed until 1934 ; it is unlikely that Picasso ever saw it. Though Picasso's athlete sits alert and the pose of the Greek youth is one of languor, the methods of drawing and the treatment of detail are similar.

This figure found on the Acropolis, dates from the sixth century B.C. There is a formal symmetry in the pose, but the decorative treatment gives it an air of sophistication.

enabled sculptors to express effects of landscape in low relief, flying draperies as in the Victory of Samothrace (page 40), and complicated groups such as the Nile god with all his tributaries personified by portrayal as children.

MIGHT OF THE ROMANS

Roman art is based on Greek art through direct imitation and, indirectly, through Etruscan art, which was similar in style to Greek sculpture in the fourth century B.C.; though possessing less grace.

In architecture the Romans were innovators and showed their practical abilities. For instance, they developed the arch and vault, which had been used by the Etruscans, but not by the Greeks. To serve the need of their vast empire and their luxury-loving populations they constructed great public works, such as bridges, aqueducts, baths and places of entertainment. The might of the Roman Empire is admirably expressed in the triumphal arches, the halls of justice and in the huge amphitheatre known as the Colosseum in Rome.

EASTERN INFLUENCE

In their sculpture the Romans showed great mastery in portraiture, in the representation of animals and in narrative reliefs, such as the illustration of the Dacian campaign on Trajan's column (page 34). Towards the end of the empire, eastern influence was strong and is seen in the art of Byzantium. Realism gave way to symbolical design and after the fifth century A.D. monumental sculpture almost ceased to be produced in Europe till the revival in the Middle Ages, known as the Romanesque period. The principal causes of the decline were the Christian reaction against paganism and its association of sculpture with the pagan vices; the dearth of patronage and of technical skill following the barbarian invasions, and the concentration of ornament within the Christian churches, where paintings and mosaics were more appropriate than sculpture.

It is less easy to follow the development of classical painting. Although Greek writers have extolled the names of many famous painters such as Apelles, Polyg-

SIMPLICITY AND DIGNITY

The Erechtheum which was completed in 408 B.C. lies to the north of the Parthenon, and is flanked by a portico where instead of columns the architect has introduced six grave and massive female figures, one of which is now in the British Museum, having been replaced by a terra-cotta copy.

notus and Zeuxis, none of their works has survived and we can judge of their skill only as it is reflected in the exquisite paintings on vases and in the later copies and imitations of Greek masterpieces found in Rome and Pompeii. In these wall paintings landscapes and figure composi-tions are treated with so much feeling for space and grouping that they look astonish-ingly modern. The masterpieces of classical architecture, painting and sculpture, have been an inspiration to classically minded artists from the time of the Renaissance to the present day.

Test Yourself

1. What are the most striking qualities of Cretan art?
2. What is the archaic smile?
3. Compare Hellenic and Hellenistic art.
4. Give some account of Greek painting and relate it to later develop-ments in European art.
5. What was the chief contribution of the Romans to art?

Answers will be found at the end of the book

GOTHIC SPIRIT IN ARCHITECTURE

This remarkable photograph of the Choir of Canterbury, taken so that the distant Chapel of the Holy Trinity is seen like a heavenly vision, brings out the character of an intensely religious age of which the Gothic cathedral was the highest tangible expression.

CHAPTER IV

ART AND RELIGION

DURING the first millennium of our era, Christianity gradually spread throughout a large part of the former Roman Empire and was eventually embraced by most of the barbarians of Northern Europe. The period of their migrations, known as the Dark Ages, produced very few artistic monuments on a grand scale in the west, and we are left to judge of its achievements from such examples of artistic craftsmanships as illuminated manuscripts, metal-work and ivory carvings.

In the Byzantine Empire, however, art continued to flourish. Magnificent churches were built at Constantinople and some of the noblest examples of Byzantine art have been preserved in Ravenna. These deserve to rank among the highest peaks in the whole history of art.

BYZANTINE DECORATION

In the fifth century A.D. Ravenna was a flourishing seaport and the seat, first of Theodoric, King of the Goths, and later of Justinian, Emperor of Constantinople. The Church of San Vitale exemplifies something of the splendour of Justinian's court. The Emperor himself is represented, with the Bishop Maximian and a group of courtiers and warriors, in a magnificent mosaic on one side of the chancel. On the other side stands the Empress Theodora, richly bejewelled, carrying the gifts she is offering to the church. The mosaic consists of small pieces of coloured glass, gold leaf under glass, and shell embedded in cement; they glitter as the light catches them from different angles, especially where the mosaic decoration covers the curved surfaces of vaults and domes. It is the richest and most splendid, as well as the most permanent, form of wall decoration ever invented by man (page 56).

In another church at Ravenna the whole nave is adorned with long processions of white-robed saints and virgin martyrs approaching the altar, and in the dome of the baptistery the twelve apostles surround St. John, who is baptizing Christ amid a wealth of foliage and symbolic ornaments.

ISLAMIC ORNAMENT

During the seventh century, Islam arose as a rival to Christianity and spread throughout the Near East and into Spain. The Arabs had no artistic tradition of their own, but as their religion forbade the representation of any living creature, they eventually developed extraordinary perfection in abstract ornament and pattern, which may be seen in their plasterwork, carvings, illuminations, pottery and textiles. From time to time, Mohammedan influence appears in Christian art, in spite of the fact that there was for long a state of war between Christianity and Islam.

The great architectural activity of the Middle Ages is generally dated from the year 1000, when the end of the world had been expected. It may have been partly inspired by the feeling of gratitude for continued existence, but other reasons contributed to make the succeeding centuries artistically great.

INTERNATIONAL INFLUENCE

The influence of the Church was universally distributed. Pilgrimages to such distant places as Rome, Compostella and Jerusalem created a religious internationalism, which counteracted to some extent the tendency of feudalism to split up society into local, mutually hostile units. This international influence inevitably spread the arts which the Church fostered.

The traditions of learning and the practice of the arts survived during the Dark Ages only in the monasteries, where, under the Benedictine rule, a certain amount of time was always allotted to the work of the hands, and the transcription of books was encouraged.

The cult of relics brought large numbers of pilgrims and rich gifts to many monastic

CLASSICAL INFLUENCES IN BYZANTINE ART

The blending of Asiatic and Greek traditions is the essence of Byzantine art. Classical elements are apparent in this ivory relief, from the Victoria and Albert Museum, in the folds of the draperies and the treatment of the hair. The facial expression, though stereotyped, is natural and sympathetic.

ARCHITECTURAL SETTING

The painter of the Virgin and Child from The Arundel Psalter emphasizes the spiritual character of his subject by an architectural setting and echoes the vertical lines and pointed arches of the cathedral to offset the charmingly natural gesture of the Child clutching his mother's veil.

55

ABSTRACT TENDENCIES IN BYZANTINE ART

The rich, jewel-like mosaic of the Empress Theodora and her court from San Vitale, Ravenna, is intended to awe and impress the spectator. The artist is not attempting to represent nature. The figures are stiff, flat and on one plane, and the empress with her tall stature and her halo has the appearance of being more divine than mortal.

churches. The desire to enlarge and adorn them was a natural consequence. Since no help could be looked for outside, the monks themselves had to be skilled in all the arts. A technical account written by the monk Theophilus, *Diversarium artium schedula*, indicates not only how many branches of art were carried on in a typical Benedictine monastery, but also that the monks had first to prepare all the materials, construct kilns and workshops and make tools. In fact, the monastic craftsman was completely self-reliant.

Since the aim of the Church in general and of the monasteries in particular was to concentrate on spiritual values rather than on the practical business of life, the aim of its art was not primarily to copy nature. The minimum of actual fact was sufficient to convey a set of doctrinal truths. Figures were used symbolically, expressiveness was sought, rather than the accurate

observation of form and detail. This avoidance of detailed naturalism led to the development of a magnificent unity of style.

ROMAN TRADITION

The word Romanesque shows the lingering power of Rome. It may be defined as the Roman tradition animated by a new spirit—and is applied to European art of the eleventh and twelfth centuries. The birth of monumental sculpture is one of the most brilliant manifestations of the Romanesque period, which also saw the perfection of many typically medieval technical processes, such as champlevé enamel and stained glass. In all its aspects, Romanesque art leads on inevitably to Gothic; but just because it is the beginning rather than the end of an artistic movement, its stimulus is sometimes unsurpassed even by the finest work of mature Gothic. The material used in medieval sculpture is

GIOTTO'S FRESCO OF ST. FRANCIS

Giotto's fresco at Assisi of St. Francis parting with his possessions is
inspired by as lofty an idealism as the mosaic on the opposite page, but it
is based upon personal observation instead of the traditions of ancient art.
A comparison of the group on the right with the attendants in the mosaic
reveals that each figure in the fresco is a study from life.

building stone. Every figure is an integral part of the building it decorates, and loses much of its significance when torn from its environment. Hence, the disadvantage of studying medieval sculpture in museums and the reason for its comparative neglect in favour of classical and Renaissance examples. Though in France such sculpture as that of Amiens and Chartres has received its due praise, in Britain there are

INVENTION IN ORNAMENT

This colourful Virgin and Child from the eighth-century Book of Kells is as richly ornamented as the Moorish architecture which is reproduced on the facing page.

still many splendid examples of medieval work which are virtually unknown.

Medieval sculpture is the result of a happy combination of two principal factors: the technical equipment of the carver who knew how to combine representation with a severe style of execution, and the wealth of religious subjects and saintly legends which the Church offered to his creative skill. The mason first ornamented his blocks of stone with zigzags, billets and other simple devices. He imitated the wood carver in his interlaced patterns with dragons and monsters of Viking and Oriental inspiration, copied pieces of classical ornament when he came across them and, finally, his hand and eye trained in these exercises, he attempted to rival the painter, the ivory carver and the metal worker in illustrating the Christian faith.

RELIGIOUS DEVOTION

The great twelfth-century abbeys of France and Spain contain some of the most interesting groups of sculpture. The "Vision of Christ in Majesty" is usually carved over the entrance door, side doors are devoted to the Virgin or the patron saint of the church and, inside, every capital tells a story from the Old or New Testament or from the life of a saint. At Poitiers and Angoulême the sculpture is not confined to the porch, but spreads over almost the whole of the west front.

The grandest achievements of medieval art are the thirteenth-century cathedrals, built by the united efforts of the community and expressing all the aspirations of that age of faith. Chartres Cathedral may be taken as the most perfect and typical example. Its three porches illustrate the full development of French sculpture from Romanesque to Gothic. The interior, with its effect of vastness and mystery, stimulates the mood of religious devotion. Immense height has been attained, great windows are filled with magnificent stained glass. Music and splendid vestments added originally to the impressive effect of the building.

GOTHIC ART

The word Gothic was a term of derision applied to medieval art during the Renaissance, when any departure from the classical standards was looked upon as a sign of barbarism. It is now more specifically applied to the art of the thirteenth-fourteenth centuries, originally known as the French style, which has certain very

58

ORNAMENT IN ARAB ART

The representation of the human figure was prohibited in Moorish art.
This limitation resulted in unusually inventive treatment of plant forms and
geometric motifs. An original feature of the rich ornamentation of the
Court of Lions in the Alhambra, Granada, is the stalactite vault.

PICTORIAL QUALITIES DETERMINED BY ARCHITECTURAL NEEDS

The stained-glass picture from Canterbury Cathedral of the Three Kings following the Star, is composed of small pieces of glass joined by strips of lead. It is a linear design on one plane with no suggestion of background, for its purpose is to decorate the cathedral and every detail is subordinated to the colour harmony resulting when light penetrates the window.

definite characteristics. In architecture these consist in the use of pointed arch, flying buttresses, rib and panel vaulting, large windows and slender, clustered shafts; in sculpture a corresponding emphasis on vertical lines, with a consequent lengthening of the figure, more naturalistic representation than in the Romanesque period, a greater individuality in figures, foliage and birds and animals in ornament. Figures now begin to detach themselves from the building and are placed on pedestals and under canopies so that they stand out against a background

of deep shadow. The recessed portals of Gothic cathedrals stress this contrast of light and shade still more.

SPIRITUAL EXPRESSION

The artist endeavours to give emotional expression to the figures through draperies, and more attention is paid to this than to the figure itself. The nude scarcely exists in Gothic sculpture. Emphasis is laid on spiritual expression rather than on physical form, though there is considerably more observation of nature than in the Romanesque period. The west front of Chartres is

SCULPTURE RELATED TO ARCHITECTURE
This head from Chartres is carved in a manner suiting coarse stone, for it is designedly of the same texture as the building itself. Though emotionally expressive, the features are conventionalized.

a typical example of the character and disposition of sculpture on a Gothic building (page 61).

In the fourteenth century the style becomes more mannered; the religious enthusiasm of the Middle Ages begins to wane. The figures are more courtly, their stance is more affected; the S-like curve of the figure, with one hip boldly projecting, is exaggerated; a mincing smile appears on many of the faces; they are sometimes clad in contemporary costumes instead of the simple tunics and draperies of the earlier styles. Tomb effigies become more realistic and the figure is not seen as a flat relief, but in the round.

In the fifteenth century mannerism gives way to realism. Figures become shorter and broader and display national and even local characteristics. Types are borrowed from the mystery plays. The grotesque element, hitherto confined to gargoyles and misericords, now affects monumental sculpture. Wood carving is extensively practised in Flanders and Germany and its intricacies are sometimes imitated in stone.

Although the Gothic of the Middle Ages might be called an international style, the different parts of Europe used it to individual purpose. Thus, the sculpture of Strasbourg shows a blend of French and German characteristics. On the whole, Gothic sculpture in Germany is much more restless, dramatic and naturalistic than in France. These qualities are seen in the sculptures of Bamberg Cathedral, which were probably influenced by Reims. Tomb effigies in Germany are usually upright, set against the wall and very realistic. Throughout the fifteenth century, sculpture in Germany was developed to a greater extent than painting, and wood was the principal material used.

In Spain, French architects and sculptors were employed to build the great Gothic cathedrals of Burgos, Leon and Toledo, and the sculpture is quite French in style. A peculiarly Spanish feature is the enclosed choir built out into the nave, the outer walls

PICTURE-PLAY OF THE BAYEUX TAPESTRY

The Bayeux tapestry, a design embroidered upon the material and not woven into it, so not really a tapestry at all, is one of the most lively and enchanting records of the Middle Ages. It was probably made in England to the order of Bishop Odo of Bayeux about twenty years after the Battle of Hastings, the culminating event of the action it so vividly portrays. The fragment reproduced shows Harold swearing an oath to Duke William upon a chest of relics on the top of which is a famous reliquary known as the Bull's Eye, while on the right Harold is returning to England.

HOMOGENEITY IN ENGLISH GOTHIC

Most English cathedrals show various periods of building and are seldom uniform in style. Salisbury was built in a comparatively short time, from 1220 to 1258, and it is an unusually organic whole. It presents a complex massing of volumes culminating in the tower with its rare, needle-like spire, which is echoed by the two tiny spires at the ends of the aisles.

being often enriched with sculpture. The painting of sculpture was more elaborately practised in Spain than in other countries, and the carved and painted retables assume enormous dimensions, often covering the whole east wall of a church. In the fifteenth century, Flemish and German craftsmen replaced the earlier French sculptors.

In Italy the influence of French Gothic was preceded by a revival of the classical spirit in sculpture at Pisa. The pulpit of Niccolo Pisano (1225-78) which stands in the baptistery dates from 1265 and is inspired by Roman and Etruscan sarcophagi. His son, Giovanni (1250-1320),

made a pulpit for the cathedral in 1310 and this reveals Gothic influence. Italian sculpture at this period is fine in quality, owing to the use of marble instead of building stone, but does not form so integral a part of the building as northern Gothic sculpture.

In Britain, Gothic architecture and sculpture is distinguished from that of France by its simplicity and restraint. Its individual character first appears in Canterbury Cathedral in the late twelfth century, and in Westminster Abbey. Salisbury (thirteenth century) has an exceptionally well-designed plan and is typical of the period. In the fourteenth century the kindred arts of architecture and sculpture reached a new and beautiful phase, as at York.

Very little medieval painting has survived except in the form of illuminated manuscripts, and these often show a wealth of imagination coupled with incredible technical skill in adorning the written page with gilding and ornament, as well as with illustrations of the subject matter. The British Isles are rich in this form of art. The *Book of Kells* (eighth century) is famous for its intricate ornament (page 58). In Anglo-Saxon times, manuscripts showed great beauty of line. In the fourteenth century, English illumination was pre-eminent in Europe.

HUMAN INTERPRETATION

During the Romanesque period the interiors of churches were often covered with wall paintings, broadly decorative and symbolic, but in the Gothic period the development of the stained-glass window and the rib and panel vault left less space for paintings on the walls and roof of the church.

One of the most exquisite examples of Gothic painting in existence is the Wilton Diptych, in the London National Gallery.

In Italy, the Byzantine tradition survived till about the thirteenth century. Meanwhile, a new impetus was given to religious life by the preaching of St. Francis, and this had a wide influence on medieval art, providing the artists with a more human interpretation of the Biblical stories and fresh subjects in the life and miracles of the saint himself.

When St. Francis died, a vast church at Assisi was raised over his tomb, comprising a shrine to guard his remains, a monastery for his order and a palace for the Popes. The building of this church was in direct opposition to his wishes, but it was a spontaneous gesture. Its builders tried to show their veneration for St. Francis by means of a visible symbol. It still remains one of the most eloquent expressions of medieval devotion. It is built in three tiers: the tomb itself, deeply embedded in the rock; the Lower Church, massive, round-arched and sombre, but covered nevertheless with fresco paintings; and the Upper Church, adorned with incomparable frescoes depicting the life of St. Francis by Giotto di Bondone (*c.* 1267-1336) (page 57). The twenty-eight scenes of this series were probably painted by Giotto and other artists during the last years of the thirteenth century. They mark the dawn of Italian painting and a sharp break with the earlier Byzantine tradition. The figures appear to be solid instead of flat; their movements are dramatic and expressive, and the background, though simplified, nevertheless suggests the appropriate setting.

Many other artists were employed in the decoration of the church. One of the earliest was probably Pietro Cavallini (*c.* 1240-1301) from Rome, who may have painted the Old Testament scenes above the life of St. Francis. Then came Giovanni Cimabue (*c.* 1240-1302), Giotto from Florence, Pietro and Ambrogio Lorenzetti and Simone Martini (*c.* 1283-1344) from Siena and probably many others whose names are not recorded. Their combined achievement has made the church a treasure-house of early Italian art, unrivalled in its significance.

Test Yourself

1. How did the traditions and practice of the arts survive during the Dark Ages?
2. Compare and contrast one of Giotto's frescoes of St. Francis at Assisi with the Byzantine mosaic of the Empress Theodora from San Vitale, Ravenna.
3. What was the most important manifestation of the Romanesque period?
4. Give an account of the main elements of the Gothic style.

Answers will be found at the end of the book

RELIGIOUS PAINTING IN THE BYZANTINE TRADITION

Duccio di Buoninsegna, an Italian painter of the Sienese school, painted The Annunciation, now in the National Gallery, early in the fourteenth century. Religious fervour and the opportunities then provided in the many church buildings being constructed combined to direct the activities of most artists to religious subjects. Duccio is regarded as the last and the greatest representative of the Byzantine tradition.

REALISM IN FLEMISH PAINTING

Arnolfini and His Wife by Jan van Eyck (1385-1441), now in the National Gallery, is one of the earliest pictures of everyday life and thus, in its subject matter, is realistic compared with the religious paintings which preceded it.

CHAPTER V

GREAT MASTERS OF THE RENAISSANCE

THE Renaissance of the fifteenth century is usually defined as a rebirth of classical art and learning; but as far as art is concerned, it might be more correct to describe it as a revival of the ancient Greek interest in the human form, tempered with the greater spiritual expression which was the legacy of the Middle Ages.

Renaissance art is far more than a mere imitation of the antique. It springs from a new attitude to life, leading to the development of the individual, greater freedom of thought and curiosity about the nature of man and the universe. Among the factors which contributed to this complex movement were the conquest of Constantinople by the Turks, which sent many Greek scholars to Italy as refugees and disseminators of learning; the invention of printing about the middle of the fifteenth century, which resulted in the substitution of printed books for manuscripts and the spread of education outside the narrow bounds of the monasteries; scientific research, which in due course led to the discovery of the solar system; the exploration of sea routes, culminating in the discovery of America, colonization, and the growth of world trade.

Although deprecated, freedom of thought was permitted by the Church, which feared the undermining of its authority. The Renaissance has sometimes been called the Age of Reason, in contrast to the earlier Age of Faith, and one of the outstanding characteristics of its principal artists was their great intellectual activity. They strove to understand the underlying structure of everything they saw and to represent it with the greatest possible force and accuracy.

In Italy the social and political situation was particularly favourable for the development of art. The country was divided into a number of small city-states ruled by merchant princes or, as in Venice, by an enlightened republican government, and it was the ambition of the Popes, princes and citizens to surround themselves with objects of beauty, or to enrich the Church with works of art. Wise patronage and lavish resources enabled them to fulfil this ambition, leaving behind them a legacy of infinite value to posterity.

In spite of the classical revival in the works of Niccolo Pisano and Giotto, the early Renaissance, largely medieval, still partook of the fervour of the preceding centuries and French Gothic influence dominated Italian art throughout the fourteenth century. The Gothic spirit, combined with Byzantine traditions, was exquisitely expressed in the art of Siena, a town which, although only thirty miles from Florence, was cut off by its situation on a high hill from the natural trade routes of Italy, and remained isolated and medieval. The great masters of Siena were Duccio di Buoninsegna (1255-1319), Simone Martini (c. 1285-1344) and Stefano di Giovanni Sassetta (1392-1450); their works are characterized by great feeling for line, tenderness, spirituality and charm of colour.

In the early fifteenth century Florence became the chief centre of artistic activity. The spirit of the early Renaissance can be studied in the works of the sculptor Donatello (1386-1466), who was the friend and contemporary of the architect Filippo Brunelleschi (1379-1446) and of the painter Masaccio (1401-28). These three brought new life into every branch of art and shared a great admiration for the antique, combining this with a close study of natural appearance and a scientific approach to the problems of form and proportion.

Donatello worked in marble, bronze and terra-cotta; he expressed a wide range of human emotions and set the example of a

TEMPERA PAINTING ON WOOD

In this detail from the small panel of Christ in Glory, in the National Gallery,
Fra Angelico attempts a subject which has seldom been convincingly
rendered in art.   He succeeds by a combination of exalted mysticism and
joy.   The impressive figure soars upward against a golden background.

ARCHITECTURAL ILLUSION

It is Signorelli's intense realism in the expression of structure which causes the central figure of this fresco from Orvieto to lean so dramatically from the painted roundel. The architectural illusion foreshadows the baroque painting of the sixteenth and seventeenth centuries.

CEILING FRESCO FROM THE SISTINE CHAPEL

Only a painter with Michelangelo's sense of the sublime could have given adequate expression to a subject like this Creation of Adam, one of the frescoes on the ceiling of the Sistine Chapel commissioned by Pope Julius II. The noble forms, even the vigorously active figure of God, have the quality of sculpture, an effect considerably enhanced by the flat background and the suggested hillside upon which Adam rests.

vivid naturalism in his statues of saints, his portraits, bas-reliefs and graceful representations of childhood. His bronze David, a nude free-standing figure, and his great equestrian statue of Gattemelata (page 242), a monument to Erasmo da Narni, a famous *condottiere* (leader of mercenary troops), were the first bronze figures of their kind to be cast since the days of antiquity.

Donatello's contemporary, Luca della Robbia (1400-82), is famous chiefly for his work in enamelled terra-cotta. This technique, which he introduced into Italy, was carried on by his family for nearly a

century and satisfied the Italian taste for colour in sculpture, both for interior and exterior decoration. Luca's forms are smooth, gentle and naturalistic.

In painting, the short-lived Masaccio was the pioneer of his generation, abandoning the restless, crowded compositions of his predecessors and developing the simple, broad forms of Giotto's designs by a still closer study of classical models. His figures appear to stand out in bold relief because he was the first painter to use cast shadows in order to give greater realism.

The eager curiosity of the Florentine painters about the visual world made them feel an urgent need for new forms in which to communicate their observations. In order to find a more adequate means of expression, the scientifically minded painters —Paolo Uccello (1397-1475), Andrea del Castagno (1397-1457), Antonio Pollaiuolo (1429-98), and Leonardo da Vinci (1452-1519)—devoted much of their time to research in perspective, geometry, anatomy and chiaroscuro (the study of light and shade). So absorbed were they in their pursuit of knowledge that, as a result of too much stress on some particular problem of perspective, or too much emphasis on the muscular tension of a figure in action, their pictures sometimes

lacked balance and repose. Nevertheless, these artists transformed painting from a language of symbols to an eloquent expression of human actions and emotions. Even the most religious painter of the Renaissance, Fra Angelico (1387-1455), used the scientific discoveries of his contemporaries to make his heavenly visions more convincing.

INTERPRETATION

Pagan subjects were often suggested to the painters by poets and men of letters (the Humanists, who made a special study of ancient literature), but the visions evoked by these were entirely different

LANDSCAPE AND FIGURES

The Venetians were the first to realize the possibilities of landscape in painting. In Giorgione's Fête Champêtre (Louvre) the landscape is not merely a background; landscape and figures are of equal importance. Stuffs and flesh, foliage and distant hills, are bound together in a rich tonal harmony to create that high summer mood, that idyllic charm and tranquillity, which are the essence of the picture.

CHARACTER OF RENAISSANCE SCULPTURE

Though Donatello's St. George was designed to fill a niche on the church of Or San Michele, it is not architectural like medieval sculpture, but is complete in itself. While it is as realistic as Hellenistic sculpture, realism is not here an end in itself, but an expression of spiritual meaning.

This study of an old man by Masaccio must be one of the earliest Renaissance portraits. To a sense of massiveness and a largeness of design as great as those of Giotto is added feeling for bodily structure and light and shade, and these are combined with that rare grasp of personality and the ability to present it objectively upon which great portraiture depends.

RENAISSANCE MERGING INTO BAROQUE

Ten architects worked upon St. Peter's, Rome, begun in 1506, but the plan is essentially that of Bramante. Raphael was among those who afterwards modified the original plans, and Michelangelo, at the age of seventy, designed the huge dome, 430 feet high, which was completed after his death. Bernini added the double colonnade, giving the piazza the appearance of a vast vestibule before the church. The colossal scale and grandiose character of the building mark the point where Renaissance merges into baroque.

from anything a Greek or Roman artist would have created. For instance, Sandro Botticelli (1444-1510), Andrea Mantegna (1431-1506), and Giorgione (1478-1510) interpreted classical themes in totally different ways.

INDIVIDUAL CHARACTERISTICS

Botticelli, furthermore, gifted with an exquisite sense of rhythm, painted a slender, wistful Venus, born to a world of flowers and fantasy, where classical and medieval grace were combined in a unique harmony (page 76). Mantegna was more absorbed with the study of classical reliefs than with poetry and his figures are heroic and austere, moving in a world which appears to be petrified. Giorgione, on the other hand, concentrated upon colour and atmosphere instead of line.

One of the remarkable things about the Italian Renaissance is that every region, almost every city, produced individual characteristics. Thus, while the Florentines

were chiefly concerned with the study of the human form in action, the Umbrian painters were more interested in the mystery of space and light. They were probably influenced by the landscape of Umbria, with its low mountains, gentle valleys and distant prospects. Some of the Umbrian painters, like Piero della Francesca (1416-92) and Raphael Sanzio (1483-1520), worked in Florence and learnt to combine their natural feeling for serene landscape with the Florentine mastery in rendering the human figure; others, like Pietro Perugino (1446-1523), remained more provincial, painting devotional pictures with contemplative figures seen against a background of infinite distance. From 1508 until his death, Raphael worked in Rome, which by that time had become the centre of artistic activity in Italy, for the rebuilding of St. Peter's and the decoration of the Vatican were attracting many of the most accomplished artists from various parts of the country.

GATES OF PARADISE

Michelangelo said of the bronze doors which Ghiberti made for the eastern entrance to the Baptistery, Florence (1425-52), that they were worthy to be the gates of Paradise. The subjects are from the Old Testament.

The characteristics of High Renaissance design consisted in symmetry, the use of broad forms, closely knit together, perfect rendering of the human figure and its complete realization in the round. The work of Michelangelo Buonarroti (1475-1564) is dominated by his passionate interest in the human form in the presentation of which he reaches a level unsurpassed by any other artist. His personal expression lay in a tragic sense of struggle, as seen in his slaves and other figures, apparently in bondage. His ambitions were only partly realized, since although he felt himself to be exclusively a sculptor, he was obliged to divide his time between sculpture, painting, architecture and occasional work on defence, besides writing

SIXTEENTH-CENTURY DESIGN

Happy Union is one of four large decorations by Veronese now in the National Gallery. The title has little significance; the artist is concerned with design for its own sake. The composition, based on an interplay of diagonals, is characteristic of the sixteenth century.

some of the finest sonnets in the Italian language.

Leonardo da Vinci (1452-1519) was even more versatile and circumstances have been even more adverse to his work. Most of his paintings remained unfinished or were subsequently damaged, and neither of the two equestrian statues he designed was ever cast in bronze, so that now it is only possible to reconstruct them from his drawings.

It is, indeed, through his drawings and his notes, consisting of more than five thousand pages, that Leonardo's remarkable mind can best be appreciated. They reveal his enthusiastic search for beauty and boundless curiosity concerning every aspect of the physical world. He spent many years in Milan and his influence dominates painting in Northern Italy at the beginning of the sixteenth century.

VENETIAN ART

In Venice, art followed a different course. Venice was isolated from the rest of Italy and closely connected by trade with the colourful Near East. St. Mark's is a Byzantine church, Oriental in atmosphere and filled with treasure brought from Constantinople. The Venetian painters, wealthy and worldly, were frankly concerned with presenting the pageantry of the scenes around them rather than with solving the abstract scientific problems which had interested the Florentines. Giorgione, Titian Vecellio (c. 1477-1576), Jacopo Robusti Tintoretto (1518-94) and Paolo Veronese (1528-88), each in his own way, brought painting nearer to the very substance of life and evoked colour harmonies, unmatched in their splendour. Pagan and religious subjects were treated as an excuse to paint beautiful women, and all the resources of oil painting were explored to convey, not only the texture of flesh and marble and brocade, but also the more fleeting effects of light and atmosphere.

An important contribution of the Venetians to painting was their rendering of nature. The figure interest was never quite eliminated, but Venetian landscape and figures were bound into a single harmony, from which it was but a step to the point where landscape could exist in its own right.

NEW CLASSICAL TASTE

The Renaissance style began to develop in the countries north of the Alps nearly a century later than in Italy. It was not a spontaneous movement, but a fashion imitated at second hand, often with exaggerations and little understanding of its essential character. In many places the native Gothic and Renaissance, or Italian, styles were used simultaneously; the more provincial centres and humbler craftsmen retaining the popular Gothic manner, while princely patrons employed those who could provide a tolerable likeness of the Italian manner. The Italian tradition spread through Europe, partly through Italian artists who found employment abroad and partly through small portable objects, such as bronze figures and plaquettes, engravings and wood carvings, which were copied and imitated. By degrees each country absorbed this new classical taste and developed a more national style, suited to local conditions. In the fifteenth century Northern Europe and Spain were still following the Gothic style, now in its final flamboyant stage, or producing very realistic work. The Italian influence came in the sixteenth century and was therefore that of the late Renaissance.

IN THE NETHERLANDS

During the fifteenth century a brilliant school of painting arose in the Netherlands. The cities of Bruges and Ghent enjoyed great prosperity under the rule of the Duke of Burgundy and carried on a flourishing cloth trade. Their civic pride found expression in the magnificent cloth halls and belfries for which Belgium is famous, and in an original school of painting which evolved from the illuminating of manuscripts and the making of stained-glass windows.

Intense realization of particular detail interested the painters more than broad generalization or decorative arrangement and they evolved a technique of transparent oil painting which enabled them vividly

EMPHASIS ON LINE

There is nothing classical in either feeling or treatment about the wistful goddess from Botticelli's Birth of Venus. The emphasis is not on form but on line; the figure is deliberately distorted to intensify the quality of the contours and curves which are echoed by the flowing hair of Venus.

TONE AND MASS

Beside Botticelli's Venus, this nude from Titian's Sacred and Profane Love is a robust, exuberant creature in perfect harmony with the pagan associations of the classical relief on the well on which she is seated. There are no sharp outlines in this realistically conceived figure.

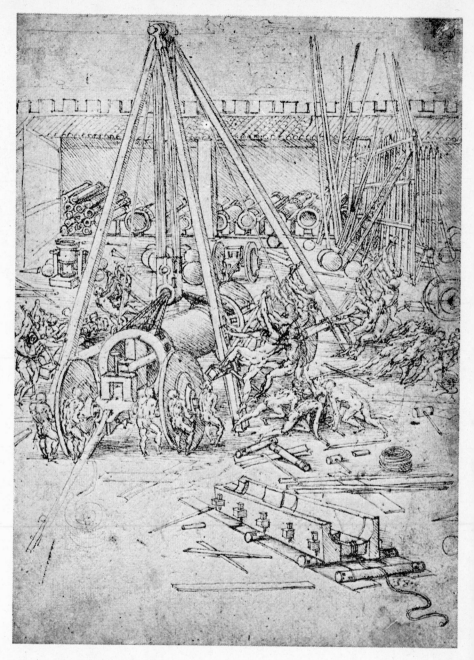

RENAISSANCE WAR MACHINES

Many Renaissance artists designed machines of war. A number of Leonardo's many drawings are of such subjects, and when he entered the service of the Duke of Milan in about 1483, he recommended himself especially to his new patron as a military engineer.

78

Albrecht Dürer shared the feeling of most German painters for line as the chief means of creating form, and it was natural that with his unparalleled technical ability he should find in engraving a perfect means of expression. *Melancholia*, reproduced below, is one of three famous copper engravings which Dürer made in 1513 and 1514, the two others being *The Knight and Death*, and *St. Jerome in His Study*. Such intense imaginative force has rarely been displayed in this form of art.

to suggest qualities of light and texture unknown to the earlier Italian painters. Their religious pictures are generally treated as scenes from their daily life rather than as heroic or imaginative compositions. Jan van Eyck (*c.* 1385-1440) and his followers excelled in portraiture and even the saints they painted were often portraits of contemporaries. However, the first masterpiece of the Flemish school, the altarpiece of the brothers van Eyck, The Adoration of the Lamb, in Ghent Cathedral, is an epitome of medieval symbolism, as well as the first fruit of the new realism.

DIGNITY AND CHARM

In France, Italian influence first appeared after the campaigns of Charles VIII, Louis XII and Francis I, who brought back not only Italian masterpieces but also some Italian artists, including Leonardo da Vinci.

During the early sixteenth century the French built themselves graceful chateaux, ornamented in the Italian Renaissance taste, though in structure they remained essentially French. Some of the sculptors such as Michel Colombe (d. 1512) and Jean Goujon (d. *c.* 1568) succeeded in combining classical dignity with French charm. The new demand for portraiture was brilliantly met by the Clouet family, while other French painters of the School of Fontainebleau tried their hand at classical composition. The religious wars of the latter part of the century put a temporary stop to this chapter of French art.

In Spain, the Moors were only defeated at the end of the fifteenth century, and there was little original artistic production until the seventeenth century. Italian, Flemish and German artists were employed when the country grew rich on the spoils from the New World. The early Renaissance style was introduced first by the silversmiths, and was given the name Plateresque.

EXPRESSION IN ART

In England, the word Renaissance can hardly be applied to the visual arts, which suffered a severe set-back from the Reformation. The Elizabethan age found its finest expression in literature and in the spirit of adventure. It is only in the realm of domestic architecture and in the applied arts, furniture, embroidery and silver that the English sense of beauty can be traced.

The German artist Hans Holbein (1497-1543) produced an incomparable portrait gallery of the personalities around the court of Henry VIII, and among his English followers the miniature painter Nicholas Hilliard stands out for his exquisite style and workmanship.

In Germany itself, sculpture and engraving were the leading arts during the Renaissance. Wood lent itself to the intricate, restless shapes in which the introspective, troubled spirit of the German people sought expression. Albrecht Dürer (1471-1528), the friend and painter of the Humanists, was trained as a goldsmith and worked largely as an engraver. When he visited Venice he was struck with the difference in the status of the artist: "Here the painter is treated as a gentleman; in Germany he is merely an artisan." Like Leonardo, Dürer devoted much of his time to scientific and mechanical problems and his paintings and engravings reveal searching intellectual qualities in which he is only equalled by the great Italian masters.

Test Yourself

1. Name, with a brief description of their work, the three most influential masters of the early Renaissance.
2. Compare briefly the arts of Florence and Siena.
3. What was the chief contribution of the Venetians to the art of painting?
4. What are the characteristics of Michelangelo's painting?
5. Compare and contrast Botticelli's and Titian's treatment of the nude.
6. Give a brief account of the Renaissance in Germany and the Netherlands.

Answers will be found at the end of the book

RAPHAEL'S TREATMENT OF LANDSCAPE

*The Vision of a Knight (National Gallery) was painted when Raphael was
but a boy of eighteen and had not left his native Umbria. Yet never again
did he create so fully developed a landscape as this, since in later years
he concentrated on the organization of figures in space. His master,
Perugino, had visited Venice and conveyed to him the Venetian conception
of the relation of figures to landscape which dominates this little picture.*

OF CLASSICAL PAINTING

a villa in Castello. Although most of the virtues of composition and draughtsmanship would still be apparent in a monochrome version, colour plays a vital part in perfecting the dream-like atmosphere of this extraordinary picture now in the Uffizi collection.

UNFINISHED TEMPERA PAINTING OF THE RENAISSANCE

The most famous Florentine artist of the Renaissance was Michelangelo (1475-1564); painter, sculptor and architect, he was one of the most versatile artists who ever lived. The Entombment (National Gallery), an unfinished painting in tempera, is an interesting example of his attitude to colour. In those parts of the picture in which the powerful modelling and drawing have been completed in monochrome but to which colour has not been added, the impression is hardly weakened by its absence, for colour plays a purely secondary part in the composition.

CHAPTER VI

ART AND THE STATE

THE term baroque is used to describe the art of the seventeenth century. It suggests the exaggeration and freedom with which the classical style then came to be treated. The eighteenth-century, or rococo, style is a final, lighter and more elegant development of this. In a certain sense, baroque marked a return to the principles of form found in Gothic art; the use of natural or organic form instead of architectural or mechanical construction, curves instead of rectangles, elaborate relief, organization in depth, restless movement and the absence of classical restraint. Classical features continued to be used, but in free, irregular combinations; columns were placed diagonally, or in clusters, and were surmounted by curved or broken pediments. The precise relationship of the individual parts of a building was no longer of import to the baroque artist; everything was subordinated to the total effect and the expression of rhythm and movement. It was a style at once grandiose, florid and imposing.

ART AND ARCHITECTURE

The arts of the baroque period must be considered in close relation to architecture. One of the most typical products of the age was the illusionistic ceiling painting with the effect of figures hovering in the clouds overhead. First attempted by Antonio Correggio (1494-1534) in Parma, this type of decoration was developed by Pozzo (active c. 1685) in Rome and was finally carried all over Europe by the Venetian painter, Giovanni Battista Tiepolo (1696-1770), who worked both in Germany and Spain. In England it was introduced by Peter Paul Rubens (1577-1640), who painted the Banqueting Hall at Whitehall, and carried on by Thornhill (1676-1754) in his decorations at Hampton Court and in the Painted Hall at Greenwich.

First developed in Rome, the baroque style found its perfect exponent in the great sculptor and architect, Lorenzo Bernini (1593-1680), but spread afterwards to all European countries. It was the accompaniment of the Counter-Reformation of the Jesuits. This sought to re-establish the predominance of the Roman Catholic Church and made an especial effort to stir the emotions and to dazzle the eye.

THREE GROUPS

Thus, Italian art of the seventeenth century aims at rendering the scenes of the Passion, or the ecstasies and martyrdoms of the saints as dramatically and convincingly as possible. It is characterized by a showy display of technical skill and theatrical realism. The Italian painters of the baroque period cannot be compared with the giants of the Renaissance. Rome, Bologna and Naples were the chief centres of activity and the painters may be divided into three main groups, according to their style. The Mannerists are those who imitated and exaggerated the peculiarities of the great masters of the High Renaissance. Thus, Parmigianino (1504-42) and Federigo Baroccio (1526-1612) emulated the sweetness of Correggio, while Guilio Romano (1492-1540) modelled himself upon Raphael. Leonardo and Michelangelo each had numerous imitators, who, lacking the inspiration of the great masters, produced empty travesties by repeating their mannerisms.

The Eclectics, as their name suggests, instead of imitating one master's style, tried to combine what they considered to be the best features of all the great masters of the Renaissance. Their ideal was a picture of Paradise with the figure of Adam drawn by Michelangelo and painted by Titian, and Eve drawn by Raphael and painted by Correggio. The Eclectic theory enjoyed a great vogue in Bologna and its principal exponents were Ludovico Carracci (1555-1619), his cousins Agostino and Annibale, Guercino (1591-1666) and Guido

FRENCH BAROQUE

The baroque style in France reflected the personal tastes of Louis XIV and XV. The Versailles bedroom with its richly ornamented bed, plaster reliefs, elaborate mirror and frames, gilded clock and Sèvres vases, makes an impression of heavy magnificence. In the salon, above, with its elegant personages the proportions are more slender, the decorations lighter; it is a thoroughly French interpretation of the baroque spirit.

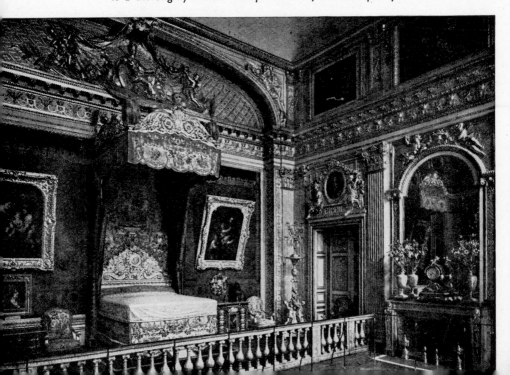

Reni (1575-1642). Carracci opened an academy at Bologna, which became the seminary of art in the seventeenth century. The technical perfection of the Eclectics leaves the spectator cold, because it is academic and borrowed from others instead of resulting from that urge to find a new means of self-expression, which had been characteristic of the Renaissance.

The most original trend of the period was naturalism, begun by Michelangelo da Caravaggio (1569-1609) in reaction to the academicism of the Eclectics and continued by various painters in Naples, including the Spaniard, Giuseppe Ribera (1588-1652). They advocated a return to nature and painted with a realism that at times approached the photographic. Caravaggio startled his contemporaries by painting biblical subjects in the setting of a Roman slum. His types were coarse but emphatic, and he used strong contrasts of light and shade and sudden effects of foreshortening to make his scenes appear more convincing.

The baroque style appealed to the religious spirit and the ardent temperament of the people of Spain, and Spanish art reached the height of its development in the seventeenth century. The country had

SCULPTURE INCLUDED IN ARCHITECTURAL DESIGN

Architecture, sculpture and water are combined in this monumental Fontana Trevi in Rome, by Niccoli Salvi. The restless movement of the water, the artificial rocks and the central figure become part of the façade, the pattern being carried up by means of columns and statuary to the intricate ornament which crowns the building.

USE OF ARTIFICIAL ILLUMINATION

The sixteenth-century Venetians had organized their pictures by means of soft, blended light and dark colour masses, but this method (chiaroscuro) was fully exploited first in the baroque period. The violent contrasts of light and shade in Caravaggio's Supper at Emmaus (National Gallery) are contrived by a carefully arranged artificial illumination. The table and the melodramatic gestures are prominent, while the remainder is in shadow.

acquired great wealth from the discovery of America, the Church was all-powerful and provided lavish patronage, particularly for sculpture. Wood, painted to look life-like in colour, was the favourite material. Some churches still possess large groups of Passion scenes, *pasos*, which are displayed and carried in procession in Holy Week. The principal sculptor at Seville was Martinez Montanez (*c.* 1580-1649), whose works are at once ascetic and brutally realistic. His pupil, Alonso Cano (1601-67), worked as sculptor and painter at Granada and was less naturalistic. Pedro de Mena (1628-88) expressed the exaggerated realism to which Spanish religious fervour sometimes led. His figures were occasionally enhanced with

actual hair and garments, and even with tears of glass. Jose Churriguera (1650-1723) gave his name to the most extravagant style of baroque architecture, the "churrigueresque."

A number of artists came to Spain from Italy in order to take part in the building and decoration of Philip II's colossal palace of the Escorial. The greatest master among these, a Greek by birth, was Domenico Theotocopulos, known as El Greco (1547-1614). He must have received his first instruction in painting in his native Crete, where the formal tradition of Byzantine art was still alive in the sixteenth century. In his work, the seemingly irreconcilable, the Byzantine and the later Italian modes are curiously combined. El Greco had left

VARIED INFLUENCES

Hollow in sentiment, The Toilet of Venus, by Guido Reni (National Gallery),
is strongly influenced by the work of both Correggio and Raphael.

EL GRECO AND THE COUNTER-REFORMATION

El Greco's original but intensely religious art was an instrument peculiarly suited to the aims of the Counter-Reformation. The Burial of Count Orgaz was painted about 1585 for San Tome, Toledo. The composition is divided in two; in the lower part St. Stephen and St. Augustine appear to take charge of the burial, while above, the count's soul is received into heaven.

The *Maids of Honour* by Velasquez, painted 1656-57, and now in the Prado, Madrid, shows the little Infanta Margarita accompanied by her maids, dwarfs and a dog, while Velasquez himself is standing before a large canvas on the left, probably painting the portraits of the king and queen who are posing outside the picture, facing the infanta, and are reflected in the mirror in the background. A figure on the steps leading from an open doorway behind pushes aside a curtain.

DIRECT METHOD OF PAINTING
Velasquez's portrait of Philip IV (National Gallery) is an
example of the painter's masterly use of pigment. It was painted
directly on to the canvas, not composed first in monochrome.

THREE-DIMENSIONAL DESIGN

Rubens presented War and Peace, now in the National Gallery, to Charles I in 1630. The richly contrasted textures of flesh, hair, satins, fruit and armour are woven into a three-dimensional design of solid masses which is carried backward and forward by sweeping diagonals.

Crete by 1570, and spent some time in Venice, where he studied the paintings of Titian and Tintoretto and may even have worked in Tintoretto's studio. Then he travelled down to Naples by way of Parma and Rome, coming into contact with the great works of Correggio and Michelangelo. Neither satisfied him entirely, and about 1576 he left Italy for Spain and spent the rest of his life in Toledo, where he found an atmosphere congenial to the expression of his emotional intensity and mysticism. Today, many of his paintings are scattered in the galleries of Europe and America, but many may still be seen in Toledo, in the cathedral, in various churches and in his house, now arranged as a museum.

No artist was further removed in temperament from El Greco than Diego Rodriguez Velasquez (1599-1660), court painter to Philip IV. Velasquez was no

visionary; his attitude towards visual appearance was cool, detached and impersonal. In his youth he declared that he would prefer to rank first as a painter of still life than second in more ambitious subjects. He spent the greater part of his life in recording objectively the Spanish royal household, with all its personalities, from the proud minister Olivares to the misshapen dwarfs who were kept for the amusement of the king. No master has ever painted portraits with more truth, restraint and dignity. In his subtle harmonies of grey and black, and the vigour and freedom of his brushwork, Velasquez seems more like a nineteenth-century painter, and was indeed a great influence on J. McNeill Whistler (1834-1903) and Edouard Manet (1832-83).

When the great Flemish master, Rubens, visited Spain in the course of his travels, which took him to Italy, France and

INFLUENCE OF CLASSICISM

The taste for antiquity at the time of the French Revolution and the Empire is apparent in the modes of furniture and dress shown in Jacques Louis David's celebrated picture of Madame Recamier (Louvre) which is more graceful than most imitations of the classical style.

England as well, he met Velasquez, and it was on his advice that Velasquez was sent on a journey to Italy by the King of Spain.

Full of exuberance and energy, Rubens was in perfect tune with his age and one of the greatest exponents of the baroque style. Religious and mythological subjects, portraits and landscapes flowed from his brush with incredible prodigality, and in addition to his painting he carried out important diplomatic functions. He knew how to flatter his princely patrons with gifts of pictures and succeeded in negotiating a peace treaty with Charles I.

Rubens organized his figure compositions in broad masses and emphasized movement in depth, using intersecting diagonals, strong verticals and swirling S-shapes. In his last years he painted a magnificent series of landscapes which became an inspiration to later painters, particularly in

England. His pupil, Anthony van Dyck (1599-1641) became court painter to Charles I and added elegance and refinement to the vigorous style of his master. Van Dyck enjoyed supreme success as an aristocratic portrait painter and left a number of followers in England who continued to work after the Restoration, depicting the beauties of Charles II's court in a somewhat heavier style.

Meanwhile, in France, conditions had not been favourable to art after the religious wars, and the two greatest French painters of the century, Claude Lorrain (1600-82) and Nicolas Poussin (1594-1665), worked in Rome, the former painting ideal landscapes and the latter mainly classical compositions in which imaginative landscape plays a great part.

Under Louis XIV the State began to encourage all the arts for the glorification of the monarchy, for it was the king and not the Church who now held the balance of power in France. The royal hunting lodge of Versailles was transformed into a huge palace, where the whole court resided and where foreign visitors were duly impressed with the magnificence of "Le Roi Soleil." Charles Le Brun (d. 1690), was entrusted with the general supervision of the interior decoration. Cabinet makers, tapestry weavers, designers of every sort were employed by the State, and they combined to create a style of pomp and splendour which was gradually imitated at all the courts of Europe. The establishment of the French Academy of Sculpture and Painting in 1648 gave official sanction to the dictates of the autocracy which ruled France during the seventeenth and eighteenth centuries.

END OF BAROQUE

In Germany, the influence of Giovanni Lorenzo Bernini (1598-1680) was very strong, especially in the production of fountains and garden ornaments. The baroque, with its virtuosity and movement, made a strong appeal to German taste, and produced some fine church architecture in Austria and southern Germany. In Bavaria, Egid Quirin Asam worked in collaboration with his brother the painter, and created a sort of operatic effect in his Assumption of the Virgin at Rohr. The development of German art in the seventeenth century was obstructed by the Thirty Years War, which devastated the country and threw civilization back by a full century.

In the eighteenth century all trace of the classical basis of baroque art vanished. Palaces as well as private houses were built on a more intimate scale; decoration became lighter, wood and metal were twisted into shapes resembling wind-blown plants, the shell became a favourite ornamental motive and the prevalent style came to be known as rocaille or rococo. It consisted in the avoidance of straight lines, angles, flat surfaces and symmetrical arrangements, and inclined towards easy curves, slender proportions, light colour and gilding and the extensive use of mirrors. As a form of interior decoration, the rococo style was eminently suited to serve as a background to the luxury and pleasure, the frivolity and sparkling light-heartedness which characterized the reign of Louis XV. French society required elegance not only in pictures but in every accessory of fashionable life, and this led to a brilliant output of fine, though rather artificial, cabinet work, veneered and enriched with gilt bronze, as well as of tapestry, porcelain and ornaments.

As this style had been so closely associated with the monarchy, it was swept aside by the French Revolution and was followed by a revival of classical taste now known as neo-classicism. This new classicism was modelled much more closely on the art of antiquity than the Renaissance had been, since excavations at Herculaneum and Pompeii had brought to light a mass of furniture and objects of everyday use of the Augustan age; but in spite, or because, of this, neo-classical art lacked the vitality and inspiration of the Renaissance. It is never possible to recapture the spirit of a past age in exactly the same form and a mere imitation of its outward appearance remains lifeless.

Test Yourself

1. Who were the Eclectics?
2. Describe briefly, with examples, the characteristics of baroque architecture.
3. Chiaroscuro was first fully developed during the baroque period. Explain this statement.
4. To what extent are the paintings of Rubens and El Greco expressive of their age?

Answers will be found at the end of the book

FRENCH ROCOCO

The Swing, by Fragonard (Wallace Collection), mirrors the gaiety, the artificiality and elegance of the court of Louis XV of France. The swirls and undulations of foliage and tree trunk, the billowing skirts of the girl on the swing, the winged children on the shell, are typical of the light, sparkling rococo spirit which found its most perfect expression in France.

CHAPTER VII

ART AND SOCIETY

DURING the Renaissance and the seventeenth century, artists received their commissions chiefly from the Church, from princes and from enlightened patrons who possessed a certain degree of scholarship and appreciated historical and mythological subjects. At the same time, a wider public was beginning to take an interest in the arts, and its requirements were naturally very different.

NATIONAL PRIDE

In Northern Europe, including a large part of Germany, Holland and England, for instance, the Reformation ended the predominance of church patronage. The new class of well-to-do *bourgeoisie* had no taste for the traditional classical or "grand style" painting, but demanded pictures which recorded their daily life and flattered their vanity, portraits, landscapes and domestic scenes. This was particularly the case in Holland, where the people felt a new pride in their country and their way of life, as a result of having won their independence from Spanish domination; and these were the circumstances which lay behind the great Dutch paintings of the seventeenth century.

DUTCH DOMESTIC PAINTING

The origins of genre paintings—that is, of scenes of everyday life—are to be found in the borders of medieval illuminated manuscripts, where little scenes occur illustrating the occupation of the months. The Venetian Carpaccio's Dream of St. Ursula, Antonella da Messina, and the Flemish painters of the fifteenth century contributed to the development of genre by painting religious subjects in the homely settings of their own day. Pieter Brueghel the Elder (1525-69), was the first to paint scenes of peasant life on a larger scale, illustrating popular proverbs, games and festivals.

Brueghel stands at the cross-roads between medieval and modern art, and his lively scenes are set in landscapes, showing his careful observation of weather, time of year and atmosphere.

The Dutch genre painters are usually less concerned in depicting an incident than in evoking the calm that reigns in their well-kept houses, where the housewife quietly superintends her maids, brings up her children, entertains visitors, attends to her correspondence or adds to her accomplishments by taking a music lesson. As the pictures were intended for private houses they were painted on a modest scale, but with extraordinary technical skill which made it possible to suggest the very texture of a satin bodice, a velvet chair cover or a Turkish carpet, used as a tablecloth, and to render the most fleeting effects of atmosphere. The light streams in through the windows and sometimes there is a glimpse through a door into another room, or on to a street beyond. The composition is usually based on simple rectangles and the colours are subdued, except in the contrast of a black bodice and a red skirt in pictures by Nicolas Maes (1632-93) and Pieter de Hooch (1629-83), or in the harmonies of blue and yellow favoured by Jan Vermeer (1632-75). The figures in these pictures represent all types of Dutch citizens.

LANDSCAPE AND PORTRAITS

The pride of the Dutch people in their native land was expressed not only in pictures of homely interiors and sober domestic scenes, but also in paintings of the Dutch countryside, with its wide skies and low horizons. The unidealized landscapes of such painters as Meindert Hobbema (1638-1709) and Ruisdael (1628-82) were of great importance in the development of this branch of art and prepared the way for the great landscape painters of the two following centuries.

A great number of portraits were

POETRY OF EVERYDAY LIFE

Subjects like the Interior of a Dutch House, by Pieter de Hooch (National Gallery), were in demand with wealthy Hollanders of the seventeenth century, proud of their recently won independence. Although so close to reality there is nothing photographic about this interior. The figures are painted with a remarkable feeling for space and serenity.

FORMAL HARMONY

In Vermeer's Lady Seated at the Virginals (National Gallery) an everyday scene is organized into a formal harmony of cool colour. The masterly design is based upon angles formed by the picture-frame and the various parts of the stringed instrument and upon the interplay of textures, the gilt of the frame, the marbled wood of the virginals, and the rich silk of the dress.

painted, both of individuals and groups of persons. The Civic Guards, who had been so successful in fighting the Spaniards, continued to forgather for annual parades and banquets, when there was no more fighting for them to do, and many of them clubbed together to have their portraits painted in large groups. Frans Hals (1580-1666) has commemorated the jovial spirit of these gatherings in the splendid series of portrait groups at Haarlem. In these compositions the figures are so placed that each is equally visible and each head is an individualized portrait.

IMAGINATIVE INTERPRETATION

Rembrandt Van Ryn (1606-69) treats similar subjects in an entirely different way. His famous Night Watch is a dramatic scene in which some of the figures are strongly illuminated while others are lost in shadow. This imaginative interpretation of the subject failed to comply with the requirements of the Dutch burghers; it was refused and the artist was eventually ruined financially. Rembrandt stands apart from all other Dutch painters in the quality of his imagination, and in his refusal to compromise with the ideals of his time he is the forerunner of the nineteenth-century painters who believed that the purpose of a picture was the expression of the artist's personal reactions as an individual. Whether he paints portraits or religious subjects, Rembrandt is always concerned with his personal thought and feelings. His biblical pictures could never have been regarded as the expression of official religion like those of his Spanish and Italian contemporaries. The essential characteristics of Rembrandt's art are his broad treatment and his unique system of illumination, whereby his forms emerge full of life and emotion, from the mystery of the deepest shadows blended by imperceptible gradations with the most brilliant light.

In France the pomp and dignity of the reign of Louis XIV had been superseded by the elegance and gaiety of the court of Louis XV.

The minor Dutch masters of the seventeenth century were popular among some Parisian collectors of this time, but their pictures were generally considered boorish and the scenes they represented too sober for French taste.

The painter who in all probability gave the most perfect expression to the spirit of the early eighteenth century was Antoine Watteau (1684-1721). Born in Valenciennes, of Flemish extraction, he was influenced to begin with by Flemish painters, though his mature work is French in the delicacy and charm of mood in his paintings of *fêtes galantes*, some of which are in the Wallace Collection.

The humbler aspects of French life were recorded in the eighteenth century by Jean Baptiste Chardin (1699-1779), as they had been in the preceding century by the Le Nain brothers. Chardin was a painter in love with his medium, who could evoke beauty out of the most ordinary object, such as a bottle of wine, a loaf of bread, or his own paintbox.

In contrast with Chardin are the painters François Boucher (1703-70) and Jean Honoré Fragonard (1732-1806). Both of these painters produced the elegant pastorals which were so much to the taste of the court. Boucher, director of the Gobelin factory, was also largely responsible for setting the style of design in textiles and porcelain. Fragonard, who was a pupil of Boucher (and for a time of Chardin), is noted not only for idylls like the famous Swing (page 92), but for his landscapes and later for scenes extolling domestic virtue.

NATIVE SCHOOL

The eighteenth century marks the beginning of a truly native school of painting in England. While Boucher was designing tapestry for La Pompadour, William Hogarth (1697-1764) was painting his narrative and strongly realistic series of pictures such as Marriage à la Mode (page 97), and The Rake's Progress. He was a moralist of a harsh and satiric kind, but a fine portraitist also and a wonderful master of technique.

Hogarth had begun his career with small conversation pieces (portraits of groups and individuals where background and

PAINTING OF THE VENETIAN SCHOOL

Tiziano Vecellio (1477-1576), better known as Titian, was one of the greatest of the Venetian school of painters. He is remarkable particularly for his colourful and sensitive rendering of flesh and the human form. As William Hazlitt wrote: "Not only do his heads seem to think—his bodies seem to feel." Noli Me Tangere (Touch Me Not), representing Christ with Mary Magdalen, is now in the National Gallery.

SEVENTEENTH-CENTURY DUTCH DOMESTIC LIFE
When Jan Vermeer van Delft (1632-75) was practising in Holland, artists'
work was more in demand among the newly risen merchant classes than,
as formerly, by the Church; consequently pictures which recorded daily
life, portraits, landscapes and domestic scenes were popular. Vermeer's
preference for lemon-yellow and blue of all shades is clearly discernible
in the Lady Standing at the Virginals (National Gallery).

EIGHTEENTH-CENTURY ENGLISH PAINTING

William Hogarth (1697-1764) may be said to have originated a truly native school of English painting. Although better known for his great series of narrative pictures, The Harlot's Progress, The Rake's Progress, and Marriage à la Mode, Hogarth had considerable success as a portrait painter. He painted many portraits of individuals or groups in congenial surroundings, a type of picture known as a conversation piece. This lively group of The Graham Children (National Gallery) is a charming example.

ENGLISH LANDSCAPE PAINTING

Early in the nineteenth century English landscape painting reached its finest achievement. The scene which inspired John Constable (1776-1837) to paint his Cottage in a Cornfield (Victoria and Albert Museum) can still be visited; it lies a short distance from where the artist was born at East Bergholt on the Manningtree Road in Suffolk.

TWO ASPECTS OF EIGHTEENTH-CENTURY SOCIETY

Boucher accepted the lighthearted gaiety of court life in rococo France. His contemporary, Hogarth, bitterly condemned the licentious state of English middle-class society in a series of paintings such as the celebrated *Marriage à la Mode*, one picture of which is shown below.

LANDSCAPE AS AN INDEPENDENT ART

Landscape first became an independent art in the seventeenth century. Hobbema's Avenue, above, is not only a faithful picture of the Dutch countryside, the artist has made a superb composition of the scraggy trees, enriching the idea of the perspective by the plantation of miniature trees on the right. In Rubens's vast landscape below, The Château de Steen, the movement of the foreground is offset by the verticals of the castle and by the quiet spaciousness and recession of the distance.

REALISTIC LANDSCAPE

In his earlier finished landscapes like Flatford Mill, in the National Gallery, Constable was in all probability much influenced by the realism of the Dutch School, while he knew and admired Rubens's Château de Steen, at that time in the collection of Sir George Beaumont. The keynote of Constable's work is his passion for nature.

setting were designed to play their part in the revelation of character). These were distinguished from the Dutch genre pictures by their lively and personal quality. His example was followed by a number of painters who had become aware of the dramatic possibilities of contemporary life, the most interesting being Joseph Highmore (1698-1780), Arthur Devis (1711-87) and Johann Zoffany (1733-1810). Another and peculiarly English tradition, which grew up at the same time as the conversation piece, was the art of sporting and animal painting. Among English sporting artists, the more important were John Wootton (1678-1765) and George

Morland (1763-1804), while George Stubbs (1724-1806) ranks among the greatest animal painters of the world.

Hogarth was followed by a generation of remarkable portrait painters, among whom Sir Joshua Reynolds (1723-92), George Romney (1734-1802) and Thomas Gainsborough (1727-88) were pre-eminent. Reynolds, despite his attempts to adopt an Italian style, immortalized the highly polished aristocracy which sat to him. He was first President of the Royal Academy and placed English painting on a solid professional basis. Like Reynolds, Gainsborough painted the fashionable people of the time, surpassing

EARLY ENGLISH LANDSCAPE

Extremely sensitive to the beauty of nature, Richard Wilson's talents were influenced by a lengthy sojourn in Italy and by the picturesque conventions of his day. When he forgot the Roman landscape and the work of Claude and painted his native Wales in the manner of this exquisite picture of Cader Idris, he achieved a most moving breadth and simplicity. Gainsborough, like Wilson, was prevented by circumstances from realizing his genius for naturalistic landscape. The stretch of Suffolk countryside behind Mr. and Mrs. Andrews, below opposite, shows something of the influence of Dutch painting, but the expression of the electric quality of the light in East Anglia is entirely original. John Crome, whose massive Slate Quarries is reproduced at top on the facing page, was not diverted from his true bent by either Italianate influences or the demands of society for portraiture. He creates a powerful spatial design by means of large masses and alternate light and dark planes.

him, however, in purely artistic qualities, in the grace and spontaneity of his art.

In his early work, such as Cornard Wood and Mr. and Mrs. Andrews, Gainsborough shows a most delicate perception of the beauties of his native Suffolk. His style, though stamped with his own originality and poetic feeling, is based on the homely realism of the Dutch tradition, which also influenced John

Crome (1768-1831), the leader of a group of landscape painters known as the Norwich School. Richard Wilson (1714-82) was inspired by Claude and his visit to Italy, but among his best landscapes are those of his native Wales, broadly painted and full of a grave and contemplative poetry. With the work of John Constable (1776-1837) and Joseph M. W. Turner (1775-1851), English landscape

LANDSCAPE COMPOSITION

*Turner has more feeling for picture-making than for Nature herself.
Crossing the Brook, in the National Gallery, shown above, is recognizable
as a view near Weir Head, Tamar, but it is more interesting as a composition than as an interpretation of nature. The figures are mere ornaments
and do not form part of the spirit of the countryside like the man adjusting
the tow-rope and the boy on the horse in Flatford Mill; and the trees on
the left do not look as if they were actually painted direct from nature.*

CONSTABLE, FORERUNNER OF IMPRESSIONISM

This small panel, from the Victoria and Albert Museum, painted about 1814, has all the elements of French Impressionism. Painted on the spot, it has the "light, dews, breezes, bloom and freshness" of nature, which were Constable's avowed aims and became characteristic of his work.

reached in the early nineteenth century its finest and most original achievement. Turner painted in both oil and water colour. Water colour drawing was a distinctively English contribution to the arts, which developed in the eighteenth century, fostered by collectors who made the grand tour and wanted records of their travels. Among a generation of gifted topographers, the most notable were Francis Towne (1740-1816), Alexander Cozens (working 1746), and his son, John Robert Cozens (1752-97). Turner, Thomas Girtin (1775-1802) and John Sell Cotman (1782-1842), who all began as topographical draughtsmen, developed the medium of water colour and used it with delicacy, magnificent breadth and decision.

In Spain, where French fashions had been introduced by the Bourbon dynasty, Francisco Goya (1746-1828) recorded the social life of his day in a series of cartoons for tapestries, preserved in the Prado. Some of his vigorous, realistic portraits reveal, consciously or unconsciously, a satirical outlook on the corrupt society of Spain. In a powerful and terrifying series of etchings, he depicted the horrors of the Peninsular War, and in another series of prints—Caprices, as he called them— satire is linked with fantastic imagination.

The French Revolution and the subsequent Napoleonic wars swept away a large part of the society which had previously encouraged the arts and the continuity of style in Europe was broken.

Test Yourself

1. How far is the character of Dutch painting the result of conditions in Holland during the seventeenth century?
2. Describe some of the ways in which the problem of portraiture can be approached.
3. Give a short account of the development of landscape as an independent art.

Answers will be found at the end of the book

SELF PORTRAIT

The self portrait, where there is no obligation to flatter the sitter, gives the painter a unique opportunity; but few artists can resist the temptation to sympathize with themselves in their portraits. Rembrandt must have painted himself more frequently than any other artist; his penetration, his keen and impersonal observation in front of his own image are extremely rare. In this moving picture of himself in the National Gallery, painted in old age, he is so absorbed in truthfully rendering outward appearances, that it is a tragic face which emerges from the canvas.

Frans Hals did not search the depths of character, but met the demands of the Dutch for pleasing likenesses, as in the Lady with a Fan (National Gallery), by interpreting a momentary expression in a bold, robust style.

REYNOLDS AND THE EUROPEAN TRADITION

In both his painting and in his famous Discourses, Reynolds attempted to bring British art into line with the great European traditions as it had been elaborated by the Italians. Like the Lely opposite, The Age of Innocence (National Gallery), is conceived in the grand manner, a manner, however, which is at variance with the subject of the picture, and gives it a false note. The charm with which the child's head is painted gives the portrait an air of unaffected dignity.

FOREIGN INFLUENCE IN ENGLISH PAINTING

A native style was slow to develop in English painting. Sir Peter Lely was of Dutch origin and came to England in 1641, where Van Dyck had been working since 1632. Lely's romantic portrait of Cowley (Dulwich Gallery) with a shepherd's pipe shows the influence of the Flemish and the Italian masters in the painting of the hands and drapery and in the shadowy landscape. It has no psychological subtlety and reveals little of the sitter's personality, but it is a fine composition with plastic qualities.

107

UNCOMMISSIONED PORTRAITS

When Hogarth forgot his social and moral aims he showed an intense delight in painting for its own sake. In contrast to Mrs. Siddons, opposite, The Shrimp Girl, in the National Gallery, was painted solely for the artist's pleasure. It is a sparkling and vivacious study.

FASHIONABLE PORTRAITS

Gainsborough, a landscape painter by inclination, was compelled by circumstance to paint portraits of the fashionable people of his time. Though it has not much depth of feeling, this picture of the celebrated Mrs. Siddons provides an example of his refined distinction.

INDEPENDENT SPIRIT

Edouard Manet was one of the most distinguished rebels against the French nineteenth-century academicians, who were still tied to Classic and Romantic traditions. La Serveuse de Bock is a fine example of his highly individual art. Broadly and directly painted, with a strong pattern of light and dark, the subject is taken from everyday life.

110

CHAPTER VIII

ART AND THE INDIVIDUAL

IN the nineteenth century the relations of the artist to his public underwent a radical change. Hitherto, he had worked for religious bodies, for the State itself, and for the "society within a society" of the aristocracy. In the nineteenth century a new order had arisen. The *bourgeoisie* or middle class, with whom the artist had no established relations, was now dominant.

COMMENT AND CRITICISM

Exhibitions seen by a wider circle than hitherto were important. After the fall of Napoleon the annual *salons* became the central point of focus in French art, while in England it was an essential condition of success to attract attention at the annual exhibition of the Academy. The practice of holding exhibitions and the growth of the Press both led to increased public comment and criticism. But though critics specializing in the visual arts now began to appear and many of them were distinguished men of letters, their judgment was often as temperamental and erratic as that of the general public. Most original artists had to face intense hostility from the Press and public opinion alike. In the early days of the French *salons*, the famous encyclopædist, Diderot, extolled the insipid sentimentality of Jean Baptiste Greuze (1725-1805) at the expense of the far greater painters Fragonard and Boucher, and in the nineteenth century the Romantic, pre-Raphaelite, Realist and Impressionist movements were all violently attacked and came to be accepted only when some more "outrageous" development diverted the attention of the critics.

INDIVIDUAL EXPRESSION

On the other hand, since definite commissions could no longer be relied on, the necessity of painting exhibition pictures often led painters to seek some sensational quality which would make their work noticed. Under the new conditions the artist was no longer a necessary part of the social organization. The old system of apprenticeship had collapsed and artists were trained in academies and art schools. This resulted in a much greater individual freedom in both choice of subject and mode of execution, which, though justified from a certain point of view, meant that the artist was regarded as an isolated unit and that painting was more and more withdrawn from the common world.

When the last phase of new classicism, known as Empire in France and Regency in England, had spent itself, it was followed by a series of short-lived revivals and hybrid combinations, culminating in the glut of ornament we know as Victorianism. The Gothic Revival, with its various ramifications, pre-Raphaelitism and similar movements on the Continent, were forms of escape from the ugliness and materialism of the Industrial Revolution. They were semi-literary movements often associated with a religious revival. The French Impressionists, on the other hand, were concerned only with visual appearance, regarding the play of light on everyday objects and scenes as of greater importance than the subject itself.

EFFECT OF THE CAMERA

By the middle of the nineteenth century the camera had made its appearance. This had a twofold effect upon serious artists. They attempted either to rival the photograph or to achieve what was impossible to the camera. Thus, the Impressionists emphasized colour, as yet unattainable in photography. Later painters have deliberately departed from "photographic detail" and attempted to make their pictures expressive of their own personal feelings.

In England the attempt to define the scope of painting in such a way as to differentiate it altogether from the photograph was made by Whistler, an American

FRENCH ROMANTICISM

*The Death of Sardanapalus was exhibited by Delacroix in the Salon of 1827,
the year of Victor Hugo's famous Preface to Cromwell which formulated
the doctrines of the French Romantics. That Delacroix has much in common
with Hugo can be seen in his love of Oriental subjects and in the temperament
expressed by the tumultuous rhythm of this composition.*

who had studied in Paris. He became a champion of "Art for Art's sake." In his own energetic and lively way he preached the subordination of subject matter in favour of Symphonies, Harmonies or Arrangements. Academic artists regarded him as an impostor, and Ruskin accused him of "flinging a pot of paint in the face of the public."

Throughout this period, Paris remained the artistic capital, as Rome had been in an earlier age, though English landscape painting was an important influence on European art.

Landscape, like genre painting, can be traced back to the illuminations of medieval manuscripts, where it was introduced as a background to figure subjects. In pictures of the sixteenth century figures were often of secondary importance, and in the following century pure landscape began to be recognized as a legitimate theme for a painting. In China it had been practised at a far earlier date as a means of expressing a religious mood or the relation of man to the universe.

The development of English landscape in the eighteenth century was outlined in the previous chapter. Of the two outstanding figures of the nineteenth century, Constable's importance lies in the vigorous originality of his style, his entirely fresh interpretation of the English countryside, his impassioned rendering of the moods of

REACTION AGAINST ROMANTICISM

Courbet, whose *Burial at Ornans* is reproduced above, and Daumier, the painter of the *Third-Class Railway Carriage* below, both reacted against the romanticism of painters like Delacroix and endeavoured to express the reality of modern life, without in any way, however, attempting to represent nature as with the eye of the camera. The *Burial at Ornans* is harshly painted and has a bold, elemental character emphasized by the abrupt lights and darks. Daumier is equally realistic and less photographic. He suggests all the atmosphere of the railway carriage and its occupants in a simple, terse manner by using large areas of light and dark and an almost monochrome palette, and by admitting no unessential detail.

IMPRESSION OF MOVEMENT

Turner's later works are almost all studies of light, atmosphere and fleeting impressions. Rain, Steam and Speed (National Gallery), painted in 1844, a remarkable feat of visual memory, is an impression of the effect of the swift movement of a train through driving rain. The structure and solidity of all objects are sacrificed to the achievement of that impression.

nature in south and eastern England, while Turner's significance consists in the new ways he found to paint light in all its immense range of effect.

The works of these English painters created a sensation when they became known in France; they were like a breath of fresh air in the artificial atmosphere of neo-classicism.

CLASSICAL PAINTERS

The chief classical painters were Louis David (1748-1825) and Jean-Dominique Ingres (1780-1867). The serenity of their art and their tendency to apply rigid canons derived from the past were unsuited to the expression of the individualism that was one of the characteristics of the century. Thus, David's principles of art

were attacked by leaders of the Romantic school, Théodore Géricault (1791-1824) and Eugène Delacroix (1799-1863). They wished to make art passionate and emotional. They tended to choose subjects which offered a wild character from the Middle Ages or the Orient, instead of from classical antiquity, and they used rich colours, strong effects of light and shade and violent rhythms. They admired Rubens, the Venetians, Constable and Turner. The impression made by Constable on Delacroix created an exciting moment in the history of European painting.

One result of the Romantic Movement in France was the rise of a new school of landscape painting known as the Barbizon school, because many of its members established themselves in a village of that

114

name in the forest of Fontainebleau. The Barbizon landscapes, like Constable's small sketches, were painted on the spot. Théodore Rousseau (1812-67) and Charles Daubigny (1817-78) were among the masters of the school, but the most outstanding of them was Jean Baptiste Corot (1796-1875) a poet painter of exquisite sensibility. Jean François Millet (1814-75), another of the Barbizon school, preached the dignity of peasant labour, while Constantine Meunier (1831-1905), a Belgian and the Millet of sculpture, emphasized the effects of physical labour in his figures of miners and artisans.

Romanticism was quickly superseded by Realism—which marked an abandon-ment of motives taken from the past and a determination to look at contemporary life. While in England the pre-Raphaelites were trying to revive the technical methods and spiritual outlook of the fifteenth-century painters, in France the realists, led by Gustave Courbet (1819-77) whose grim Burial at Ornans was once said to be "the funeral of Romanticism," prepared the way for the Impressionists. Edouard Manet (1833-84) is a link between the two schools, which indeed had much in common. Impressionists had no use for literary subjects or for elaborately reconstructed historical scenes. They were interested in the visual world around them, even when it was crude, harsh or ugly.

IMPRESSION OF LIGHT

Turner expressed light by using a thick pigment with some broken colour rather smoothly applied. In Claude Monet's Summer, the effect of shimmering light is produced by streaks and dabs of pigment so accurately placed that shapes are suggested. That the rough surface of the paint catches the light can be seen in the reproduction.

THREE ROMANTICS

*Géricault, Corot and Millet were all part of the French Romantic Movement.
Théodore Géricault, who, with Delacroix, was one of the leaders of the
opposition to the classicists David and Ingres, harboured a fatal passion
for horses, for he died as the result of a riding accident. His own turbulent
spirit looks out from the rolling eye of the storm-stricken creature he
paints with such mastery. Millet and Corot are less obviously romantic.
They represent the new attitude towards nature and peasant life which
was a by-product of Romanticism. Both were among the first in France
to carry painting from the studio to the fields. The composition of Corot's
Bridge at Mantes is as carefully constructed as a Poussin. Millet senti-
mentalized the peasants, who were the chief subjects of his painting, but
The Woodsawyers is a magnificent composition and as realistic in its
approach as a Dutch genre picture or a Courbet.*

Manet learnt much from the Spanish masters, Goya and Velasquez, and it was only in his later work that he turned, like his friends Claude Monet (1840-1926) and Pierre Renoir (1841-1919), to the painting of open-air effects. These painters sacrificed academic composition and conventional detail in order to capture the brilliance of sunlight, and they tried to reproduce the diffused effect of a whole scene, when embraced in a momentary glance, instead of examining each object separately. Other Impressionist painters were Alfred Sisley (1840-99), Camille Pissarro (1830-1903)

METHOD KNOWN AS POINTILLISM

This picture by Georges Seurat is painted in tiny roundish dots of equal size arranged with mathematical precision to give an illusion of light, form and pattern; a slow, difficult undertaking, as disciplined as the Impressionistic method is spontaneous.

and Berthe Morisot (1840-95). By the end of the nineteenth century, however, this new Impressionist method of painting had spread to every country in Europe and America. In France there was a galaxy of great masters, each of whom brought a personal contribution to modern art. Edgar Degas (1834-1917) was fascinated not by the play of light but by the unpremeditated gestures of everyday life and painted the momentary poses of ballet dancers, racehorses and laundresses, combining a calculated design with the impression of something casually seen. Renoir made use of the Impressionist palette to express his absorbing interest in the human figure, his sheer delight in unaffected feminine

charm. Georges Seurat (1859-91) invented a new technique of painting in dots of pure colour and worked out an elaborate analysis of the emotional value of lines and colours. Paul Cézanne (1834-1906) realized the danger of allowing painting to become so much absorbed in the pursuit of transient effects of atmosphere that it lost in substance. As a precaution, he therefore attempted to solve the problem of representing the solidity of objects by the control of colour alone. A satirical viewpoint, a passion for observing life and wonderful skill as a draughtsman are the characteristics of Toulouse-Lautrec (1864-1901) the pictorial interpreter of the cafés and dance-halls of Montmartre. The

DESIGN AND THE CASUAL MOMENT

Both Degas, in the ballet scene above, and Renoir in *Le Moulin de la Galette* record a casual moment, but neither is a copy of objective vision. In the Renoir, the diverse elements are united; with Degas, on the other hand, the dancers are but incidents in a balanced composition.

CHARACTERISTICS OF PRE-RAPHAELITE DRAWING

Two aspects of pre-Raphaelitism are shown here. In Ford Madox Brown's work, a photographic view of Heath Street, Hampstead, is seen that extraordinary desire to record life with the accuracy of the camera which was the result of a violent reaction against the mawkish sentiment and unreality into which English painting had degenerated, and due also to the invention of photography. No detail of the scene is omitted, however extraneous to the main theme. Rossetti's passionately felt and equally detailed drawing on the left springs from a romantic love of the Middle Ages which was characteristic of part of the pre-Raphaelite movement.

Dutchman, Vincent van Gogh (1853-90), after absorbing all the new ideas and aims of the Impressionist circle in Paris, poured out the ecstasy and anguish of his troubled spirit in a series of vibrating canvases inspired by his brief sojourn in the south of France. Here, until their temperaments hopelessly clashed he worked with Paul Gauguin (1848-1903) who also had lived among the Impressionists in Paris. Gauguin ended his days in the South Sea Islands, living among the natives and painting not only people themselves in their tropical setting, but his interpretation of their primitive character. He revived the principles of decorative composition, painting large areas of smooth, flat, rich colour.

Realism and Impressionism had an influence on sculpture as well as on paint-ing, suggesting new subjects and freer treatment. The practice of working in clay, and of leaving the execution of the marble to skilled carvers became general; versions of the same model were often reproduced both in marble and in bronze without regard to the necessity of designing for a specific material.

Auguste Rodin (1840-1917), the outstanding sculptor of the nineteenth century, carried to extremes the expression of movement and of emotion by means of broad generalization of form. The first reaction against his "impressionism" was a return to considerations of solidity rather than of surface.

In a sense this may well be called a return to classical principles, but instead of copying the outward form of the classical

NATURE AND GEOMETRIC FORM

Nothing could be further removed from pre-Raphaelite painting than the Mont Sainte Victoire by Cézanne, from which everything extraneous has been eliminated. Forms, their mass, solidity and relation to each other are expressed with an economy of detail which reduces them to something almost geometric: "Everything in nature adheres to the cone, the cylinder and the cube," as Cézanne once remarked.

DECORATIVE FLOWER PAINTING BY FRENCH ARTISTS

The flowerpiece on the opposite page was painted by Ignace Henri Fantin-Latour (1836-1904) when he was thirty years old. He is at his best in studies of still-life, usually showing a simple vase of flowers against a neutral background. In this picture the flowers have been painted with sensitive precision, though it is mainly by the richness of his colour orchestrations and the quality of the pigment itself that he achieves enduring charm. The flowerpiece below was painted by Paul Gauguin (1848-1903), who, though a contemporary of Fantin-Latour, was very different in his approach. He was concerned less with the effect of light and the impression of three-dimensional form—with the portrayal of the natural appearance of his subject-matter—than with colourful pattern. He, more than any other artist, severed all connexion with ties and responsibilities of life in his search for complete individual freedom. Strindberg wrote to him: ". . . you are a man who takes pleasure in the antipathy you excite, so anxious are you to keep your personality untouched."

masterpieces, modern sculptors try to grasp their inner structure, to observe the laws of balance and proportion and, above all, to attain stability. Another feature of modern work has been the sculptor's insistence on direct carving as opposed to Rodin's practice of working largely in clay. This in its turn led to experiment with different kinds of material—the different textures of stone, wood and metal suggesting different kinds of treatment.

New influences came to bear on modern art. The study of medieval, archaic, oriental and savage art greatly enlarged the repertory of form and led to an emphasis on the mode of treatment rather than on the thing represented. The aim of modern sculpture is to reject the psychological element, which played a great part in Rodin's work, and to seek beauty of form for its own sake. Instead of aiming at reproducing natural forms, the sculptor creates shapes that are pleasing in themselves and fit into their architectural setting.

Test Yourself

1. How did the relations of artist and public in the nineteenth century differ from those which had obtained in previous ages?
2. What was the effect of the camera upon painting?
3. What were the aims of the Impressionists?
4. Compare the work of Cézanne and Seurat.

Answers will be found at the end of the book

PAINTING MOONLIGHT USING JAPANESE COLOUR-PRINT TECHNIQUE

Whistler achieves the rare effect of moonlight in Battersea Bridge (Tate Gallery) by using a subdued and narrow range of colour.

VAN GOGH AND THE JAPANESE PRINT
Japanese colour prints also impressed Van Gogh. In this Self Portrait their influence is apparent in the effect of emphatic, nervous line and silhouette.

MASK-LIKE SELF PORTRAIT

Cézanne's portrait of himself, painted about 1900 and now in the Tate Gallery, has a mask-like quality; every trace of psychology and feeling has been eliminated. It is not indeed a portrait in the ordinary sense: the painter's own head means no more to him than an apple in his search for solidity and structure and his concentration on the minutest details of colour relation.

AN IMPERSONAL ATTITUDE

Degas's *Self Portrait* (National Gallery) discloses as little of himself as that of Cézanne on the opposite page, though for different reasons. Degas reveals nothing of himself, humorously choosing a pose as fleeting as if caught by the camera. Cézanne strives for new means of expression; except for the dress Degas's portrait might be by a Renaissance painter.

SATIRICAL PORTRAIT

    The coarse, solemn features of the Dancer from Montmartre (Tate Gallery),
her frowziness and air of boredom are tersely and caustically recorded by
Toulouse-Lautrec and rendered more striking by the contrast afforded by
the foliage and the suggestion of the open air in the background. The
unusual viewpoint and the harsh linear quality of the painting suggest the
probable influence of the Japanese colour print.

MODELLING BY MEANS OF COLOUR

Before Paul Cézanne (1839-1906), painters rendered form by interpreting the light and shade of an object in varying tones of the same colour. For example, the mountains of Raphael (facing page 80) are simple masses of light and dark blue. Cézanne sensed that shadows were composed of colours rather than mere tone. The mountain in this picture of Mont St. Victoire retains its form although painted in a variety of pure colours.

FOST-IMPRESSIONIST PAINTING

Vincent van Gogh (1853-90) was a Dutch painter of the post-Impressionist school; he worked for much of his life in France. Dissatisfied with the limitations of the Impressionists he sought to secure more personal and vivid representation by distorting to some extent the forms of Nature. This picture of Suresnes (private collection) seems at first glance to have been painted in a rush of impetuosity. The canvas has been covered thickly in dots and streaks with fierce energetic strokes, but the buildings have been drawn with the utmost care.

COLOUR IN THE JAPANESE PRINT
The subject of this coloured woodcut, the Interior of a Saki Shop, by Utamaro
(1753-1806) is a scene from contemporary everyday life of the Japanese
people. It is now in the Victoria and Albert Museum.

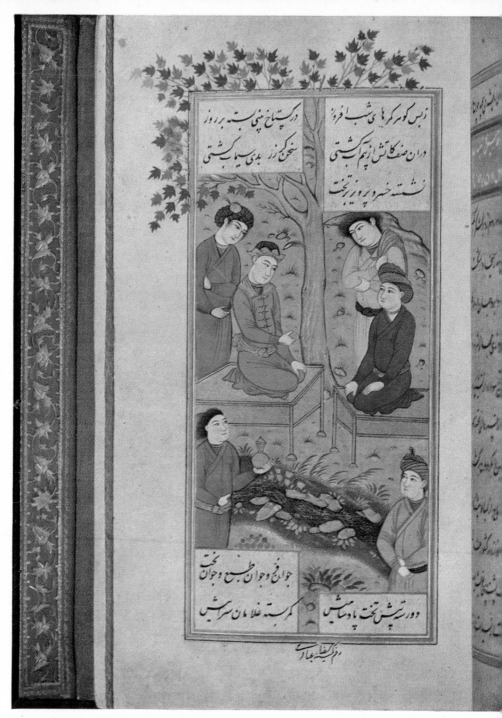

PERSIAN MINIATURE PAINTING

Remarkable wealth of detail is introduced into this miniature painted by Bihzad (c. 1440-1520) as an illustration to a poem by the famous twelfth-century poet Nazami. Bihzad is the greatest master of Persian painting.

CHAPTER IX

THE WIDENING HORIZON: ORIENTAL AND PRIMITIVE ART

EACH new development of creative art brings with it a new orientation towards the past. In the last half-century, in particular, there has been an immense expansion in the appreciation of art. Oriental art has become more widely known and more justly appreciated, while the high æsthetic quality of primitive art has been recognized within the last fifty years.

The Venetian traveller, Marco Polo, found his way to China as far back as the thirteenth century and ever since then European traders have been bringing goods from the Far East, including some works of art, which were much admired and imitated in Europe. Chinese lacquer, porcelain and embroidery have been familiar in Europe for the last three centuries, and Chinese designs were copied to such an extent that the word "chinoiserie" was coined to describe the fashionable style of the eighteenth century.

IN CHINA

Nevertheless, Chinese art was not for a long time taken very seriously in Europe. The Chinese and Japanese were admired for their exquisite craftsmanship and their fantastic and playful ornament, but little was known about their painting and sculpture. It was only after the first Japanese prints found their way into the studios of Paris in the second half of the nineteenth century that the real nature of oriental art began to be understood. Since then, the East, from Central Asia to Japan, has been a field of great discoveries.

We now know that Chinese civilization is more than four thousand years old. The Chinese sense of form can be seen in one of the earliest and most characteristic expressions of the race, the ancient sacrificial bronze vessels, often decorated with monster masks and sometimes made in the shape of birds and animals. They were probably used in the rites of ancestor worship.

Sculpture in China before the advent of Buddhism was connected with the service of the dead. Stone sculpture decorated the tombs which were often guarded by stone lions or chimerical figures, while tomb chambers were ornamented with reliefs representing processions of horsemen and chariots. Buddhism was brought to China by missionaries who had gradually been establishing their monasteries farther and farther eastwards, especially in eastern Turkestan, which was a Chinese protectorate. Here in the first century A.D. the religion of India fuses with the culture of China.

At first a Greek type was used to represent the Buddha and from about 50 B.C. to c. A.D. 500 a vast quantity of sculpture was produced in the local greystone. A fixed series of incidents from the life of the Buddha became current (Birth, Departure, Temptation, Enlightenment, Great Miracle, Sermon, Death) and single images were carved in high-relief. Artistically this Greco-Buddhist sculpture is inferior to the best Indian or Chinese work.

During the first century A.D. when northern China was ruled by the Wei Tartars, many cave temples were excavated and carved with colossal figures of Buddhas and the Bodhisattvas. Many of them show a remarkable elongation, not unlike European Gothic figures.

In the T'ang Dynasty (A.D. 618-907), a golden age in all the arts, Chinese sculpture reached the highest point in development. Work on the cave temples was continued and many Buddhist figures were produced, and also some secular figures of animals guarding tombs. The contours of the figures are rounded, the faces have a gentle

PAINTING CLOSELY CONNECTED WITH CALLIGRAPHY

The graceful signature forms part of the design in this sensitive painting of a bamboo shoot. Chinese calligraphy and painting were indeed intimately connected: the same brushes, inks and silks or paper were used for both, and both were characterized by the same simplification and abstraction.

beatific expression, they are surrounded by circular or flame-shaped haloes, richly carved. The folds of garments tend towards naturalism, though the sculptors never surrendered their traditional ideal of conventional, abstract form.

The casting of images in bronze continued to be practised. It was a field in which the Chinese had been skilful from remote antiquity. Glazed pottery was also used for large as well as small figures, and

quantities of terra-cotta figures have been found in tombs. These are very lively in movement and illustrate every aspect of Chinese life, soldiers, women, dancers, polo-players, horses and all the animals of a farmyard. The pliability of clay lends itself to such vivid naturalism, and these Chinese tomb figures have been often compared with Greek Tanagra statuettes.

During the Sung Dynasty (960-1280) painting was the supreme art, and sculpture

LANDSCAPE AND THE HUMAN FIGURE

*Whereas in European painting landscape was for centuries
subordinated to the human interest, the reverse was true of
Chinese art.   This Ming painting is a typical example.*

131

CHINESE INFLUENCE IN EUROPEAN ART

Chinese art was brought by traders to Europe early in the eighteenth century and the Chinese designs were freely copied. Of the many imitations those made at Delft were among the most successful; the plate with the exotic Chinese flower-and-bird design is characteristic.

gradually declined, though carvings in ivory, jade and various semi-precious stones continued to be made, showing all the invention and skill of the Chinese craftsmen.

It is, however, in painting that China possesses most interest for the West. The greatest painters in China were poets, philosophers or priests and a literary education was common to them all. Painting was thus closely allied to calligraphy.

PHILOSOPHY AND ART

Since Chinese writing was always done with a brush and was really a pictorial script, the Chinese painters enjoyed unique facility and relied on brushwork and tone far more than on colour (p. 130). Their paintings were usually on silk or paper, though the Chinese knew and practised the art of wall painting. The artist memorized his subject, sometimes selecting only a tiny fragment of natural appearance —a branch of plum blossom or a reed of bamboo—instead of trying to represent everything he saw in nature. For this reason he omitted anything that appeared to him too obvious or unimportant. There are never any shadows in Chinese paintings. When European portraits were first brought to China, the Chinese asked why the Western barbarians washed only half their face—they could not understand the meaning of light and shade. Backgrounds are seldom more than slightly indicated. Balance and the value of empty space played an important part in Chinese philosophy and this is reflected in their paintings.

MAN AND NATURE

The painter as well as the poet recognized all life as a unit and celebrated in their works the essential kinship of man and nature. They were inspired not only by an intimate knowledge of nature but by a proud love for it.

"From what motive springs the love of high-minded men for landscape? In his very nature man loves to be in a garden, with hills and streams whose water makes a cheerful music as it glides among the stones. What delight does one derive

ENERGY AND CONTEMPLATION
Full of energy beneath the contemplative pose, this T'ang figure gives an impression of gravity and simplicity.

from the sight of a fisherman engaging in his leisurely occupation in a sequestered nook, or of a woodman felling a tree in a secluded spot, or of mountain scenery with sporting monkeys and cranes? Nothing is so distasteful as the bustle and turmoil of a city, and one naturally envies the lot of sages and hermits who always abide amid the beauty of nature. To meet this want artists have endeavoured to represent landscapes so that people may be able to behold the grandeur of nature without stepping

work was in wood or metal, though clay, painted and lacquered, was also used. In subject matter Japanese sculpture resembles the Chinese.

COLOUR PRINTS

A unique decorative quality appears in the Japanese colour print which reached such a high level in the eighteenth and early nineteenth centuries. It afforded a cheap means of reproducing portraits of popular actors and beauties. These were collected

CONTROLLED ENERGY

The terra-cotta horses of the T'ang period (A.D. 618-907) make an impression of controlled exuberance. They are full of life and character and tremendous energy is expressed in their movements, held in check, however, by the formal treatment of individual features such as manes and trappings.

out of their houses." Thus wrote Kuo Hsi, a Chinese landscape painter, who lived in the eleventh century.

The Japanese have always looked to China as the source of their inspiration, but as they are a more active and warlike race, their art is more dramatic and restless than that of China.

JAPANESE ART

The best Japanese painting was done in the Fujiwara period (A.D. 900-1190) and was largely secular, consisting of portraiture and variations on the social and military life of the aristocracy. The decorated screen, which served as a folding partition in the Japanese home, was a typically Japanese form of painting.

The character of Japanese sculpture was determined by the materials; there was no stone available in Japan and most of the

by their admirers just as photographs of film stars are collected today. In the work of Hokusai (1760-1849) and Hiroshige (1797-1858) landscape became a dominant theme in Japanese colour prints. These prints were not regarded as the finest art by the Japanese themselves, but their design and colour were a revelation to European painters and had a great influence on the French Impressionists.

In India the earliest surviving monuments date from the third century B.C., and are mounds commemorating Buddhist sacred rites surrounded by rails with four gates at the cardinal points. They are exact imitations in stone of the earlier wooden originals, carved with reliefs on the pillars and gates. The subjects are historical events, scenes from the life of the Buddha and illustrations of the Jatakas (stories of his previous incarnation in animal form).

In the decoration of those early Buddhist structures the characteristics of Indian ornament are already apparent—exuberance and feeling for rhythm.

Animals are treated with remarkable naturalism, winged griffins and human forms fill all the available spaces, and sometimes there are full-breasted female figures, carved in the round, swinging from the architrave of the gateways. In the earlier stupas at Bharhut and Sanchi, the Buddha does not appear in human form. His presence is symbolized by the empty throne, or the footprint. This avoidance of representation may be compared with early Christian illustration when the sacred monogram or the fish was used as a symbol for Christ. In the second century A.D. the figure of the Buddha appears in its true Indian form, seated cross-legged, forming almost a geometric triangle, a perfect symbol of composure and meditation.

BUDDHIST PAINTING

The golden age of Buddhist art in India began with the rise of the Gupta Dynasty in A.D. 320, and lasted until about A.D. 600. In spite of the Brahminical revival, Buddhists still enjoyed rich patronage. The Buddha image of this period is purely Indian in facial and bodily type. The figure has wide shoulders, a narrow waist, the limbs are almost cylindrical with no indications of bony or muscular projections. The beauty of these figures should not be judged by European standards of realism; they are attempts to represent the spiritual state to which the Buddha attained.

Buddhist painting consisted of frescoes in cave temples; it is well illustrated by the painting in the caves at Ajanta (executed first to seventh centuries A.D.). They represent scenes from contemporary court life, and are commanding in scale, monumental, rhythmic and rich in detail.

From the time of the Ajanta frescoes until the middle of the sixteenth century no Indian paintings have survived. The later paintings fall into two classes, Rajput and Mughal. Rajput painting, in some ways, seems to continue the traditions of the Ajanta frescoes; they are large in design although small in size, and portray scenes from the lives of the gods or of secular life.

When Buddhism was finally absorbed in India by the Brahminical revival, the artistic tradition spread to Ceylon, Burma, Siam, Java, Tibet, and China, and the Brahminites themselves borrowed sculptural forms from Buddhist art to represent their divinities Siva and Vishnu as in the great rock-cut temples at Ellora, Elephanta and Mamallapuram, in the seventh century, A.D.

In India it is difficult to distinguish between architecture and sculpture, as the buildings are covered all over with carving inside and out. The southern Indian temples of the medieval period (eighth to thirteenth centuries) dedicated to Siva are particularly profusely decorated. Examples are the temples at Tanjore and in the provinces of Orissa and Mysore.

The most original creation of southern India is the popular image Siva as Lord of the Dance. The finest images are in copper, cast by the *cire perdue* process (p. 255), and express the dynamic idea of movement. The idea behind the image is that when Siva danced with drum and fire he awakened the powers of nature to life. The four arms of these figures sometimes shock Europeans, but they are no more a deformity than the addition of wings, and they help to express the rhythm of the dance.

PERSIAN ART

Reference has already been made to the rise of Mohammedan art. This spread throughout the Near East to Persia and India. The ban on figure representation was gradually relaxed and a delightful school of illumination arose in Persia. The Persians love gardens, and their painters often depicted the fountains and canals with which they watered their dry land, and the whiteness of fruit blossom against the dark green of a cypress tree. The pages of their books are filled with battle and hunting scenes, flowers, feasting and romance. Like the Chinese, the Persians never painted shadows nor had they any knowledge of perspective, but they used the most brilliant colours and often painted

the sky gold to suggest the dazzle of sunlight.

When the Moghuls conquered India they brought Persian painters with them, and these gradually trained native Indian artists to work in the court style. Indian miniatures are, as a rule, more realistic than the Persian ones; the artists excelled in portraits and absorbed a certain amount of European influence.

The discovery of Eastern art led to further exploration. It was found that native American art had certain similarities with Far Eastern forms. Objects of strange beauty were discovered in the Pacific islands, objects of everyday use made of wood, bone or shell, richly decorative and sometimes symbolic.

At the beginning of the present century, Negro art was discovered by artists in Paris, and became as fashionable as Japanese art had been earlier. Negroes worked mainly in wood and to a limited extent in metal, as in the celebrated bronze figures of Benin. Negro carvings have little to do with the imitation of natural appearances, they are three-dimensional, based upon a cylindrical mass of summary form. They are of superb craftsmanship and striking in their vitality. Study of this form of art, which may be called primitive, like the study of Eastern art has encouraged the twentieth-century artist to disregard "photographic" imitations of nature, and to separate emotional expression from the elevated ideas and types once thought indispensable.

INFLUENCE OF NEGRO ART

If the head by Picasso, on the opposite page, is compared with the sculpture from Africa shown on the right, it is clear that one derives much from the other. The shape of the Picasso head, the long neck, the simplification and emphasis of the features all bear witness to the influence of Negro forms. It is no copy however; it equals the African head in force and vitality.

Test Yourself

1. What was the effect upon Chinese painting of its close association with calligraphy?
2. What is the importance in the history of European art of:
   (a) the Japanese colour print, and
   (b) Negro sculpture?
3. Give some account of the character of Persian painting.

Answers will be found at the end of the book

DESIGN INFLUENCED BY COLOUR AND TEXTILES OF THE EAST

Matisse calls this picture Decorative Composition; the title is significant, for the subject matter is subordinated to design.

138

CHAPTER X

THE MODERN OUTLOOK: ABSTRACT AND REPRESENTATIONAL ART

AT the beginning of the present century the most advanced group of French painters was called in derision the "Fauves" or "wild creatures," on account of the strange distortions and unconventionality of their work. Subsequently, these men—Henri Matisse (b. 1869), André Derain (b. 1880), Maurice de Vlaminck (b. 1876), Georges Braque (b. 1882), Georges Rouault (b. 1871), Raoul Dufy (b. 1879), Othon Friesz (b. 1879), and André Segonzac (b. 1885)—became acknowledged as leading masters of French art. Their work is strong, individual, colourful, and subject matter is subordinated in favour of interest in design.

In England the influence of Impressionism produced the "New English" school, among whom the foremost were Steer and Sickert. This was followed by a vigorous group of painters led by Augustus John (b. 1875). During the First World War a number of more imaginative painters appeared, among whom Stanley Spencer (b. 1891) and Paul Nash (1889-1946) are outstanding. On the whole, English artists have shown more restraint in their experiments than some of their contemporaries on the Continent, and they usually show a particular feeling for the beauty of landscape.

Modern Russian art has had a considerable influence on Western Europe through the theatre and ballet, for which many of the best artists have designed. The exotic flavour in the works of Leon Bakst (1886-1924), Alexander Benois (b. 1870), Michael Larionov (b. 1881) and Nathalie Goncharova (b. 1881) made a great impression in Paris at the time when primitive and oriental art were becoming popular.

A recent discovery is the art of children and of untutored persons, such as the Sunday Painter, Henri Rousseau (1844-1910), who was a customs official and painted for his own pleasure when he was not playing the violin. Rousseau, despite his simplicity, had extraordinary feeling for shapes, colour and pattern. Drawings by children, primitive people and self-taught artists have a good deal in common. They generally represent imaginative conceptions instead of visual appearances, for the eye has to be trained to see the world as it is, and the hand has to be equally trained to represent what the eye sees, or what the imagination perceives. There is a fresh, naïve charm in the drawings of children before they have been taught to draw from the object, and their outlook is particularly appreciated today because it is the antithesis of the objective, photographic record.

It is important to understand the difference between representational and non-representational art, though in many works both are combined. During the Renaissance, when Vasari laid so much stress on close verisimilitude to nature, the principle that nature should be expressed in beautiful proportions and selective compositions was still implicit. The continual study of nature, especially of the human form, was pursued with the object of discovering perfection—an ideal form, such as the Greeks had sought. It was only in the nineteenth century that all other considerations were sacrificed in the pursuit of mere truth to nature with the frequent result of a very superficial realism. The appearance of abstract art was the inevitable reaction to naturalism and the camera.

Paul Cézanne (1839-1906) had declared that all natural forms could be reduced to spheres, cylinders and cubes, and this theory was developed by Pablo Picasso (b. 1881), the leader of the cubist move-

RELIGIOUS SIGNIFICANCE

To Stanley Spencer the everyday happenings of life in an English village have religious significance; it is natural to him that the Resurrection should take place in the village churchyard where he has studied every tombstone.

ment. He began with the simplification of natural forms, or variations of such forms, composed like musical variations. He then launched further into exploration in the world of pure form, unhampered by the need to associate it with recognizable organic objects or to convey specific ideas.

This aspect of modern art is not new, and may be related to the recurrent phases of geometric art in the past, such as Neolithic, Celtic, Islamic. Abstract art is far removed from the individualism of the nineteenth century; it is part of the pattern of the age which has produced skyscrapers, steel and concrete factories and aeroplanes. Here, again, there is a close relation between art and science, though the forms are naturally different. Sculpture lent itself to abstraction, and Constantin Brancusi (b. 1876), for example, began producing shapes designed simply to convey their own interest as early as 1908. In England, Henry Moore (b. 1898) and Barbara Hepworth (b. 1903) pursued abstract sculpture and Ben Nicholson (b. 1894), among others, abstract painting.

The Constructivist movement began in Moscow in 1920. Several of its exponents, later, worked in England : Naum Gabo (b. 1890), Antoine Pevsner (b. 1886),

SIMPLIFICATION OF FORM

Modigliani's treatment of human form resembles that of Botticelli.

L. Moholy-Nagy, Principal of the Chicago Institute of Design. They produced "constructions in space," composed of a variety of materials, including celluloid and metal. The American, Alexander Calder (b. 1898), produced what he called "mobiles," delicately balanced constructions of spheres and wires, which revolve in a current of air. These were almost like a kind of astronomical instrument and

MUSIC AND PAINTING

In his striking portrait of Madame Suggia (Tate Gallery) Augustus John conveys all the vigour and impetuosity of her playing. The folds in the curtain behind and the sweep of the dress echo the movement of the bow and the pleasing, flowing curves of the instrument.

again illustrate the parallel course of modern art and science. Similar tendencies may be traced in every branch of life.

Surrealism presented a complete contrast to cubism. It was a reaction to extreme individualism. It also closely linked up with modern psychological research or at least the modern state of mind. The theories of Freud, concerning the world of dreams and the subconscious, are parallel with its productions. Instead of painting the world as they saw it, the surrealists evoked visions and represented the most inconsistent combinations of objects. At the same time, they painted every detail with the minutest accuracy in order to make it as real as possible; in fact, more real than reality. This, too, is not an entirely new manifestation in art. The monsters of primitive art, the gargoyles and drolleries of the Middle Ages, the fantastic devilries painted by Bosch in the

LINKS BETWEEN FRANCE AND ENGLAND

Of all English artists Sickert had the closest connexion with French painting. The Belvedere, Bath (Tate Gallery), is treated in a free Impressionist manner, and the painter's knowledge of Degas is revealed in the linear style and in the way the frame cuts the figure of the driver of the horse and cart.

UNTUTORED ART

Henri Rousseau le Douanier was an isolated and untrained artist who painted in his spare time. This jungle scene with apes is a memory of his experience as a youth in the tropical forests of Mexico. It is a flat pattern of great aesthetic power, painted with the directness and freshness of a child.

sixteenth century, the visions of Blake and of Odilon Redon (1842-1916) belong to the same world. Modern surrealists often show a very morbid strain, a taste for decay and decomposition. Leaders of the movement were the German Max Ernst (b. 1891), the Italian Giorgio di Chirico (b. 1888) and the Spaniards Joan Miro (b. 1893) and Salvador Dali (b. 1908). Picasso has also painted in the surrealist manner at times.

Without attempting to define all the various tendencies of early twentieth-century art, which included Futurism, Vorticism, Expressionism and Dadaism, it may be said that some of them were extremely ephemeral. It must be added, however, that their existence shows the vitality, as well as illustrating the theoretical character, of the age. Even those painters who continued to work on more or less traditional lines benefited by the experiments of the pioneers.

Throughout the ages the artist has been ahead of his generation in seeing beauty and significance. Being more sensitive than the ordinary man, he may be said to have his fingers on the pulse of life. For this reason, it is just as important to appreciate the modern aims as it is to pay homage to old masters.

Test Yourself

1. What is abstract art?
2. Suggest reasons for the great divergencies in aim and outlook in twentieth-century painting.

Answers will be found at the end of the book

143

OIL ON CANVAS

This romantic head from Titian's Concert (Pitti Palace, Florence) shows
the soft, enveloping blurring and richness of tone made possible by the
use of the oil medium, especially on canvas.

CHAPTER XI

PICTURE-MAKING AND COMPOSITION

WHEN Michelangelo said, "Painting is a music and a melody which intellect only can appreciate and with great difficulty," he left us with a thought which is worth the deepest attention. The comparison is striking, and while analogies may not be pressed too far, it throws brilliant light on the subject.

Assuming that the artist has something to express which he feels with a special intensity; whatever his subject, it will be transferred to paper or canvas in terms of shapes, colours and tones. Their precise arrangement or organization within the picture is what we mean by the term composition. There are, however, great varieties and complications of pictorial expression—not always easy to grasp at first sight. To study some of the important elements of composition, and to form some broad idea of their function in picture-making, is of considerable value to all who look at pictures.

TEMPERAMENT

We look to the work of art to move us through that indefinable something we call beauty, and for most people this beauty is conceived as some aspect of Nature which the artist is especially gifted to perceive and record. It has to be expressed, however, within the confined and limited shape of the picture, in which process the artist has to make certain arbitrary decisions of selection and arrangement which vitally affect the character of his work. As a simple example, we may imagine an artist before a landscape which has given him the impulse to paint; its various features—trees, fields, buildings, hills, sky —can be placed on the canvas in an endless number of ways, while remaining strictly truthful to appearance. We can imagine other artists inspired by precisely the same scene, yet all producing quite different compositions in whose individual treat-

ment we should recognize the expression of temperamental bias or personal vision. Nature is a storehouse of rich material from which the artist freely takes what his imagination needs. (Matthew Arnold once defined art as, "Nature seen through a temperament.") This individuality is expressed through acts of selection, emphasis, suppression and arrangement which enable us to recognize the works of different artists, simply by reference to their characteristic use of certain shapes, colours and rhythms.

ORGANIZATION

We may now attempt a rough definition by saying that composition is the art of organizing shapes, colours, forms, so that they will give a moving effect to the artist's imagination. This organization is not simply a matter of clear or logical presentation, but is a sort of elemental force acting through the power of shades, colours and forms to stir us without regard to any objects they may happen to represent. Composition is the *music* of painting, and pursuing this analogy we may look for such qualities as rhythm, melodic shape, development of theme, tone contrasts and the like—to find their parallels in visual art.

MEANS OF EXPRESSION

But, it may be objected, there are so many different styles and means of expression, how are we to avoid confusion? And certainly there is nothing more sterile and confusing than judging works of art by standards at which they do not aim. It may therefore be helpful to note, very broadly, some of the main forms of pictorial art, and to distinguish the means of expression peculiar to them. The historical approach is perhaps the most convenient, and it has the advantage that we are able to proceed from the simple to the complex; from the highly conven-

BUSHMAN'S USE OF THE SILHOUETTE

There is no evidence of a deliberate, decorative purpose in this South African bushman's drawing of a cattle raid. The scene of exaggerated movement is presented in all its variety and confusion. Lucid statement is, however, given to actual appearance by the use of the silhouette.

tionalized rendering of Nature characteristic of Oriental and early Christian art, to the realism of Western painting, and so to the changes which have come about in modern art.

In Oriental and early Christian art, Nature is subjected to wilful distortions which are obvious devices of visual rhythm; and these affect us in a way that may be likened to the pleasure we derive from the movements of dancers in a ballet. Thus the folds of Buddha's garment in a Chinese work of art are clearly not realistic, but are made to flow and serve the interests of the *design*. Likewise, in medieval illuminations the folds and limbs are forced into rhythmic patterns, where the movement of line plays a vital part relative to the main shapes of the figures, and Nature is reduced to flat shapes animated by striking linear rhythms.

GROWING REALISM

Towards the close of the medieval period we find a softening of these linear rhythms and somewhat less stylized rendering of Nature, but there is still a great insistence on the value of silhouette enriched by decorative details. Composi-

tion is still mainly concerned with designing flat shapes and there is virtually no regard to light and shade or the suggestion of space and solidity.

By the beginning of the fourteenth century a new development is on the way. The objects in a picture are represented as being solid by means of light and shade; the conception of recession in space is introduced; the eye is now invited to move *into* the picture and *round* objects. Composition, while still attaching importance to silhouette and linear rhythm, is no longer solely concerned with designing flat shapes, but also becomes the art of organizing solid forms in space; it leads the eye to perceive rhythmic relations not only across the surface of the picture, but also *within* the picture.

Thereafter, and until the end of the nineteenth century, realism in painting steadily grows, and composition becomes more complex and audacious in its organization of light and shade, movement in space, colour and atmospheric suggestion. Ultimately, the preoccupation with realism tends to become an end in itself, neglecting the finer powers of imaginative design, and it is largely out of dissatisfaction with this tendency that the modern movements arise.

It will be our endeavour to show that in all of these different approaches the place of composition is fundamental. This will also help us to examine more closely what we mean when we use such terms as rhythm, balance, harmony of shape, and so on.

One of our most instinctive demands in design is the sense of balance, to which the obvious answer is symmetry; that is, the more or less exact repetition of shapes or pattern round a central point or line of axis. The Greek vase (page 47) shows a central figure flanked by two sets of similar though not identical figures, so poised that balance is maintained. The symmetry is not one of exact repetition, but these variations only serve to enliven the design. This is also an excellent example of rhythmic movement in the bold pattern of bodies, playing in angle against one another. Richness of effect is achieved through the contrast of light and dark.

BALANCE

The next step is to the freely composed asymmetrical design reproduced on page 173. By means of a subtle distribution of shapes, accents of tone and colours, balance is maintained and the eye is satisfied that no part is overweighted at the expense of the whole. And just as we follow the development of a musical phrase, noting how it re-appears in varied forms, so in the picture we see the main shapes echoed throughout the design, or given those variations of form which add richness to the work, while unity of effect is secured. One should note, too, that the distribution

EGYPTIAN DRAWING CONVENTIONS

The representation of frontal shoulders on a profile body is characteristic of Egyptian painting and appears in the figures in the top row of this banqueting scene from a Theban tomb (British Museum). In the lower section, however, two figures are shown full face, and the enchanting little slaves, one of whom is bending forward to adjust her lady's headdress, are drawn in complete profile. The usual conventions of Egyptian drawing must, therefore, have been quite conscious, voluntary and methodical.

EMPHASIS ON PATTERN

This twelfth-century English wall painting is characterized by precision in the outline of the figure, but its most striking peculiarity is the pattern of loops and whorls in the drapery and along the upper edge of the picture.

of tone (range of light to dark) and colour, accentuating different parts in varying degrees, plays an important role in achieving balance, rhythm and variation.

So far we have dealt with works conceived as designs without suggestion of solidity or recession in space; but once the artist feels the need to explore these latter possibilities, composition has to extend its scope so as to include the elements of light and shade and the sense of movement in space. We may study this by comparing the Giotto fresco (page 149) with the Fra Angelico Annunciation (page 20). The effect of the latter will depend on the highly conventionalized design of the main

148

Giotto's celebrated fresco from Assisi of St. Francis feeding the birds, shows an entirely different attitude to painting from the English wall picture on the opposite page. There the tendency is towards abstract pattern: here, on the other hand, the forms are constructed with direct reference to actual appearances, and the tendency is towards naturalism.

TECHNIQUE OF FRESCO PAINTING

In true fresco painting the pigments are mixed with water and applied to moist plaster, with which they become chemically incorporated. This means that nothing in the painting can be altered or removed, and that the work must be done with considerable rapidity. The fourteenth-century painting of the Triumph of Death by an unknown artist in the Campo Santo, Pisa, full of lively observation and intricate detail, gives some idea of the technical skill the method demands.

figure. The whole conception is flat in character, despite the slight shading of folds and other forms. Whereas in the Giotto, the figures and rocky landscape appear more solid, and seem to be standing in space, in both there is insistence on the design of large shapes, flatly considered, with echoes and rhythms of forms clearly emphasized; but in Giotto we have a new emotional effect, due to the expression of weight and depth.

SPACE-COMPOSITION

With increased knowledge of perspective, this kind of space-composition gradually affirms itself. The Fra Angelico (page 70) affords a most interesting comparison with the same subject treated by Duccio. The figures are still designed somewhat as silhouettes, but are placed in an architectural setting of depth; and this setting largely determines the serenity of the work by its simple emphasis of the verticals in the columns, the various horizontal lines, the semicircles of the arches echoed in the receding arcade. Another valuable point this work serves to bring out is that the placing of any prominent feature in a picture sets up certain divisions of space, whose proportions may be felt as bearing a harmonious relation to each other. In our example we have the various compartments set up by the verticals of the columns. Thus the choice of a horizon line, the placing of trees etc., can set up divisions of space which are given special value.

In striking contrast is the Uccello battle-piece (page 30). While in the Angelico we find peace and stability in the repose of vertical and horizontal, here, everything moves in a state of excitement and turmoil clearly expressed in the clash of direction

150

in the lances and the rhythms of the rearing horses moving across the picture in bold alternations of light and dark. Unity is maintained as between the upper and lower parts by the lines of the hills echoing those of the horses. The whole effect is enhanced by great vivacity of colour and tone contrasts.

As the representation of space is mastered, the eye is led into the picture and moves about in such a way that space is given a kind of dynamic expression. As

example, let us take the Giovanni Bellini (1429-1507) Agony in the Garden (page 168). The main statement of the picture lies on a diagonal line rising from left to right, culminating in the figure of Christ. All the figures and the rock comprised in this group are set at very decided angles to each other, giving a sense of dramatic tension. Beginning in the right foreground is a hurdle threading its way zigzag fashion into the landscape, then continuing in a jagged path, and finally released into a

151

EARLY FLEMISH OIL PAINTING

Oil painting was in use before the time of Jan van Eyck; he perfected it and made it practical. This detail from Arnolfini and His Wife (National Gallery) shows the lustrous, hard surface he obtained, probably by adding with fine hair brushes coats of glazes over a groundwork of gesso (fine plaster mixed with glue) on a panel, and the precision with which he was able to translate into his painting all the minute detail of the scene before him.

winding road leading up to the hill on the extreme right. A similar movement may be observed on the left, carrying the eye to the hill-town. Then, as if to steady so much restless tension, we have the almost horizontal lines of road and paths in the middle distance. Again, we may note the dramatic use of contrasts in light and shade and tone.

One of the greatest masters of space composition is Raphael, and it will be helpful to examine one of his important works, The School of Athens (page 26). We are first struck by the large central archway echoing the shape of the lunette. This arch stands above a flight of steps,

giving horizontal lines of support to the verticals of the background. Within this framework come the figures; first, the upper group—whose heads fall roughly into another horizontal line, and thus far greater stability is ensured.

In the foreground, established by bold squares of paving, we have two other groups in great variety of pose. Both these lower groups seem to move inwards creating a kind of hollow, leading the eye into space; two rather isolated figures set at angles help to link the two levels. The scale of the figures, in relation to the whole, also gives a sense of space, which is extended

TEMPERA PAINTING

This detail from Michelangelo's *Madonna and Child, St. John and Angels* in the National Gallery, shows a tempera painting in an unfinished state. The basis is a panel coated with gesso. The pigments in dry powder form were mixed with egg and slightly thinned, and then the design was painted in green. This underpainting is visible in the Virgin's headdress and in the head on the left. The local colours were added to the monochrome design in rather small strokes, resulting in an enamel-like surface.

WAX PAINTING

This lively Greco-Roman portrait of about A.D. 50 from the case of a mummy discovered in the Fayum, Egypt, was painted in a medium of gum-resin to which wax, emulsified by lime or some other alkali, was added. The finished painting was heated so that the wax and resin melted and formed with the colours a homogeneous surface of a most durable nature. The method which was prevalent throughout the ancient world is known as encaustic.

into the distance by receding arches. Tradition develops as each school of painting brings fresh qualities of vision; to Venice we look for richness and a sensuous delight in nature. Our example is from Titian's The Concert (page 144).

Classical composition is here enveloped in a warm glow of colour and atmosphere. All parts of the picture nestle beautifully together; the shapes of the figures—their harmony of curve and angle—find echo and variation in the landscape beyond, in the line of hill, of trees and path, and the whole is fused by broad passages of light and shade into a composition of extra-ordinary loveliness. With the Venetians the bold, dramatic use of light and shade is carried to great lengths in the work of Tintoretto. His Last Supper (page 167) —impetuous and virile though it be—is nevertheless controlled by a sense of design, in which great energy is expressed by insistence on diagonal lines. The power of composition in depth is quite astounding; figures not only move diagonally across the picture, but also inwards—by means of audacious foreshortening, as in the flying figures above.

The late sixteenth century abounds in these virtuoso flights, where every licence is taken to stir the emotions. El Greco's (1542-1614) The Burial of Count Orgaz (page 86) is a striking example of this exalted intensity, with its violent swirl of cloud, figure and drapery above—balanced by the dispositions of the group below. There is great movement and yet ultimate restraint. So, too, treating a more homely theme, Rubens shows himself a great master of the swirling composition, violent yet controlled (page 98).

During the sixteenth and seventeenth centuries, Flemish and Dutch painters gradually turn from sacred or heroic themes, to find inspiration in the everyday life about them. Jan Vermeer's (1632-75) The Artist's Studio (Czernin Gallery, Vienna) is reproduced as a frontispiece to this book but as the illustration is in monochrome it cannot convey this great artist's very personal and lovely sense of colour. It is possible, however, to appreciate the characteristically natural feeling for arrangement which contributes so much to the calm serenity of his work.

Rembrandt is one of the great exponents of composition in light and shade, and his Philosopher is an example none the less

With El Greco, who was about thirty-five when Titian died, the possibilities of oil painting are realized to an even greater degree than in the work of the Venetian master. El Greco used the actual pigment in much the same way as Van Gogh three hundred years later to express emotional intensity. This detail from the Laocoon shows the thickness of the rapid application of colour and the nervous criss-cross brush strokes.

PORTRAIT PAINTING OF VELASQUEZ

Diego Rodriguez de Silva y Velasquez (1599-1660), one of the greatest Spanish painters who ever lived, was court painter to Philip IV of Spain and painted the monarch many times. In this detail from the portrait, in the National Gallery, of the king as an old man the artist's brilliant handling of paint is immediately apparent.

The head of Christina of Denmark, from Holbein's portrait in the National Gallery, reveals an attitude entirely opposed to that of Velasquez. It is drawn rather than painted. Details such as the eyes and the ruff are carefully outlined. The head does not emerge softly from the background like that of Philip IV, but forms a flat pattern against it.

striking because it is very simple (page 176). Notice how breadth is given by the diagonal descent of light across the picture and how the small figure cutting sharply into the light holds attention in spite of the surrounding dark masses.

In Spain, Velasquez combines court portraiture with the exploitation of the fascinating possibilities of light and shade, space and movement (page 87); while his French contemporaries, Poussin and Claude, were perfecting the classical landscape and figure composition.

But if composition can be rich in emotional appeal, it can also decline into a cold, scholarly imitation of classical art.

The rigid convention resulting was approved by official *salons* at the beginning of the nineteenth century, such remote and pompous painting was out of touch with the teeming energy of the age. In England and France there came a vigorous revival of landscape painting and of an interest in simple everyday life.

This mood of realism developed at last into an excessive concern for accuracy of appearance to the neglect of composition. And though Impressionism, in the '70s did achieve a real breadth of approach in its intense feeling for vibrant colour, light and atmosphere, nevertheless, in aiming at this freshness of impression it tended to

SPONTANIETY AND BRILLIANCE

In this brilliant detail from Lawrence's Queen Charlotte (National Gallery) the effect is gained, almost fortuitously, by the spontaneous, impetuous handling of the pigment. The filmy folds in the muslin dress, the glittering jewels, have not been carefully studied, they are suggested by a rapidly manipulated impasto (i.e. laying colours on thickly) which, where it is particularly thick, imprisons the sparkle of light.

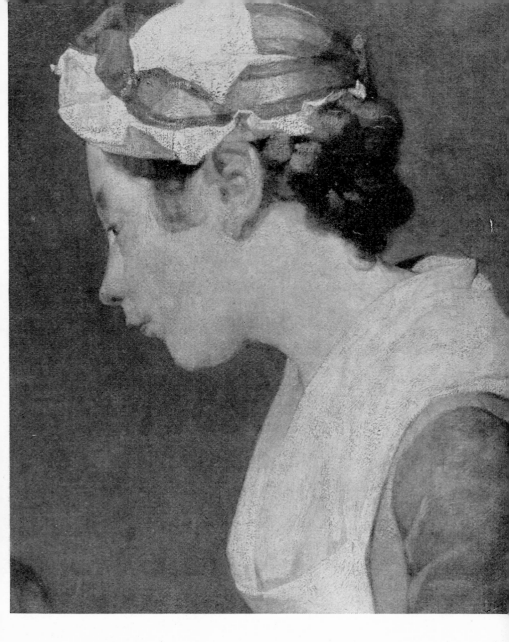

CARE AND DELIBERATION

The delightful head of the little girl by Chardin from *The Lesson* (*National Gallery*), is painted in a quite different manner from the Lawrence on the opposite page. It is the result of sober deliberation. The hand of Queen Charlotte will not bear close scrutiny; it is wooden, weak in construction. Every detail in the Chardin—the ribbons on the cap, the ear, the curve of the chin, the folds in the sleeve—is painted with the utmost care and with regard for its place in the whole design.

neglect the form in which it was expressed.

Towards the end of the nineteenth century came the reaction. The artist still finds his subject-matter in ordinary, every-day scenes, but now he is concerned to transform what might be called photo-graphic appearance into shapes and colours; and these he subjects to a more or less arbitrary conception of design. While not ignoring Nature, he seeks to extract from it those visual elements on which his imagination can play, and to create a work which is enjoyed for *itself*, valid in its own world of forms.

In the Degas (page 164), an ordinary subject is transformed into a most carefully contrived design. By deliberate placing and simplification, he unites the shapes of the woman combing her hair with those of the servant bringing coffee, on which is imposed the contour of the vase, echoed again in the patterns of the table. If this is still realism, it is of a kind powerfully dominated by the artist's will to design.

And it is not long before the artist takes the next step. Contact with Nature is still essential for Cézanne; its colour and forms give spur to his imagination. But when these are transposed to canvas, they assume an independent existence of shape and colour on which the artist imposes his will. The sensation set up in his mind by the actual group of objects goes beyond their literal appearance; and to express this, Cézanne simplifies geometrically the shapes of the original forms where the interests of his composition demand it.

Again for Van Gogh, Nature was recognizably the starting point, inspiring the artist to a lyrical intensity expressed through the rhythmic shapes of trees, hills and clouds. Similarly, Gauguin regarded the figures in his paintings as shapes in a bold design.

The painting by Seurat (page 30) shows a most interesting treatment of natural appearance, in which an everyday scene is transformed into a very closely articulated design. The large figures on the extreme right set the note: the contour of the woman's back and bustle skirt, the arc of the parasol, are echoed in different ways right across the picture. Every feature—figure, animal, tree, shadow—is simplified and reduced to its essential function as a shape very deliberately placed in the picture.

FREEDOM IN EXPRESSION

Finally, we reach a point where the artist creates freely, without any aim of naturalis-tic representation. For example, in paint-ings by Picasso, the suggested snatches, or distortions, of recognizable objects have no significance other than through their value as shape and colour. To adapt or distort Nature is not necessarily to be regarded as an act of sedition undermining law and order, but simply as the freedom to create what we have called the music of painting.

One last point, by way of conclusion: in dwelling so closely on the value of composition, it is not suggested that the associations of subject matter should be ignored. Painting, like literature, is an art of complex appeal; nevertheless, the vital task for the artist remains to express himself in that special form, that "music and melody," without which the art of painting remains incomplete.

Test Yourself

1. Attempt, with a few examples, a rough definition of composition.
2. Compare the rendering of The Annunciation by Duccio (facing page 64) and Fra Angelico (page 20).
3. Analyse the composition of The Last Supper by Tintoretto (page 167) and Agony in the Garden by Giovanni Bellini (page 168).
4. Differentiate between the painterly and the linear approach in art, giving examples.
5. What is the difference in technique between van Eyck's Arnolfini and His Wife (facing page 65) and Titian's Concert (page 144)?

Answers will be found at the end of the book

RICHNESS IN REMBRANDT'S PORTRAITURE

So penetrating is the portrayal of character in portraits by Rembrandt van Ryn (1606-69), the great artist of the Dutch school, that the richness and subtlety of his colour is apt to be overlooked. His *Portrait of a Woman* (National Gallery), painted about 1666, is a fine example of the mellowness of colour and technique he developed in later life.

RENOIR'S USE OF COLOUR
Auguste Renoir (1841-1919) is sometimes included amongst the Impressionists but in Les Parapluies, in the National Gallery, he displays a feeling for composition in colour quite foreign to painters like Monet and Sisley.

CHAPTER XII

THE PAINTER'S
MATERIALS AND METHODS

THE researches of archæologists and anthropologists, together with evidence to be found in ancient buildings and in collections of works of art, lead us to conclude that the mediums and pigments used today are in many respects as they have been throughout the ages. It is a debatable point whether, in his efforts either to create or imitate objects of interest, carving or drawing and painting was man's first means of expression.

Primitive man, like young children today, probably first scribbled or scratched mental images, and this he would naturally do with flint or bone on the rock face or with his finger in the sand.

If we go back for evidence thousands of years, to the Aurignacian period some twenty thousand to thirty thousand years ago, we find drawings of animals scratched upon bone, carved in stone and upon rocks, and astonishingly well drawn and painted animals scattered upon the walls of caves. The most notable of the cave paintings are those found at Altamira, in Spain, and in the Dordogne. The recent discovery of the primitive work of bushmen in South Africa by Professor Leo Frobenius and others (page 146) confirms the fact that primitive man of today is still using the same materials as his ancient ancestors.

EARLY COLOURS

His pigments were coloured earths and vegetable juices. Those that have survived the test of time are the earth colours and black. The earth colours were white, yellow and a reddish brown; black was obtained from burnt wood and bone. Marrow was used as a medium with which to apply them and the use of urine has been traced by one authority.

The silhouette—one of the earliest forms of expression—was followed by drawing

in a single colour, red earth; and this by the use of a red, black and white. To these colours brown and yellow were added at a later stage. Shells and the blade bones of animals were used as palettes. No evidence has been discovered that brushes were used by primitive man. There is little doubt, however, that a flat bone was used as a spatula to spread the paint and that free use was made of the fingers and thumb.

When considering methods and materials used in the ancient world, thoughts turn naturally to the art of Egypt: rich evidence of the work of this period has been discovered and preserved.

EGYPTIAN DISCOVERIES

A knowledge of the methods and materials used by Egyptian painters spread to Assyria, Babylonia, Persia, India and the Far East. In Europe it influenced first the work of Greek artists and through them spread to Rome and to other parts of Europe. It is true to say that even today we owe much of our knowledge to the discoveries made by the ancient Egyptian. The Egyptians discovered mediums with which to apply and to bind colour to canvas, wood, mortar and stone. They mixed their colours with gums, size, honey, milk, egg and wax. For wall paintings they mixed their pigments in water and applied them direct on to the wet lime surface from which their wall plaster was made. This method, later named fresco, the Italian word for fresh, has been used throughout the centuries and is still unrivalled for its durability.

The Egyptians used seven colours, mostly mineral in origin—red, yellow, brown, green, black, white and a blue-green. Their paintings, which are still fresh and vivid in colour, are formalized in style (page 147), no attempt, for instance,

WATER-COLOUR ART
   Cotman's Study of Trees shows how the medium of water colour should be used. It is painted in untouched, flat washes of colour.

being made to foreshorten objects or figures represented.

Relative importance is given by greater or lesser proportions, just as young children still do in their drawings and paintings.

Painting and sculpture were developed at the same time through the colouring of both low relief and sculpture. The actual or local colour of figures and objects was painted in a flat wash and no attempt made to represent form other than by the use of an incised outline with a rounded edge. Women, for example, were painted yellow and men brown.

EVIDENCE FROM THE PAST

Recent discoveries have informed us that colours were made in cakes, kept in bags made of skin or in hollowed reeds. Palettes made of pottery in various shapes have been found and also brushes made of reeds.

Of Greek painting, little trace survives. For our knowledge of the methods and materials used we are indebted to descriptions and writings that have been discovered and to the paintings found on contemporary pottery.

The perfection of Greek sculpture, which was brilliantly coloured, provides evidence of a profound knowledge of form, craftsmanship and draughtsmanship. We know that the Greeks, like the Egyptians, worked in distemper and fresco. Their methods of expression, however, differed considerably. For example, the outlines of their figures were not incised but drawn with a brush and filled in with colour. The earliest examples are silhouettes painted in black. These were followed by objects and figures outlined in black and filled in with local colour in a manner similar to the Egyptian paintings. Women were painted in white, however, instead of yellow. Few colours were used—only white, yellow, red, black, and a dull green produced by mixing yellow and black. The Greeks, by burning ivory, gave us ivory black, and by subliming together sulphur and mercury produced

FINISHED PICTURE IN WATER COLOUR

In The Ploughed Field, John Sell Cotman (1782-1842) achieved a finished picture in monochrome, a method the old masters used chiefly for making rapid sketches and notes of light and shade. By developing his technique of direct washes he retains the charm and freshness of this medium.

LINEAR DESIGN IN PASTEL

The chalky texture of pastel is admirably suited to the strong linear design which underlies all Degas's seeming informality. Here the servant's head is cut off as in a snapshot, but this enables the artist to concentrate on the line of the arm which carries the eye along the line made by the arms and head of the central figure. The vase is cut in two by the edge of the picture, but the remaining contour is stressed to echo the pattern on the tablecloth and the curves of the figures on the vase.

vermilion. Unlike the Egyptian, the Greek painters broke away from the silhouette and introduced foreshortening into their work.

We are told by Greek historians that Zeuxis (420-390 B.C.) painted in grisaille; that is, the representation of form in tones of one colour, grey. He developed from this method the *camaieu*, a painting in two tints, an imitation of the cameo or bas-relief, a monochrome in one on a background of another. Early Greek painting in monochrome is the first known attempt by the painter to represent form on a two-dimensional surface: this resulted from attempts to represent the effect of light and shade upon objects, a method subsequently described by Italians by the term chiaroscuro. We also learn from their historians that Apelles introduced the painting of form in colour. Apelles (fourth century B.C.) himself has left evidence that the process of fresco painting was known to the Greeks and that panels were painted and afterwards fixed to walls as decorations.

Encaustic painting was also practised in Greece from the Alexandrian period. This method of painting is recorded, although the process is not described. It is known, however, that wax and pigments were mixed and applied heated; they were then blended and modelled with heated irons. Portraits of the dead or mummy cases survive from the Greco-Roman period in Egypt and were carried out by this method.

ROMAN PAINTING

Roman art was copied from Greek art and consequently lacked its vitality; it retained, however, its character. Roman painting is, therefore, a means by which we can appraise that of the Greeks. The fine examples of Roman painting found buried under the lava of Vesuvius at Herculaneum and Pompeii are vigorous and full of light, with a rich variety of colour. We learn from the writings of Pliny that the Romans introduced many new and bright colours to the artist's palette, notably pure purple.

The methods and materials used by the Greek painters and their classical style of painting united to a Roman tendency to realism, influenced the form which European art of the Middle Ages was finally to take.

Early Christian art found in the Catacombs carried on the classical tradition. The recognition of the Christian religion by the Emperor Constantine in the year 312 led to the decoration of churches with religious subjects.

These decorations were executed in tempera fresco and mosaic. When considering the methods and materials used by the painter in the Middle Ages, the influence of the Byzantine mosaics on the Italian painters of the Middle Ages whom we call Primitives cannot be overlooked. These mosaics were patterns and pictures made by cementing together small cubes (called tesseræ) cut from many brightly coloured materials such as coloured glass, some with gold in it. The word Primitive as here used should not be confused with the word used previously in connexion with work of primitive man at the beginning

of this chapter. It is used here to denote work of a pioneer character; in this instance, the Italian school at the time of Duccio of Siena, Cimabue and Giotto. Two methods were then used by the artist, tempera and fresco.

The use of gold, copied from the work of the mosaic artists, was extensive; it was used not only as a background to subject matter, but as a ground to paint on by both the Italian Primitives and the Flemish, German and Russian artists of the same period. Mention should also be made here of the wealth and vitality of English twelfth-century wall-painting (page 148), probably derived from Greek and Roman painting, so fully described by Professor E. W. Tristram in his book, *Treasure Trove*.

Cennino Cennini, a painter who lived in the fifteenth century, describes contemporary methods used in fresco and tempera painting in a treatise entitled *Trattato della Pittura*. The exact date of the discovery of the use of oil as a medium for painting is not known, although the use of vegetable drying oil was first described in a fifth-century manuscript. Vasari claims that the process was invented by the Van Eycks in 1410, and that the medium was probably perfected by them.

FRESCOES

Oil painting sprang into immediate favour in the north of Italy, whilst the painters in the south continued to use tempera and fresco. New light was thrown on methods used in fresco painting during the Middle Ages by an examination of the damage done, during the retreat of the Germans through Italy, to the famous frescoes by Orcagna, Gozzoli and others in the Campo Santo of Pisa (page 150).

In the earliest examples of oil paintings flat oil glazes of local colours of the same tone were spread over a monochrome painted in tempera in which the drawing and the modelling of form was first completed.

Vasari also records in his writings that Arezzo, who lived in the thirteenth century, was the inventor of painting on canvas; but we know that the Egyptians made use of canvas as a ground, which they first

SIGNIFICANCE OF DETAIL

In Botticelli's Primavera, painted about 1478 for Lorenzo di Pier Francesco de' Medici, the central figure of Venus dominates the composition; but our attention is also attracted by the three Graces, by Mercury, by the figure of Spring wafted by Zephyrus, by Flora or by the myriads of exquisite leaves and flowers. The magical effect of the whole does not depend upon any of the usual devices of composition. It springs from the intensity with which every detail has been painted; each one is significant.

covered with plaster, for the decorations of sarcophagi.

The colours used in the Middle Ages differ little from those used latterly in the ancient world, a notable exception being ultramarine, a deep rich blue much favoured for its beauty and permanence. It was made from lapis lazuli. The colours in use were the earth pigments, yellow and red ochre, raw and burnt sienna, Venetian and Indian red, terre-verte, raw and burnt umber and, in addition, vermilion, orpine, cinnabar, malachite, verdigris, whiting and white lead, charcoal and ivory black. Colours were made by the artist in his studio and kept in bladders or jars, in different tones of each colour. The use of gesso, a plaster composition, for ornament in relief and attempts to represent relief in painting are said to have led to the dis-

covery of the science of perspective by Paolo Uccello (1397-1475). Whether he should be given such credit is debatable, although his work shows that he was absorbed by its study. The method favoured during the fourteenth and fifteenth centuries of using an underpainting, a monochrome usually in grey or brown, led to a close study of painting in light and shade. Leonardo da Vinci, in his *Treatise on Painting*, gives useful information on the aims of the painter in his day. He says, "The first aim of the painter is to make it appear that a round body in relief is presented upon the flat surface of his picture." Although many of the secrets of the methods of the Van Eycks have been lost, it seems probable from the writings of Cennini that they painted in oil colours mixed with varnish over a tempera monochrome, the transitional method between tempera and oil painting (page 152). This method was introduced into Italy by Antonello de Messina. During the fifteenth century, Cennini mentions that oil painting of a similar nature was practised in Germany at the same time and he advocated glazing in oil over tempera. The work of the Flemish painters, following the traditions of the Van Eycks, was noted for its fine craftsmanship and durability. Guilds of master painters were set up which insisted upon the use of materials of good quality and durability. Their work was linked with the work of the painters of the Netherlands, Italy and Spain.

During the fifteenth century, white grounds gave place to coloured primings. Titian, for example, used red. The fresco masterpieces of Michelangelo and the fine craftsmanship of such painters as Raphael for some time influenced and imposed restraint upon methods of oil painting, but this medium, less dependent upon careful preparations, encouraged painters to draw direct inspirations from Nature and attempt to copy her varying colours and effects. Towards their close, at the end of the fifteenth century, the Middle Ages included not only the period when the craft was perfected, but the most creative years in the history of painting.

DUTCH PORTRAIT PAINTERS

Although the Flemish and Dutch schools worked in close physical proximity, the two schools were very different in outlook. Instead of concentrating upon religious subjects, the Dutch became a school of genre and portrait painters exemplified by such great masters as Vermeer and Rembrandt. They followed the early methods of the Flemish school and research has shown that they developed them in much the same way, although little written evidence has come down to us.

RELIGIOUS PAINTING OF THE VENETIAN SCHOOL

The son of a Venetian dyer, Jacopo Robusti (1518-94) is better known by his nickname " The Little Dyer," Tintoretto. One of the greatest painters of the Venetian school and a man of phenomenal energy, he painted a large number of religious subjects. The dramatic rendering of The Last Supper is enhanced by startling contrasts of light and dark.

SPACE AND VOLUME

In The Agony in the Garden (National Gallery) Bellini creates an impression of space and volume by the sculpturesque treatment of the figures and by the S-shapes winding into the background, balanced by the verticals of tree, rock and far-off tower, and by the straight lines in the middle distance.

The painting by Vermeer of himself at work in his studio (frontispiece) is enlightening and is evidence that he used on occasion the alla prima method—that is, direct painting in colour.

The practice of oil painting and its unsuitability for direct mural painting led to the use of canvas specially primed for the purpose which allowed the artist to work in his studio. This practice in turn started the painting of easel pictures. The oil medium freed the artist from the restrictive method of tempera and fresco painting when he ceased to work over a tempera underpainting; alterations could be freely made in the medium and consequently liberties were taken with the craft. In addition to this, the use of oil led to the introduction of varnishes to preserve the richness and depth of newly finished work. The full possibilities of the medium were first exploited by such masters of oil painting as Rubens, Van Dyck and Rembrandt van Ryn, who often used a rich impasto—i.e. application of thick layers of paint—instead of working in the traditional method; that is, on a tracing of a carefully prepared cartoon. Rembrandt, trained to work in the careful manner of the Van Eycks, strayed further from traditional ties by making alterations by means of glazing and using his palette knife impulsively as well as his brush.

PERSONAL TREATMENT

The practice of composing pictures in oil colours encouraged the artist in a personal method of treatment. The earlier manner which advanced methodically from the carefully considered cartoon to the monochrome and final full-colour effect required the artist first to visualize his subject, then through well-defined stages to keep in view the original aim until the desired result was obtained. Between the Flemish and Dutch and the Spanish schools lay that of France, which had no effective existence until the seventeenth century. It followed the methods, however, of the oil painters of Northern Italy. French art at this time was a mere copy, and consequently showed a lack of initiative. Drawing was lifeless and painting was influenced by the red and brown tones of old masters.

ACCOMPLISHED TECHNIQUE

During the eighteenth century, when portrait painting became the vogue, however, French painters were obliged to reproduce faithfully the colour of their sitters and thus the prejudice against true colour was overcome. Their respect for the work of such masters of portraiture as Rubens, Rembrandt and Velasquez (page 156), particularly for their brilliant technique, led to a striving for accomplish-ment in brushwork for its own sake. The smooth character of classical painting gave place to loaded and uneven impasto, painted in a warm-coloured monochrome and subsequently glazed with transparent colour, after the manner of the Venetian school. Connoisseurs of the time looked for accomplished technique rather than good design, form and colour in art, consequently painting became comparable with the artificial display of rhetoric. Although pastel, the art of "painting" in coloured chalks, was invented during the seventeenth century, it was first made popular by the French artist, Chardin, who, nonetheless, also painted brilliantly in oils (page 159). Not only did the oil painter copy the broken spots of pure bright

LIGHT AND RECESSION

The Classical buildings in Claude's Seaport are a framework for the opening through which we are carried beyond the romantic tower and the moored vessel into infinite recessions of luminous space. The light is most intensely concentrated on the distant horizon and thence radiates throughout the picture uniting all the various parts of the subject.

CHARACTER AND TECHNIQUE

The most striking thing about this Chinese Polo Match (Victoria and Albert Museum) is the amount of expression achieved by a limited means. There is no background, no shading and little colour. The sense of structure and movement, the liveliness in the faces and gestures are conveyed by a sure, unfaltering use of line. The character of the work depends on the technique. The figures are painted with a brush in Chinese ink on silk, the same materials being used for writing, itself a linear art requiring a skill only attained after long and untiring practice.

colours, but imitated the broken colour and soft effects which are characteristic of work in pastel. Another noteworthy influence upon the painters' materials at this time was the imitating in oils of the soft shades of the tapestry weavers' yarns, which added greys, pinks and lilacs to the painters' colour range. Pastel shades became the vogue in painting and led to the use of gouache, a body colour, a mixture of water colour and white. Gouache was the medium used by the illuminators of oriental manuscripts and in the missals of the Middle Ages.

During the eighteenth century, various experiments were made in painting and there was a danger of the value of craftsmanship being almost ignored. Towards the end of this century the English painter, Reynolds (1723-92), after studying art in

Italy, advocated the study of traditional methods, although the present state of his work suggests that he failed to discover many of the secrets of the old masters. One of the most destructive materials used in his time in an effort to obtain the warm mellow tone of their work was bitumen. For many years artists had ceased to make their own colours and relied upon colour manufacturers for their supply, without inquiring into the nature of the colours or their permanence. They were supplied in skin bags. Tin-tacks were used to pierce them when colour was required and to seal them after use. Colour so packed quickly dried, and because of this failing an Englishman invented in 1824 the tin tubes which are in use today.

Eugêne Delacroix (1798-1863) led a revolt against traditional methods. Hi spirited method of painting often relied upon completing it in one sitting, a method of hit or miss which does not permit of either the careful thought or preparation associated with sound craftsmanship.

FRENCH IMPRESSIONISTS

Contemporary with Delacroix lived the English painter, Joseph M. W. Turner (1775-1851), who at first worked in the classic manner of Claude Lorraine (1600-82). He became in turn the inspirer of the French impressionist school. Turner began his career as a water-colour painter and developed this medium by substituting mineral for vegetable pigments. This change led to the transparent quality of water-colour painting, a quality for which the English school of water colour is famous. The technique used by Turner for oil painting was unsound. His worship of sunlight led to the extensive use of chrome yellow. This fugitive colour and the lack of knowledge of his craft will lead in time to the destruction of much of his work.

The French impressionist school—led by Claude Monet, a landscape painter, and Edouard Manet, a figure painter—towards the close of the nineteenth century, finally cast aside the old traditional formulas and painted Nature as they saw it. The Impressionists became somewhat obsessed with the broken colour effects in Nature and made the rendering of them their principal aim. By closely observing and analysing the rich variety of colour to be found in sunlight and shadow, they concluded that these could not be represented by flat washes of colour alone. They found that by placing small areas of pure unmixed colour side by side, a truer effect could be obtained, when viewed from the correct focal distance. The debt owed to these two painters and their followers for this discovery is now acknowledged.

An historical survey of this kind would not be complete without a mention of the pre-Raphaelite Brotherhood, whose work stands out of the dull level of the unsound craftsmanship of the nineteenth century (page 120). Their passion for detail led them to study the work of the Flemish and Italian Primitives and to admire their craftsmanship. Their method of procedure was as follows: On a hard, stone-like ground made of a mixture of white lead and copal varnish, the passage to be painted was drawn. This was covered with a thin coat of white paint, from which all superfluous oil had been extracted and to which a drop of copal varnish had been added. Through this thin coat the drawing could be seen. Over this wet ground the colours, transparent and semi-transparent, were laid with a sable brush, care being taken not to disturb but to blend colours with the ground. The absence of cracking and the well-sustained brightness of the colours is a testimony to the soundness of their method. It has been pointed out that since the introduction of oil paint as a medium, there has been a growing tendency to neglect the study of materials and the craft of painting. This, together with the regrettable practice of varnishing pictures for exhibition purposes before they are thoroughly dry, will inevitably lead to the destruction of many paintings produced since this practice has obtained.

MODES OF EXPRESSION

Finally, it should be said that selected materials can be obtained from reliable colour manufacturers today that are as permanent as any used by the old masters. It is to be hoped, therefore, that artists will return to the study of their materials and craft and so produce works in the future that will compare favourably with those produced by the old masters, and will, with them, stand the test of time.

Having broadly indicated the history of the artists' means of expression, let us now look a little more closely at the qualities which give us pleasure in each.

Drawing and painting have a common feature in that they both provide the artist with a free and flowing mode of expression. They differ, however, in that drawing is executed in a hard substance and painting in a fluid mixture.

Painting has drawing for its foundation, but it is a combination of three elements—sound drawing, design and colour.

Of the various methods of painting already mentioned in the order of their discovery in the preceding historical survey —distemper, fresco, tempera, encaustic, oil tempera, oil painting, pastel, gouache, water colour—each has a characteristic quality of its own. The following descriptions of the materials used and the method of their application will help to distinguish them.

INTERIOR DECORATION

Distemper may be said to be the earliest medium used by civilized man. The term should not be confused with the French word *détrempe*, which is used to describe both distemper and tempera. Distemper is made by mixing coloured powder or pigment with a solution of gum or size and water.

The amount of size or gum-arabic used is sufficient to fix the colour when dry. Too much of either will cause the paint to crack and flake away from the ground. The tones of distemper in the wet and dry states differ considerably. Distemper, when dry, is much lighter in tone. It is rarely used today for picture-making, but is still used for some forms of interior decoration and for scene painting. The use of caseine as a fixative for distemper paint is a modern discovery. When it is used in solution with pigment, the distemper dries almost the same tone as when it is wet.

Fresco, a method of painting in pigment mixed with water, direct on to wet plaster, was discovered by the ancient Egyptians. They found that by allowing the carbonate of lime in the plaster to crystallize by combining with the carbonic acid gas in the air, a lasting and perfect binding was made. This method, which has been used throughout the centuries, has been found unsuitable for use in Britain owing to the damp climate and harmful fumes in the air of modern cities. Earth colours only are suitable for fresco. As the painting has to be completed while the plaster is wet, the work has to be done in sections. In old frescoes it is possible to recognize the joints of the sections of the work completed by the artist each day.

Tempera, a kind of distemper, was used almost universally in Italy during the Middle Ages. The excellent condition of the tone and colour of pictures painted during this period is proof of its lasting quality.

The pigment is mixed with an egg medium instead of size. The medium, an emulsion, is made of yolk of egg mixed with water and vinegar; the latter is added to prevent decay. An equal quantity of this emulsion and pigment is generally used, but the correct amount of each colour to medium can be measured only through experience.

Tempera painting differs considerably in appearance according to the priming over which it is painted. It can be used to produce an opaque or transparent effect, consequently it is often difficult to distinguish it from either fresco or oil painting, particularly from oil painting when tempera is varnished with white of egg or polished.

In encaustic or wax painting, pigment and wax are mixed and applied whilst warm to a panel of wood. For this method of painting, the palette is made of metal, which is also kept warm. Heated irons are used to blend the colours and produce the effect of form. Encaustic painting was extensively practised in the ancient world and is very durable.

This particular process is laborious and difficult and in consequence rarely used today. It has the rich appearance and range of tone of oil painting and the advantage of being impervious to damp, the chief enemy of all other forms of painting.

TEMPERA PAINTING

Oil tempera, a transitional method between tempera and oil painting, was the method mainly practised towards the end of the Middle Ages. The foundations of oil tempera painting were usually laid in a tempera monochrome in grey, terre-verte, or a warm tone such as brown or red, and completed in colour by glazes of a pigment mixed with oil.

Because of the opaque and lasting quality of the underpainting in tempera, it can often be seen, particularly when alterations have been made in the overpainting, through the pigments ground in oil, which becomes more translucent with time. The name given to these faults or corrections is "pentimento," the Italian word for repentance.

Oil painting is the most popular method of painting today. Although the technique, which has already been described, has varied considerably, the materials used have varied little in character since the method was first invented. Oil paints are made from pigments ground with either poppy or linseed oil. The direct method of painting in colour, known as alla prima, as opposed to painting over a monotone

with glazes and scumbles is almost universally practised today. The procedure is as follows:—

A canvas which has already been primed —that is, covered with a mixture of white lead and oil—is purchased either in roll form or attached to a wooden frame called a stretcher. Wooden panels are sometimes used, but are apt to warp or split.

The subject is first drawn in charcoal, in outline or tone; the drawing is then fixed, to prevent it from rubbing or mixing with the paint, by means of a spray diffuser.

ARRANGEMENT IN GREY AND BLACK

This is the title Whistler gave to the portrait of his mother reproduced below. It was a protest against the realistic, anecdotal painting of his day, and emphasized his predominant interest in pattern and tone. The use of black and neutral colours reveals the influence of Velasquez, while in details such as the picture frame cut off by the edge of the picture, Whistler has much in common with Degas.

PAINTING ENTERS THE SPHERE OF ARCHITECTURE

In this ceiling decoration by Tiepolo the illusionistic effect observed in the fresco by Signorelli (on page 67), is carried to extremes.

174

The fixative used is made from shellac dissolved in methylated spirit. If the painting is to be finished at a sitting, the medium or vehicle used with the paint is sometimes a mixture of turpentine, oil and varnish in equal proportions. Reference to other mediums used will be made at a later stage in this book.

The medium used for first stages of a more protracted work is turpentine, which dries with a flat surface. Before proceeding with the painting between each stage, therefore, it is necessary to give the surface a thin coat of linseed oil, a process known as "oiling out," to restore the richness and true tones of the colours and to blend and fix them with fresh coats of paint. The finished work, when thoroughly dry, is given a coat of varnish to which is added, as occasion demands, transparent colour to enrich the darker passages.

OPAQUE PAINTING

Pastel is a form of opaque painting done with a crayon (page 164). The crayon is made from a coloured powder mixed with an agglutinant of pipe-clay or gum dissolved in water. There are three kinds of pastel—hard, medium and soft. Pastel drawings are made on a coarse tinted paper which provides a tooth to hold the powder and a middle tone of colour suitable to the subjects concerned. Great care has to be taken with the handling of a pastel on account of its fragility, as a pastel cannot be fixed without a consequent loss of colour and tone.

For this reason, therefore, pastels are generally mounted on a wooden stretcher with a woollen shock absorber placed between the stretcher and the frame.

Gouache is a form of body colour paint made from a mixture of pigment and gum-arabic. There is little difference between gouache and distemper. The former is coloured pigment and white used on paper and the latter for wall decoration.

Gouache painting can be traced back to the ancient Egyptians, but was most popular for picture-making in the eighteenth century. Paintings in this medium are light in tone and have a pastel effect. When used today it is generally made from a mixture of water colour and Chinese white. Water colour shares the popularity of oil paint in modern practice. Watercolour paints are made of pigment ground in gum-arabic, which is a vegetable gum soluble in water, obtained from the acacia arabica. The gum, which is very durable, forms a means of attaching the pigment to paper. In the past water colour was prepared only in cake form and a little honey was added to keep it moist. Cakes are still used but there is a more general demand for water colour in a moister condition. It is packed for convenience in pans and tubes and the artist's colourman uses glycerine as a medium. The modern form of preparation has the unfortunate tendency to attract moisture, which attacks the water-colour paper. The paper used is specially prepared and of high quality; the best being a rag paper prepared from linen fibre to which a little size is added. Size prevents the pigments from soaking into the paper, instead of staining and retaining its transparency on the surface.

In the purest form of water-colour painting the white of the paper is preserved and used to give the lightest tones. There is a tendency today, however, to use Chinese white to obtain the highlights. The English painter has excelled in the water-colour medium and the reader is referred to the work of the Norwich school—to Cotman in particular—for examples of water-colour painting in its purest form (pages 162 and 163).

Although all forms of wall decoration are, in fact, mural paintings, the term is usually applied to modern forms. It has already been pointed out that fresco is an unsuitable method for use in northern climes and modern cities. Experiments have, therefore, been made with other media. Perhaps the most successful has been the use of oil paint used direct on to canvas which is afterwards fixed to the wall.

Although the latter type are executed in the studio, the aims in a mural painting differ from those of an easel picture. A mural painting should not have the effect of piercing the wall by representing distance realistically, but whilst enriching and decorating it should preserve the plane of

LIGHT AS A MEANS OF EXPRESSION

Light is Rembrandt's basic means of expression. In The Philosopher (National Gallery) he has developed its possibilities superbly. There is little doubt that in this respect he was deeply impressed, and to some extent influenced, by the dramatic effects of light and shade which were first developed in Italy by Caravaggio and conveyed to Holland by travelling Dutch artists.

176

the wall. The most noted mural painter of modern times was Puvis de Chavannes, and his most successful efforts the mural paintings in the auditorium of the Sorbonne and in the Panthéon in Paris.

The painter has at his command today a wealth of materials and media for picture-making. Various materials have been used for painting upon in oils such as plaster, metal, wood, paper and canvas, but special mention should be made of the priming—that is, the painting surface—particularly those applied to wood and canvas, the latter almost exclusively used for oil painting in modern times. The best priming for wooden panels is gesso.

PRIMING

Gesso was used in the Middle Ages, not only as a priming but for raised ornament. It was either polished to an ivory finish or gilded when used for the latter purpose. It is made from slaked plaster of Paris and glue. Originally, parchment glue was used, but this has been replaced by carpenter's glue diluted with water. Canvas used for oil painting should be made of pure unbleached flax fibre of various meshes, according to the texture of the surface required. Gesso priming, which is the purest white known for this purpose, can be used, but is apt to crack owing to the flexibility of canvas. Because this is so, oil priming has replaced gesso on canvas supplied by artists' colourmen. Canvas so primed can be sold either stretched or in roll form. Before the priming is applied the canvas is given a coat of size to protect the fibre from oil. The usual oil priming is a mixture of white lead and linseed oil, although poppy and walnut oils are sometimes used.

Since the painter has ceased to make his own colours and has relied upon the manufacturer, the number and variety of colours offered have steadily increased.

A colour manufacturer of repute offers no less than two hundred and twenty-five different colours in his latest catalogue. Yet it is true to say that the best colour combinations are made from the simplest palette. The simplest palette recommended by experienced teachers carries the follow-ing range of colours for figure painting: flake white, yellow ochre, light red and blue-black. It is interesting to note the similarity of this range of colour to that used by primitive man. This range is enlarged to the following, which is not exceeded by most experienced painters: flake white, yellow ochre, raw sienna, light red, burnt sienna, oxide of chromium (green), ultramarine, blue-black or ivory black.

The most elaborate range that should be found necessary is: flake white, cadmium yellow, yellow ochre, raw sienna, raw umber, burnt sienna, vermilion, light red, rose madder, terre-verte or oxide of chromium, cobalt blue, ultramarine blue, blue-black, ivory black.

Colours are divided into two main groups, warm and cold. Painters trained in their craft place their colours on their palette in an orderly and consistent manner.

All the colours mentioned have the advantage of being permanent, many being natural earth. The materials from which they are made are given opposite their names below:—

Flake white	Basic carbonate of lead—white lead
Cadmium yellow	Sulphide of cadmium.
Yellow ochre .	Natural earth.
Raw sienna .	Natural earth.
Raw umber .	Natural earth.
Burnt sienna .	Earth colour, calcined raw sienna.
Vermilion . .	Mercuric sulphide.
Light red . .	Earth colour, calcined yellow ochre.
Rose madder .	Prepared madder root.
Terre-verte .	Natural earth.
Oxide of chromium	The washed product obtained by heating together sodium bichromate and boracic acid.
Cobalt blue .	Alumina tinctured with oxide of cobalt.
Blue-black .	Carbon black obtained from charred wood.
Ivory black .	Charred ivory.
Ultramarine .	Extract of lapis lazuli, or from a permanent artificial ultramarine made by heating together silica soda, sulphur and coal, owing to the high cost of the former.

Water colours are made from the same materials as oil colours, but Chinese white,

When the morning Stars sang together. & all the
Sons of God shouted for joy

W Blake inv & sc

VISIONARY ART

William Blake was not concerned with the rendering of visual experience;
he drew entirely upon his imagination to convey the vast, primeval concepts
of Hebrew poetry. The general impression of this engraved illustration to
The Book of Job is reminiscent of a page from a Celtic manuscript; the
only eighteenth-century element is the style of drawing common to artists
of that time, who, like Fuseli, attempted the heroic manner.

which is made from oxide of zinc, is used in place of flake white. Many kinds of vehicle are on the market for mixing with and applying oil paint to canvas or wood. Paint as supplied in tubes and tins is too stiff for use without a diluent; that is, unless a loaded thick impasto is required. The most commonly used are the following: turpentine or rectified petroleum, linseed oil and poppy oil.

If a matt surface is required, turpentine alone is used. For general purposes a mixture of rectified petroleum, linseed oil and copal varnish in equal parts is advised. Oil paintings should not be varnished until they have been allowed to dry for at least six months. There are several varieties of varnish, the two most reliable being mastic varnish and copal varnish. Of these, mastic varnish is the more generally used as it has the advantage of being easily removed if it cracks or darkens. Mastic varnish is made from mastic resin dissolved in spirits of turpentine, and copal varnish from tree fossil copal dissolved in slightly heated oil of turpentine and diluted with spirits of turpentine. Both of these varnishes are liable to crack and darken: mastic in long cracks and copal in short ones.

A better protective surface for an oil painting than varnish is wax dissolved in spirits of turpentine. A thin layer of wax spread over a painting will dry with a matt surface, but it will polish with a wad—made of linen over cotton wool—to as brilliant a surface as that obtained by a varnish.

The great advantage of a polished wax surface is that it will never crack and can easily be removed. Paraffin wax is much more durable than beeswax, and Professor Laurie, late professor of chemistry at the Royal Academy of Arts, London, claims that a mixture of melted wax and resin is the best protection for canvas yet discovered.

There are four kinds of brush in common use for oil and two for water-colour painting. For oil painting, three shapes made of hogs' hair and one of sable for fine touches are recommended. Water-colour brushes are made of both camel hair and sable. Those made of sable are to be preferred, as they have resilience and keep their shape better than camel-hair brushes.

What is known as a dipper in two partitions, one for holding turpentine and one for the vehicle, or medium for mixing the pigment used, is attached to the artist's palette. The only other articles of the artist's equipment that remain to be mentioned, in addition to his easel, are palette knives—one for mixing colour and keeping the palette clean and one for painting and laying on heavy impasto.

Test Yourself

1. Compare the use which Claude and Rembrandt make of light as a method of organizing composition.

2. Describe the following techniques:
   (a) encaustic
   (b) tempera
   (c) fresco.

3. What is the method of oil painting known as alla prima?

4. What is gouache?

5. Name the materials generally used for painting upon in oils. What is the most satisfactory priming for use in this connexion?

6. State the types of brush used for oil and water-colour painting respectively. What materials are used for each and what are the individual advantages

Answers will be found at the end of the book

STUDIES IN CHALK

This is one of the studies Holbein made for portraits painted for the English Court of Henry VIII. It is drawn in chalk with an extremely light touch.

CHAPTER XIII

THE GRAPHIC ARTS

A CHILD, engrossed in the exciting task of making pictures, was once asked to explain how he was able to make such wonderful things, and his reply was, "Oh, it is quite easy. I just think a think and then put a line round it."

This is, perhaps, a quite good definition of graphic art. Albrecht Dürer (1471-1528) when contemplating the perplexing visions of St. John on the Island of Patmos, attempted to visualize what John described, and then he drew a line round it. The result is seen in the amazing designs of his woodcuts of the Apocalypse. In a similar way, Rembrandt saw the human drama of the Life of Jesus in the Gospels, and drew lines to express his visions. Other great graphic artists such as Meryon (1821-68), Goya (1746-1828) and Blake (1757-1827), though their methods have varied, have all in their own way followed the same principle.

The art of drawing a line to enclose or express an idea is a creative art. It is the formation of a convention, a method of writing down something that has first been seen in the mind, a selection from a multitude of forms and then a translation into a new language—the language of lines and tones. The power to express thoughts in this way is a primitive instinct and can be seen in the markings, by ancient man, on cave walls, rocks and clay, etc. From the ability to make such drawings, there arises later the desire to multiply them so that they may be distributed and thus reach a larger audience, hence the activity in devising various methods of producing prints and the development of the graphic processes.

PRODUCING PRINTS

This activity appears to date, in Europe, from about the time of the invention of printing with movable types (i.e. about 1450) and as wood was used for making the early forms of type so wood blocks were used for cutting out the first illustrations for printed books. Other methods followed —engraving, etching and lithography.

Great enjoyment can be obtained from the examination of prints and an understanding of their particular qualities, for each method possesses its own unique and attractive character. History owes much to the engraver's art; our knowledge of many things and events of the past is due to the fact that these have been recorded for us in one of the graphic processes.

HISTORIC RECORDS

Thus Albrecht Dürer, in his line engravings and woodcuts, has left a wonderful interpretation of New Testament scenes: Wenzel Hollar (1607-77) in his etchings has given an exact record of the appearance of London in the seventeenth century and of the costumes of the time. Thomas Bewick (1753-1828), in his wood engravings, provides delightful studies of British birds and animals: Goya, in his aquatints, has dramatically rendered the horrors of war: Daumier (1808-79), in his lithographs, gives a whole picture of French social and political life: Turner (1775-1851), in his mezzotints, a magnificent series of landscape compositions.

It will be seen that in the history of prints, from which we have taken outstanding examples, there is a richness of subject matter of every kind. They convey the character and flavour of a period: but each process has also a quality of its own which is so much a part of the finished result, that to appreciate this fully we must also know something of how the print is made. The soft, velvety tone of a mezzotint, the crisp line of the etching, the "white line" of the wood-engraving can be readily distinguished when the student has grasped the main technical principles behind each process.

These processes indeed are like instruments in an orchestra, each having its own particular beauty and limitation. Just as a violin produces a quite different quality of sound from a cornet, or a 'cello

BRUSH AND CHALK MEDIUMS

These two drawings are very similar in subject though the style is entirely different. The one above of the girls playing knucklebones, which comes from Herculaneum and dates from the first century B.C., is drawn with a fine brush in red monochrome and is based on feeling for pure line. In the chalk drawing on the opposite page, by Watteau, the eighteenth-century French artist, the outline is composed of sensitive, frequently broken, lines, the general effect of the shapes recalling the curving, shell-like forms which are associated with the rococo style.

from a flute, so does an engraving differ from an etching and a lithograph from a mezzotint.

But first of all let us consider drawing itself, apart from the various fascinating ways of making prints. Various materials are employed and each has its own special quality and bearing on the finished result. The materials and implements which graphic artists use include: silverpoint, goldpoint, pencil, pen, chalk, charcoal, pastel and brush.

Drawing with a silverpoint or goldpoint was a method favoured by some of the old masters, but rather neglected now, perhaps because its quiet gentle tone is out of keeping with the present hurrying, vigorous and noisy age. Its quality possesses a subtle charm like a faint echo of some delightful vision remembered in moments of calm. It has been used in modern times with much skill by A. Legros (1837-1911), and W. Strang (1859-1921).

The silverpoint or goldpoint is fixed in a holder like a pencil and the drawing is made on a sheet of paper prepared with a coating of zinc white. The pale, crisp line is like the line made by a graver and has a wonderful delicacy. Pencil is a favourite method now and is much in use because of its quality and its convenience. No medium is more easily carried about or so quickly used. Superb examples of portraiture in this medium were produced by the French master, Ingres (1780-1867), one of which is reproduced on page 186.

Pen drawing with the quill or reed pen was much used by the old masters. The drawings by Rembrandt (1606-69), give an idea of the flexibility of this method, especially when it is reinforced by wash. With the invention of the steel pen, this kind of drawing has tended to disappear and pen drawing is now used mainly for purposes of process reproduction. It is, however, a useful implement to assist in the definition of form in drawings with chalk and other material.

Chalk is a valuable medium for broad and vigorous effects. It is much used by

PURPOSES OF DRAWING

Drawings are usually made for one of two purposes: either to be in themselves complete works, like the Dürer on the opposite page, or as studies for paintings. Dürer's magnificent portrait of a woman demonstrates the possibilities of pen drawing, especially when reinforced by wash. This drawing by Michelangelo (1475-1564) is a study for the figure of Adam in the Sistine Chapel fresco. The artist has concentrated on the modelling of the torso, and the drawing reveals knowledge and intense study of the movements and relation of the muscles which underly the much simplified form in the finished painting, a photograph of which is reproduced on page 68.

painters and sculptors. Red chalk was used by many of the old masters in their preliminary studies for their pictures (p. 182). The nineteenth-century English artist, Alfred Stevens, may be mentioned as an eminent later practitioner of this old master method.

Charcoal is also greatly in favour for bold and strong work and is suited for rapid definition and the expression of vigorous effects. Pastel may also be used in a similar way and possesses great charm.

Brush drawing has been used with much skill from the time of the ancient Chinese and Japanese draughtsmen until the present day. It can be seen and with good effect in the drawings of Low and Derrick and many other modern draughtsmen. It has a flexibility which other methods do not possess and a range of touch denied to the pen and other implements.

Drawings are endless in their number, variety and beauty and here we can touch on only the fringes of the subject. They have the quality of bringing us into as direct a contact as possible with the artist

PENCIL DRAWING

Ingres was one of the greatest masters of lead-pencil drawing; a close
follower of the Classic style as a painter, he reveals himself in his drawings
as a nervous, subtle draughtsman, using the pencil more ably than any
other artist of his age—the first half of the nineteenth century.

and even those which the artist did not complete, or intended only as working sketches for some more elaborate production, are fascinating as they show the workings of his mind and the freshness of his first thought.

But in addition many artists have turned to methods of drawing, by means of various implements, on wood, metal or stone, in such a way that prints may be made from them. The ways of preparing these materials for printing purposes are numerous but, though so many, the prints obtained from them can be roughly divided into two classes—known as "surface" and "intaglio" prints respectively.

Surface prints are made by the application of printers' ink to the surface of the wood block, metal plate or stone, in which

WOOD ENGRAVING

Comparison of Bewick's vignette from The Chase, by Somerville, above, with the Holbein woodcut on this page reveals the main difference between woodcuts and wood engravings. In the latter both white and black lines are used, whereas in the former all the lines are in black on a light background.

the portions of the design not requiring to be printed are cut away, leaving the design in relief, or rendered inactive (as in the case of lithography). A sheet of paper is then pressed firmly to the inked block, plate or stone, and a print is obtained from the inked surface.

Intaglio prints are made in a different way, by removing the ink from the surface and forcing it into the lines or hollows which have been cut or etched into the surface of the metal plate. When the sheet of paper is placed on the surface of such a plate very severe pressure is applied so that the paper is forced into the cuts or lines which are holding the ink, thus producing the print.

The kind of pressure required for a surface print is a firm and steady contact, in some cases rubbing on the back of the

HOLBEIN'S DANCE OF DEATH

Holbein's forty-one woodcuts known as the Dance of Death, of which this is one, disclose remarkable dramatic power and exuberance. Death is here playing his part with grim irony as he mockingly clutches his unwilling victim.

187

paper with a burnisher or pad is sufficient, but in the case of an intaglio print very heavy pressure is needed and therefore a different type of printing press is used.

Surface prints include woodcuts, wood engravings, lino cuts, lithographs and some forms of etching. Intaglio prints comprise engravings, etchings, aquatints, drypoints and mezzotints.

The woodcut is the oldest of these methods of reproduction. About 1450, the inventors of printing with movable types made use of wooden types, and to illustrate their printed books they utilized wooden blocks which could be inked and printed in the same way as the type.

Various kinds of soft wood were chosen for this purpose, pear, maple, sycamore, cherry, apple; and the wood was usually cut lengthwise with the grain. Today, for ease in working, linoleum is sometimes used.

The design or picture was drawn on the surface of the wooden block or plank with a pen or brush and then the white portions of the picture were cut away by means of a knife or chisel, leaving the lines of the picture in relief. Ink was then applied to the surface of the block by means of an ink roller, so that all the parts of the surface remaining after the cutting away was completed could receive the ink. Paper was

Sir William Nicholson's woodcut of Queen Victoria on the opposite page is made to appear almost in a different medium from that used in the Holbein on the preceding page. Whereas Holbein's is an intricate work, every one of his innumerable lines requiring many cuts, Sir William relies on simple, solid masses left in relief, the white portions of the picture being cut away. In his Daphinis and Chloe, below, Charles Ricketts creates a snow scene by cutting away the foreground and leaving the sky dark.

CALVERT'S ENGRAVING

Edward Calvert, a follower of William Blake, was a master of wood engraving, using it to express his romantic dreams of a pastoral golden age. The Chamber Idyll, shown above, is a fine example of his power to suggest a variety of textures, contrasts of light and dark, and the mystery of night.

then laid upon the inked surface, pressure applied to it and a print obtained. The quality and strength of the black ink in a woodcut remains the same throughout, and the general effect is bright and lively. It is a rather laborious task to cut the blocks, especially when much intricate work has to be cut away and every single line requires many separate cuts, the ground surrounding it being removed before the block is ready for printing. Some of the finest examples of woodcuts have been made by Dürer, Altdorfer (1480-1538) and Holbein (1497-1543) (p. 187). The method is still in constant use for the illustration of books, and for other purposes.

Multicolour prints are made in the same way but in this case larger surfaces are left uncut and several blocks are used so that one tint may be imprinted over another.

Japanese woodcuts are also made in a similar way and several blocks are used for separate colours.

Beautiful woodcuts have also been produced by Italian and French book illustrators; and in Britain by Millais, Sandys, Morris, Burne-Jones, Charles Ricketts and Sir William Nicholson (p. 188). The main characteristics to be appreciated in a woodcut are the clean black lines and simplicity of effect.

Wood engraving is a later development from the woodcut method and came into extensive use about 1800. A hard boxwood is used, cut across the grain and polished smoothly. Whereas in the woodcut method much labour was expended in cutting away the light parts of the picture and leaving the lines black, in this process the reverse way of working is used. An instrument called the graver cuts the lines white from the dark ground, and the result is a method of working white on dark, instead of dark on white. It is a quicker and more direct and natural method of working and is much used at the present time. Both methods are used in combination by some artists. The material used is boxwood, the tools include graver, chisel and knife.

A classic exponent of the " white line "

MODERN WOOD ENGRAVING

The astonishing dexterity and intensity of feeling which characterize the work of Eric Ravilious are apparent in this wood engraving.

is Thomas Bewick. Wood engravers of today are numerous. The characteristics to look for in wood engraving are white lines instead of black, or a mixture of both, sharper definition, more minute detail and greater variety of pattern than are to be found in woodcuts.

LITHOGRAPHY

If the woodcut was the earliest method to be used, lithography has been the most recent to be discovered and developed. Its discovery dates from the year 1796 and was the work of a man named Senefelder who was born in Prague in 1771. While living in Munich he perfected his discovery between 1796 and 1798. Senefelder found that by writing with a greasy chalk on a certain kind of limestone it was possible to obtain a print from it, if the remaining portions of the stone were kept wet during the process of inking, as the ink adhered only to the parts which had been marked with the greasy chalk.

This discovery was developed rapidly and is now used extensively for many purposes, especially for the illustration of books and the making of posters. A certain kind of limestone from quarries in Germany was found most suitable for the purpose, but other kinds are now used, as is also prepared zinc, which is more easily manipulated.

The surface of the stone is roughened with sand and the design drawn on the prepared surface with a certain kind of chalk composed of soap, tallow-wax, shellac and black. The porous nature of the stone causes it to absorb the grease from the chalk and when the stone is inked with a roller and the surface of the stone kept wet, the ink from the roller will take only where the chalk has marked the stone. To aid the design when printing, the stone is treated with a solution of gum, weak acid and powdered resin. This reinforces the marked portions of the stone and causes a chemical change to occur in the nature of the unmarked parts which enables it to reject the ink. The print obtained is therefore a surface print, as the ink lies on the surface of the stone and is prevented from adhering to the remaining parts of the surface, not by cutting away the stone but by rendering it inactive through the natural antagonism of grease to water.

The print is obtained by the application of a firm, scraping pressure to the back of the paper when placed down on the surface of the inked stone, and a special type of printing press is used for this purpose. When it is required to print in colour, separate stones are used for each, the different colours then being printed over each other.

The stone can be prepared with a rough or smooth surface so that very firm, minute work may be done, or, if desired, a rough coarser treatment can be obtained. Instead of chalk, an ink or wash can be used when made from the same ingredients as the chalk. The chalk drawing may also be made on a special transfer paper and then transferred to the stone by running it through the press. In the printing trade, great developments have been made with this process but the general principle of the work remains the same.

Many artists have taken pleasure in the peculiar freedom of draughtsmanship which lithography permits. One may mention for instance Daumier, Gavarni, Forain, Whistler, and Toulouse-Lautrec.

The characteristics of a lithograph are a rough, coarse texture like a chalk drawing. Very minute definition can also be obtained with a pen. It provides a great range of tones from a delicate grey to rich dark, and a wide range of colour combinations.

COLOUR PRINTING

Great variety is also obtained in gradation and mixture in colour woodcuts. A separate block is used for each colour.

Japanese prints show a wonderful sense of pattern and colour and have had considerable influence on Western art since the middle of the nineteenth century. Their appeal is largely due to this unusual sense of pattern, their disregard for a prosaic imitation of nature and their reliance on a daring selection of form and detail. The woodcuts by the Japanese artists, Hokusai, Utamaro, Hiroshige and others are worth study. Several European artists have adopted their method.

FREEDOM OF LITHOGRAPHY

In lithography the drawing is made either directly on the stone or on a transfer paper, thus giving the artist complete freedom of draughtsmanship. Forain's lithograph of a scene in a court of justice, a favourite subject with him, is a well-balanced mass of light and dark which, while full of subtlety in the characterization, is treated in a free, impressionist manner that would be impossible with any other method of making a print.

A special instance of colour printing is provided by William Blake's (1757-1827) relief etchings. These were made on metal plates and the portions of the design requiring to be printed were painted with a varnish. When this was dry the plate was bitten in acid and the unprotected parts of the plate were eaten away and the surface lowered so that when inked by the ink roller only the protected surface portions of the plate received the ink. This method is the reverse of ordinary etching and was used by Blake to illustrate some of his poems, for instance, "Songs of Innocence."

The goldsmith's craft is believed to have been the source from which the method of engraving was evolved. It is the earliest form of working in metal for the purpose of print-making, as this type of print is made, not from wood or stone, but from a metal plate, highly polished and about the thickness of a penny. Many kinds of metal have been used: copper, brass, zinc, pewter, iron, steel, but the most useful for the purpose is copper, as it is strong and not too hard for cutting into.

The picture or design is cut into the surface of the metal plate by means of a sharp-pointed instrument called a burin or graver. This instrument is set in a handle of boxwood shaped like a half mushroom, which fits into the palm of the hand and enables the craftsman to push the point of the steel blade or graver into the surface of the metal plate. As the work proceeds the burin or graver cuts a V-shaped furrow into the plate and a thin curl of copper is displaced. If the graver is sharpened correctly there should be no rough edge to the cut line.

To assist cutting, the plate is placed on a flat leather sandbag which enables the plate to be turned towards the graver. Great skill is needed in controlling the action of this tool and as the method is a push stroke it is rather restricted in its action. If delicate lines are required, the cut is gentle but if stronger definition is needed, then greater force is used. Tones and shadows are obtained by means of crossing lines in various directions or by means of short lines and dots or a combination of them. The particular qualities of engraving are purity of definition and a certain severity of form.

The method flourished in Germany and the Low Countries and in Italy. Among the classic engravers are Dürer, Schongauer (1440-91), Lucas van Leyden (1494-1533), and the Amsterdam masters; in Italy, Marcantonio (1480-1530) and Mantegna (1431-1506). Afterwards the process was used extensively in France, then it was neglected and used mainly for the purpose of making large reproductions of paintings. In this century, however, there has been some revival in its use.

Almost at the same time that engraving was first being practised, a new method of making prints, which is called etching, from the Dutch word *eten*—to eat, was discovered and developed. In this process a material is used similar to that for line engraving—a plate of highly polished

ENGRAVING BY MANTEGNA

Engraving, the cutting of a picture into the surface of a metal plate by means of a sharp-pointed instrument called a burin, was particularly suited to the genius of Mantegna. The cleanness of line and severity of form characteristic of the process were congenial to a painter trained at Padua where sculpturesque harshness and rigidity were insisted upon in the treatment not only of the human figure but of rocks and landscape.

ENGRAVING BY SCHONGAUER

Schongauer, of much more gentle nature than Mantegna, makes delightful use of engraving on copper in this heraldic roundel, adapting the sternness of the medium to a Gothic stiffness and formality in the pose of the lady and in the folds of her cloak, the curves of which are echoed by the twisting leaves of the plant.

copper, brass, iron or zinc. The surface of the metal plate is protected with a thin coating of hard wax (a mixture of beeswax, asphaltum and pitch). On this waxed surface the picture is drawn by means of a sharp point, which is held quite lightly. The drawing is made freely and sufficiently firm to pierce only the wax coating and expose the surface of the metal, the same pressure being used in all parts of the design. Since a draw stroke, and not a push stroke as in engraving, is used, as much freedom as in drawing with a pen is possible.

When the design is completed, the back of the plate is usually protected by giving it a coating of "stopping-out" varnish and the plate is then placed into a porcelain bath containing a corrosive acid. In general use are nitric acid, or a mixture of hydrochloric acid and chlorate of potash, or perchloride of iron. The acid at once begins to eat into the metal wherever it has been exposed by the action of the sharp point. When a certain portion of the design is considered to have been etched sufficiently, the plate is taken out of the acid bath, rinsed and dried, and this portion is painted out with a quick-drying varnish. The plate is then returned to the acid bath and the etching of the other portions continued. This stopping-out process is repeated with the other parts of the design until the darkest parts are considered completed.

The waxed surface of the plate is then cleaned off by means of turpentine when the design is found to be eaten or etched into the polished surface. Corrections to the plate can be made by a burnisher and scraper. The ink used for printing is a mixture of burnt linseed oil and various black carbons. After the whole of the plate has been covered with ink the surface is wiped clean by the printing muslin and by hand, leaving the ink embedded in the

TOPOGRAPHICAL ETCHING

Hollar was a topographical artist who imitated the precise line of the engraving tool by using the more easily handled needle and acid of the etching process, the subject being recorded with almost photographic fidelity. The interest of the etching shown here lies in the precise image it gives of seventeenth-century London with old St. Paul's dominating the scene and the bare hills of Hampstead and Highgate in the background.

IMAGINATIVE ENGRAVING

Dürer's magnificent engraving of Death and the Knight, above, forms a striking contrast to Hollar's etching on the opposite page. Whereas Hollar's salient feature is the accuracy of representation, Dürer's imaginative power almost overwhelms his technical skill and knowledge of form.

INSPIRATION TO ETCHERS

Lucas Vorstemann, an etching with a fine suggestion of rich colour and virile drawing, is one among many of Van Dyck's portrait prints which have been a source of inspiration to etchers.

198

MODERN PORTRAIT ETCHING

The remarkable portrait etching shown here, Renan by Anders Zorn, one of the most outstanding of modern etchers, has a forceful, rugged, vibrating line which well bears comparison with the work of Van Dyck opposite.

lines on the plate. A sheet of paper is then placed on the inked plate and this passes between the heavy rollers of the printing press where it receives such severe pressure that the paper is pressed well into the etched lines to receive the ink remaining there. This method of printing is similar to that used for the printing of engravings and all intaglio prints.

The process of etching permits the greatest freedom of all the methods of expression in a clear and sensitive line of even thickness, and has a wonderful range of delicacy and strength. Many masters have been attracted to it, among whom Rembrandt stands out supreme.

A variant of the etching method is the soft-ground etching which resembles a strong pencil drawing. A wax ground is used in this case which is a mixture of the ordinary wax ground and equal parts of tallow or lard which makes it soft to the

touch. A sheet of paper is placed over the prepared plate and the picture is drawn firmly or gently on this as required with a pencil. When the paper is removed, the soft wax adheres to the paper wherever the pencil has pressed, thus exposing that part of the metal plate to the action of acid. The line has the same quality as a pencil line and can also be influenced by the grain of the paper used. When the plate is placed in the acid bath the acid attacks it in the same way as in ordinary etching. It is also printed in the same way.

Many artists find it difficult to express themselves in terms of line, and prefer to make use of tones for this purpose, and because of this, many experiments have been made to discover a method of etching in tone. Such a method, called aquatint, provides a grained texture of surface.

The most satisfactory way of obtaining this effect of tone is by means of a deposit

LIGHT AND DARK IN ETCHING

*In this etching by Auguste Lepère, remarkable both for the drawing of the
crowd and for the treatment of the façade of Amiens Cathedral, the darkest
parts are the result of the longer action of the acid on the plate, the lighter
portions being protected from the further effects of the acid.*

CHANGES IN ETCHING

Alphonse Legros made several changes in this etching, La Mort du Vagabond. Originally it showed two men on the left pulling the tree and a man chopping the base. Legros then burnished out all but the tree and etched a standing figure in the right foreground. Next he changed it for the existing design.

VITALITY AND TRUTH

The Shepherd Girl Spinning is a typical example of J. F. Millet's fine qualities as a graphic artist. The homely subject is treated in a manner which reveals an artist who has shared the arduous life and labour of the peasants. The picture is a woodcut from a drawing made by Millet himself.

of resin dust or asphaltum dust. This is a process developed by a Frenchman, Jean Baptiste le Prince, about 1750, and also by the Englishman, Paul Sandby, about the same period, and the latter is believed to be the originator of the somewhat misleading name of aquatinta.

The method is roughly as follows: Resin dust or asphaltum dust is sprinkled or powdered evenly over the surface of a metal plate. This is then heated sufficiently to cause the particles of dust to adhere to the plate, and is then allowed to cool. On examination, it will be discovered that the surface of the metal plate is exposed between each minute particle of dust. When this is placed in the acid bath, the acid can eat into the metal between these particles of dust and thus a granulated bitten surface is obtained which can be filled with ink to print the required tone.

There are various alternatives to the process described above, consisting in different ways of laying the grained ground. But enough has been said to enable the reader to grasp the essentials of the process. The quality to look for in an aquatint is tone with a grained surface, luminous in effect and showing delicate gradations It was used by Goya and Rowlandson on a line foundation. Turner used it successfully to render sky effects in his mezzotint plates.

A process in which no acid is used is drypoint. If a strong sharp-pointed instrument be drawn firmly on the surface of a metal plate, two things occur. An incision is made in the plate which will hold ink and at the same time a rough edge or fringe is made to the incision by the metal displaced in its making, for this is not cut away, as in the case of engraving, neither is it eaten away by acid, as in the case of etching. This rough edge or fringe is called burr and it collects the ink when being printed and thus gives an added richness to the effect of the printed line. It is this velvety richness which gives the peculiar charm to drypoint work.

The same materials are used as in etching except that acid is not required. Copper is the most suitable metal. Zinc is a little soft for the purpose. The needle point has to be strong and unyielding, for considerable strength in the fingers is required when making the incisions.

Clearness in definition is sometimes sacrificed in drypoint, but an unusual richness of effect is obtained in its place by means of the beautiful quality of the burr. The line has a tapering quality, but when the burr is removed it has not much depth.

Drypoint has been practised by such great artists as Rembrandt, Dürer and Whistler (1834-1903).

For richness and power of tone and perfection of gradation, a process without rival is mezzotint. In its character it is a combination of the rich burr quality of drypoint and the minute incision of the point of a graver. No acid is used in its production, unless a preliminary line etching is bitten to assist the definition of certain forms in the design, as seen in Turner's plates of landscapes.

In other methods of engraving, the work proceeds from light to dark but in mezzotint engraving it is the reverse. The surface of the metal plate, usually copper, is roughened, by the action of rocking, evenly all over it, a tool like a broad chisel with a curved edge, its face being grooved into ridges. On being ground-off at an angle from the back, each ridge makes a point called a tooth and there are from fifty to a hundred teeth to each inch, according to the fineness of the tool. This grounding tool is held nearly vertically in contact with the plate and is rocked evenly in parallel directions across the plate, beginning at the lower edge.

When one set or direction is finished the plate is moved slightly and a new direction rocked, until the surface of the plate has been covered, sometimes forty different ways. Each movement of the grounding tool presses the sharp teeth into the surface of the plate and makes an incision and also raises burr. When the rocking is finished, the surface of the plate is roughened all over with this burr and has the appearance of a pile of velvet. If inked at this stage it would print a rich, full dark tone. On this surface of dark tone the work commences and the lighter tones are scraped away carefully by means of a sharp, steel blade rather like a pocket knife, the lightest parts being left until the last.

An etched line is used, if desired, on the plate before the mezzotint ground is prepared, to give definition and strength to the composition. Turner is one of the most famous artists to employ mezzotint, but the method has also been used by many well-known engravers; for example, John Raphael Smith.

The foregoing will have given you enough technical data to distinguish between different kinds of print, and whether or not some are beyond your reach, a print collection can be made without undue expense, and is worthy of care.

An excellent way of keeping prints is to have them mounted in a stock-size mount kept in print boxes.

Beware of damp walls. If prints become wavy strain them out again by slightly damping the back and pasting the edges only, fastening them to a strong board in this way for about two days. Then cut them off the board and put them back on their mounts. If white mildew spots appear on mezzotint proofs, touch the spot gently with a soft rag and lemon juice, but do not rub them. The acid of the lemon will destroy the fungus on the spot.

If prints are dirty or soiled with age rub them very gently with soft bread crumbs, and if that does not remove the dirt, soak them in a dish of clean water and then gently strain out again. Iron mould and brown spots require expert treatment.

Prints taken on hand-made linen paper are very durable and the ink used for printing is fadeless. They improve in appearance with age as the paper absorbs the oil from the ink. Old paper is likely to show dark spots when damped. This is due to the absence of size in the paper and will disappear as the paper dries.

Test Yourself

1. What is the difference between a woodcut and a wood engraving?
2. Describe the processes of metal engraving and etching, naming some of the artists who have used these mediums.
3. What is a mezzotint?

Answers will be found at the end of the book.

CHAPTER XIV

METHODS OF REPRODUCTION

THE invention and development of printing added greatly to the use and the possibilities of graphic art.

In the preceding chapter an account has been given of the various methods of reproduction by means of which artists have been able to make a number of copies of their own handiwork—these including woodcuts and wood engraving, etching, engraving on metal, and lithography.

All these reproductive methods have lent themselves to and been used for the illustration of books and in conjunction with the printed word.

Reproduction, in fact, has gone hand-in-hand with the growth of modern civilization. In the Middle Ages, when every page of a book had to be written by a skilled hand and every illustration drawn and painted on the page, books were a luxury to be enjoyed only by the privileged few, and were the unique treasures of the monasteries in which they were produced.

NEW FORM OF ART

With the invention of printing in the fifteenth century there came not only the opportunity for more people to read, but also a new form of popular art. The first books were made from wood blocks, and the page was printed just like a complete picture. When movable type was devised, woodcut illustrations were naturally still used and harmonized perfectly with the printed characters from which a surface impression was obtained in exactly the same way.

In the seventeenth and eighteenth centuries, when it was desired to obtain a more elaborate effect than the wood block provided, engravings on metal were used. Sometimes they were engraved by the artist himself. But there grew up also the custom of using professional engravers who reproduced or interpreted the work of an artist.

This practice reached its height in the Victorian Age. The graphic arts were not used as a direct form of expression. The engraver was now an established middleman and the artist himself no longer worked for reproduction but left that function to his "interpreter." For the purposes of the illustrated journals which were founded in this period, *Punch* and the *Illustrated London News*, for example, groups of professional engravers, such as the celebrated Dalziel brothers, came into being and fulfilled the duty of the commercial blockmaker today.

DEVELOPMENTS IN PRODUCTION

The wood engravings then used aimed at the effect of tone and this entailed a long and tedious process of imitating the light and shade of a wash drawing or painting by fine lines cut out or engraved. It was a mechanical method. When speed of production required it, a large block was cut into squares and divided among as many as two dozen engravers, and finally morticed together like a jig-saw puzzle.

There were two main flaws in this procedure. It could not retain the quality of the artists' own handiwork. At the same time, it was not a true mechanical form of reproduction.

Improvement in the latter respect was brought about by the invention of photography and the photographic methods of reproduction whereby a photographic print could be etched on metal. At first, photography was used only to transfer the image of the original design on to the wood block, thus enabling the engraver to make a more exact copy. Later, with the full development of the new method, the engraver middleman was eliminated and the craft was completely revolutionized.

At the same time the artist illustrator enjoyed a new freedom. A pen drawing, for example, could now appear, line for line, just as he had drawn it and the end of the nineteenth century saw a new liveliness

Cupid

The Cunning Beggar

COPPERPLATE ENGRAVING

At first sight this copperplate engraving by Stephen Gooden might be mistaken for a wood engraving. A close inspection will reveal the characteristics of an intaglio process.

of technique, as in the drawings of Phil May, which were deliberately designed to make the most of the original line quality.

With the development of the half-tone process, by which various tones can be reproduced by breaking up the image into a number of graduated dots, the artist's attitude to print was completely revised. It was now not so much a method of translation as of producing a large number of copies of an original, using the new mechanical methods as a medium.

Since the latter half of the nineteenth century this has been one main factor in the use of graphic art. The other has been a tendency for the artist to revive and recover the spirit of the early days of the

printed book, when the artist was his own engraver. This was the aim of William Morris, in his beautiful Kelmscott Press books which have had so great an influence and have given rise to a number of private presses whose publications are examples of fine handicraft. Such books are usually costly and limited in edition, but have been the vehicle of much distinguished illustration.

MECHANICAL REPRODUCTION

Newspapers and periodicals, of course, now require completely mechanical means of reproduction. Each type of publication has certain advantages and limitations governed largely by the quality of paper on which it is printed and by its general make-up. The make-up, or in other words, the relative emphasis which the words and pictures are given, is as important in the production of any publication as the punctuation of a well-constructed sentence or the inflexions in the voice of a public speaker.

The artist can turn the limitations of any medium to his advantage. Thus the political cartoon of a newspaper may gain even from the coarseness of newsprint, by the bold and emphatic forms and simple treatment which this demands. The cartoon is also usually the focal point of the page on which it appears. This is another very good reason for its boldness of black-and-white effect.

SPECIAL QUALITIES

The variety of purposes for which publications are designed demands special qualities in the artist. It is not enough to be a magnificent draughtsman. For example, a good cartoonist is a journalist and a social commentator who is closely informed about current political developments and is able to condense half a dozen columns of editorial matter into one pictorial idea. The coarse vein of eighteenth century satire to be seen in the work of Rowlandson and Gillray has in more recent times given place to an economical form of wit, dependent not on an attached description in words, but on the quality of the drawing itself. This takes such

ETCHING AND DRYPOINT

On the opposite page is shown one of the earliest of Whistler's etchings, made in France. James McNeill Whistler (1834-1903), the Anglo-American master, expressed himself more completely in etching than in any other medium. In technique, variety of texture and the treatment of light and shadow he is the close rival of Rembrandt. Sir Muirhead Bone's accuracy as a draughtsman is well exhibited in drypoint, a method in which lines are scratched directly on the plate with a steel needle or a diamond mounted in a handle, the ridge thrown up on both sides of the line giving a rich quality to the print. The above reproduction is a characteristic example of his work in this medium illustrating his care for detail and composition.

varied forms as the political cartoons of David Low or the literary portraits of Sir Max Beerbohm.

In fact, illustration for newspapers and magazines is as varied as the periodicals in which it appears. Each publication has its own standard, but the artist can transcend this standard according to his own ability. The *Punch* drawings of Charles Keene are an example of first-rate graphic art which went far beyond its ostensible humorous purpose.

On the whole, however, the illustration and decoration of books gives most scope to the graphic artist. The illustrator adds observation and comment to the author's words. Occasionally the co-operation of illustrator and author produces remarkable results, such as the illustrations of George Cruikshank and Hablot K. Browne ("Phiz") to the novels of Dickens, and Sir John Tenniel's illustrations to *Alice in Wonderland*. Here the fusion of two minds is so complete that it is impossible to think of the book without visualizing it through the original pictures it contained.

Modern illustration has not produced anything quite comparable with these examples of the last century; but on the other hand, it shows a greater sense of decorative value and of that harmony of drawing and typography which adds

SATIRICAL ETCHING

Goya, the finest etcher of the eighteenth century, used the medium to satirize the political and social conditions of Spain. The subjects of his great series of etchings are the weakness of the state, the greed and corruption of the Church, the hypocrisies of the people, the social rottenness, the horrors and miseries of war. His draughtsmanship is as incisive as his satire is biting. With economy of line he has set forth in black, white and subtle tone the significance of the terrible situation which is the subject of the etching from the Disasters of War shown below. The print is typical of Goya's work and it illustrates his lucidity and dramatic power. The bayonets pointed at the group of victims by unseen hands tend to inspire an atmosphere of horror. Goya has followed his usual practice of reinforcing the etching with strong contrasts of tone obtained with aquatint.

MEZZOTINT WITH AN ETCHED LINE

In this mezzotint after a picture by Turner, Sir Frank Short used an etched line to give strength to the composition before the mezzotint was begun. The surface of the plate then having been roughened all over by the rocker, the instrument used in preparing a mezzotint ground, the lighter tones were carefully scraped away by means of a sharp steel blade, the lightest parts being left until last.

dignity to the appearance of the printed page.

It has been said earlier, that the artist's own use of graphic processes of reproduction is limited to luxuriously produced and expensive editions. There is one interesting exception today, in the form of lithography (pp. 214, 215). The lithograph has several advantages. It gives an exact reproduction of the work of the artist's own hand. If colour is used, the artist can control it and obtain exactly the effect intended without submitting to the element of chance and the mechanical screen effect which is inseparable from the process colour reproduction usually employed. Moreover, a lithograph can be printed on uncoated paper, thus avoiding the shiny surface of the clay-coated "art" paper which is one of the necessary evils of fine-screen mechanical reproduction. Much admirable work has been done in this medium, especially in children's books.

Just as the tremendous growth of printing has created a new function for the artist, so also has the growth of commerce and industry. There are two aspects to this new function. One is the design of things we use. It is only by a very narrow convention that we identify the artist exclusively with the painter of easel pictures. It is a convention which grew up in the last hundred years, during which the productions of industry were given little attention from the viewpoint of appearance, or else were made to copy, often very unsuitably, the work of the old hand craftsman. But many great artists in the past were designers first and only incidentally painters of pictures;

ENGRAVER AS MIDDLEMAN

*Sandys did not himself prepare this wood engraving for reproduction; the
actual engraving was done by one of the Dalziel brothers.*

MASTER OF ALL ETCHING

Rembrandt's expert use of the acid process has never been surpassed and no one has ever depicted the gamut of human experience in the medium of etching so triumphantly as this great master. Diana Bathing is an extraordinary feat of craftsmanship, but it is still more remarkable for its intensely imaginative qualities. The etching is infinitely richer in tone, the characterization more subtle, the drawing and modelling more delicate, than in the painting of the same subject.

"He heapeth up riches and knoweth not who shall gather them."

RURAL CRAFTSMANSHIP

Stanley Anderson shows in this engraving the British craftsman making a chair by hand without the machine-operated tools of a factory.

212

and in the twentieth century there is a revived interest in design and in the ability of the artist to work with society as a designer instead of remaining aloof in another world of his own.

This process of development has been much handicapped by the wars of the century. One cannot say more than that the artist has begun to apply his mind to a new problem. It is sufficient to say that this form of design does not mean the application of as much ornament as possible to any given surface—and that it implies as much sympathy with the process of industrial production as the illustrator must possess with printing processes.

Akin to this function is the further extension of graphic art in the form of posters and advertisements. It is akin because it implies, likewise, the solution of a special problem of design with exacting conditions which the artist must satisfy. Until recently a poster was regarded as a sort of inferior easel picture, with only a chance bearing on the product it represented. This accidental approach evaded the essential problem and the special qualities of design obtainable.

SIMPLICITY

The value of a poster depends on a capacity to tell a story or deliver a message in the simplest pictorial terms that will seize and hold the attention of the observer. This result may be achieved by a dozen artists in a dozen different ways, depending on their particular imagery and type of skill, but in the final analysis it must depend upon æsthetic factors. A picture conveys its message more quickly than words and the pictorial image will be assimilated before the text; and thus the designer stands or falls by the clarity with which he conveys the message.

PROPAGANDA

Classic examples of the poster were provided at the end of the nineteenth and the beginning of the twentieth century by Toulouse-Lautrec in France, in Britain by William Nicholson and James Pryde (who used the pseudonym The Beggarstaff Brothers). Since then the graphic arts of propaganda have greatly extended in other ways—in advertisements in newspapers and magazines, in brochures and in the design of packages and containers. They are all seen under different conditions and in different surroundings and each is a separate problem that, nevertheless, must take its due part in a logical sequence of announcements.

To combine the illustration and the typography of a press advertisement into an harmonious unity is a serious discipline, which, when successfully maintained, can produce results of an almost classic dignity.

In package design is another problem like that of the poster, demanding restraint and simplicity, and a sense of colour and form that will most readily catch the eye, together with an awareness of economy in the printing process used.

In all these forms, graphic art is not necessarily rendered inferior because it serves a useful purpose. It is adapted to special conditions, but in fulfilling these conditions most adequately, it is true to basic principles of art.

Test Yourself

1. The graphic arts were not often used as a direct form of expression in the Victorian Age. Discuss this statement.

2. What are the advantages of lithography as a method of reproduction?

3. Describe some of the purposes for which the graphic arts are used commercially today.

Answers will be found at the end of the book

LITHOGRAPHY AND CARICATURE

Lithography in the time of Honoré Daumier (1808-79) was a comparatively new technique, and this great artist soon proved himself one of the greatest lithographers. His output included a number of lithographs dealing with artists and connoisseurs. The subject above, Two Artists Examining the Work of a Rival, appeared in "Charivari" in 1852. To the same paper he contributed many caricatures savagely attacking King Louis-Philippe and his government, on account of which the paper was on several occasions suppressed by the police. His political thrusts were appreciated but his very personal style of drawing was not popular, so that he never realized good prices for these illustrations which have been so much appreciated since.

Some of Toulouse-Lautrec's masterpieces were the posters he executed in colour lithography. This example shows how, with a few lines, he catches a characteristic pose, exaggerated to form a striking design, and illustrates his preference for strong silhouette.

LIMESTONE STATUE FROM A TOMB IN ANCIENT EGYPT

The Seated Scribe, keen, shrewd and alert, square of jaw and thin of lip, belongs to the Egyptian Fifth Dynasty. Whereas the legs, back and arms are treated as large formal masses, more careful attention is paid to the details of the shoulders and head. The statue is now in the Louvre. The colossal ram on the opposite page is one of many which, all alike and regularly spaced, line the avenue of approach to the famous temple at Karnak; it is seen as a simple architectural mass forming part of the plan of the building and makes a striking contrast to the brilliant Egyptian sky.

CHAPTER XV

APPRECIATION OF SCULPTURE

SCULPTURE is the language of shapes as music is the language of sounds. Since the dawn of civilization, man has made things in clay; from earthenware vessels for his use, to idols for his worship. He has cut things in stone for utility and non-utility purposes. He uses it to grind corn, to make roads and houses, he has burnt it for lime and made implements from it. But it is rather that other use, the non-utility, with which we are now to deal. To make statues of his gods and heroes, to commemorate great deeds, to embellish his architecture, to record his doings and feelings, man has cut and carved stone. He has moulded clay for the same purposes.

The sculptor still uses these two materials to express his thoughts. He models in clay or similar substance; this is called the plastic method. He carves in stone, wood and other materials; this is called the glyptic method. Sometimes a combination of these two methods may be used, as, for instance, in cast concrete which may be finished by chiselling.

In the plastic approach the sculptor applies piece upon piece of clay or wax until he makes a desired shape. In the glyptic approach he starts with a mass of material and cuts it away piece by piece until he arrives at his design. These, the only two ways of making sculpture, are also known respectively as modelling and carving. Whatever new materials may in the future be discovered or invented they could only be used by the sculptor to mould or carve, for these are the twin methods of communicating the language of form.

Sculpture is a universal art which can be understood by everyone. We can all see that one person is more beautiful, that is, more shapely, than another, though we may disagree as to which is which: the delicate shapes of a baby's hands affect us differently from those of a "horny handed son of toil." We can all appreciate

the difference between one teapot and another and one may please us more than the other. Most people get pleasure from seeing the shapeliness of a horse or a dog or a cat, and we all notice when a friend has grown thinner or fatter. We are affected by shapes, though perhaps we do not think of it quite in that way, and so we hold the key to the understanding of the sculptors' language.

Many protest that they do not understand sculpture. The reason is that they have either sought in the wrong way to understand it, or have not sought to understand it at all. Which is the right way and which the wrong? The right way is to look for shapes and forms, to encourage our eyes and mind to compare one shape

EGYPTIAN CHARACTERIZATION

The smiling face, individual nose and strong mouth of the head reproduced below, express a distinct personality. The head belongs to the Twelfth Dynasty and is carved in obsidian, a stone so hard that it requires the greatest skill in cutting, grinding and polishing.

with another and so appraise its peculiar virtue.

Sculpture can be appraised only through its appearance, by the way in which the light falls on it here and is more or less excluded there. Keep your mind open to receive the physical rendering of its meaning. People often ask "ought I to like the sculpture of so and so?" the answer to which is "yes, if you do and no, if you don't; but be sure you really do or don't." For there is not one right outlook only but many and they depend on the individual spectator, on his particular ego, on his artistic, mental, psychological and even on biological development.

The only sure foundation on which to build a sound appreciation of the visual arts is that of first of all looking and liking because new shapes seem lovely to our eyes and mind. Most of us have the capacity to enjoy shapes and can strengthen that ability; and when the awareness is strong, a new richness is added to life. We shall then wonder why we did not discover it before. Imagine how much poorer life would be if bereft of songs and symphonies, how impoverished if books vanished. Yet to many the pleasure which the appreciation of shapes gives is feeble indeed; the potentiality is there but not the awareness.

Look at the shape of things around us, in the room in which we are reading. Is one piece of furniture more pleasant to the eye than another? Does the shape of our teacups please or annoy us, or does it affect us not at all? Why do we like the shape of one friend's nose better than that of another, or why does the shape of his hand seem more, or less, expressive than our own? Cultivate the habit of examining shapes of natural objects and compare them with man-made things.

As a general rule the more nearly the latter resemble the former in quality the better. That is why the delicate shape of the leg of a Chippendale chair (a shape which cannot be reproduced on a drawing-board with a compass and set-square) is finer than the legs of most late Victorian furniture which are much more mechanical.

All this is delving into the language of

EGYPTIAN PORTRAIT STATUES

Dating from about 2800 B.C., the portrait statues of a priest and his wife are seated in the rigid frontal pose typical of Egyptian sculpture. Though the individual features are generalized the headdresses and pleated garments, fashionable at the time, are treated realistically.

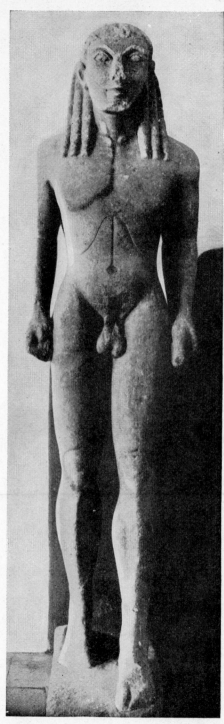

form which a sculptor uses when he carves stone or moulds clay in order to pass on his ideas and comments on life and things. By learning that language we can more easily understand the works of the great masters of sculpture.

The flowering of the leading historic styles of sculpture was the outcome of a steady tradition which took, in most cases, several centuries to mature. Tradition forms style, which may be a little modified by local conditions—the Greek style, the Roman style, the Renaissance style, the Gothic style, the modern style. But what is the modern style? The more or less steady flow of tradition, which, in the past formed the model for the sculptors (and this applies equally to painters) has been disturbed by the influx of hundreds of new ideas pouring into the main stream from sources all over the world. This is due to the camera, means of rapid transit, and the general overflowing of national ideas and ideals beyond political frontiers. The speedy developments of science and the machine besides, have shaken the steady working of the world violently out of gear. It is generally admitted that civilization the world over is in the melting pot, and sculpture, ever a mirror of the times, has the same symptoms of disturbance.

These are years of experiment. New ideas, new techniques are being tried out. Strange new forms are appearing in modern sculpture so that the average person is bewildered and confused; simple tradition has been overwhelmed by the welter of new material which has descended upon us. A style which meets with general acceptance does not exist, because we find here a sculptor whose ideas and style are

GREEK SCULPTURE OF 600 B.C.
The Apollo (left) from the Athens Museum, dates from about 600 B.C.; the figure is characterized by protruding eyes, a mouth with upturned corners and conventional hair style. The rigid pose with the left foot advanced is typical of many Egyptian statues of the period.

NATURALISM AND CONVENTION

The bronze Charioteer of Delphi (below) dates from about 480 B.C. The hair curls naturally round the headband, the hands and feet are life-like; the eyes, made of glass, are shaded by lashes of fine bronze strips. Yet the figure has the quality of a fluted column.

EXPRESSION OF PERSONALITY

The statue of Hermes (250 B.C.) (above) has been definitely identified as the work of the Greek master Praxiteles. It was described by a contemporary writer and found 1,500 years later buried on the site named. The ease and grace of the pose are particularly striking.

still moulded by Renaissance art and there a sculptor whose work is made in bold new shapes bearing little resemblance to these natural forms which most historic sculptors have employed. It may be with sculpture as with other things in this fast-moving world, that entirely new ideas will be born in this century.

Isaac Newton has given way to Einstein, and Michelangelo may have to give way before Einstein's counterpart in art, but that does not mean that the older men were not great. A new revelation does not make a former one less significant. Different forms of loveliness may be accepted when the birth pangs of the new age are over.

Let it be said, however, that the present period of experiment is good. The best historic sculpture has been, in the main, static in character, but these days are

FORMAL EFFECT

This head of Apollo (early fifth century B.C.) represents the climax of Greek sculpture. The formal, simplified treatment, gives the effect of neither stone nor flesh.

NATURAL DETAIL

Once part of a full-length statue of Athena, by Pheidias (fifth century B.C.) which stood on the Acropolis at Athens, the detail shown above has a more natural appearance than the Apollo on the left.

difficult for the production of sculpture of that quiet and settled order which characterizes so much of the best work of days gone by. To many, modern sculpture seems ugly and it certainly runs contrary to that kind of beauty which our Victorian grandfathers understood. But sculpture together with other spiritual activities of man, when the present conditions of life pass, will settle down into some new and vigorous style, and consequently into a condition necessary for the best expression of its art. Meanwhile sculpture will persist. There is something inevitable about its existence. Man always has and always will carve stone, marbles, woods, and ivories and mould bronzes into lovely and expressive shapes.

Sculpture irresistibly reflects the times of its production. During the seventeen-hundreds sculpture was imbued with eighteenth-century grace; the nineteenth century produced dull, mechanical stuff; twentieth-century sculpture is experimental and perturbed. On the whole, it will always tell succeeding generations what manner of men we are.

The lesson we learn from historic sculpture is that in its finest manifestations it is not, in the photographic sense, representative of natural forms. The sculpture of these days realizes that forms of nature, admirably limited as they are to their material in the human figure of flesh and blood, need transcribing into stone and bronze forms, so that in the resultant sculpture, the material used and the natural forms on which it is based have partnership in determining the final result.

In other words, a stone or marble statue of a man should show flesh forms transmitted into stone ones. Stone, bronze, wood etc., have a dignity and character of their own and a sculptor neglects these at his peril. So that if it were possible to make a perfectly life-like man in stone or bronze the result would not necessarily be a work of art, because it had not been seen by the eye and passed through the mind of the artist. Photographic likeness does not produce art. Art must be a comment on nature and not a copy of it. If we remember this it will help us towards understanding much which may seem puzzling in modern work.

Test Yourself

1. Name the two ways in which sculpture can be made.
2. In its finest manifestations sculpture is not representative of natural forms. Discuss this statement briefly.

Answers will be found at the end of the book

FIFTH-CENTURY PARTHENON FRIEZE

Although in this bas-relief from the Parthenon, built about the fifth century B.C., only the essential details of both horse and rider are included and no attempt has been made to disguise the texture of the marble, the work has a most lively appearance.

CHAPTER XVI

HISTORY OF SCULPTURE

THE advent of the true sculptor in the history of art is foreshadowed by the animal carvings of Palæolithic man, but his art is first fully realized in the cultures of the ancient Near East. Like architecture, sculpture in Egypt was bound up with the desire to perpetuate or to serve the dead, with the idea of duration. This accounts for the immense size of much Egyptian sculpture and the impression of monotonous uniformity it makes as a whole. Throughout its long history (4500-1090 B.C.) Egyptian sculpture never entirely succeeded in throwing off the trammels of certain conventions, conspicuous among which is what is known as the law of frontality. All the figures, standing or sitting, confront the spectator; there is no inclination to the right or to the left. In portrait statues of the Pharaohs, the characterization is generalized to make an impression of imperturbable calm and monumentality, and to express what was more significant than individual traits, the enduring power of the Pharaohs, the abstract idea of sovereignty. In statues of the lower classes, such as the limestone Seated Scribe (page 216), the type often gives way to the individual. But Egyptian sculpture is never truly three-dimensional; most of the statues are distinctly four-sided, like four reliefs carved on the four sides of the block of stone, and do not give an impression of visual unity and massive harmony.

The civilizations of the Tigris-Euphrates valley produced comparatively little sculpture in the round, probably because of the lack of stone in that rich agricultural territory. The chief monuments of Chaldean art, discovered at the palaces of Tello and Susa, are all in the Louvre. They are bas-reliefs and great statues of black diorite, eight of which bear the name of Gudea, Prince of Sirpoula, and one of which is reproduced on page 35. This statue reveals a stylized treatment of detail very suited to the material in which it is made. It is of monumental dignity, but shows a conception of the human form directly opposed to that of the Egyptians. The Egyptian sculptor tends to elongate his figures and attenuate detail; the Chaldean artist prefers a sturdy, robust type with salient muscles and broad shoulders.

Assyrian sculpture is less interesting; very few figures in the round were made, and those were rigid and conventional (page 32). But among the reliefs with which the Assyrians decorated their palaces are some magnificent expressions of animal life (page 38). Babylonian and early Persian art also produced remarkable animal studies. The masterpiece of early Persian art, the celebrated Frieze of Archers in the Louvre from the palace at Susa, reveals not only an Assyrian origin, but a delicacy and sobriety of drawing probably due to the proximity of Greek artists.

Sculpture did not interest the Ægean peoples except for small figurines, or statuettes. It was with the Greeks that the art became of supreme importance. To the Greeks, sculpture was the art which called for the highest talent in the artist and the greatest sensibility in the spectator. And it was not only important to the Greeks themselves; it has been a dominating influence in the development of Western art and civilization. It falls into three periods, Archaic, Hellenic and Hellenistic, and covers the centuries from 1100 to about 100 B.C. The object of much early Greek sculpture, both in relief and in the round, was architectural decoration, though independent statues were made for commemorative purposes.

In these so-called archaic statues the forms are simple, almost geometrical, the various parts being based upon conventional devices rather than visual experience. One of the most ancient marble statues discovered in Greece is an Artemis excavated at Delos, dating from about

PHYSICAL SUFFERING PORTRAYED IN STONE

The famous Laocoon group in the Vatican was executed by three Rhodian sculptors about 50 B.C. The raised right arm is evidently a reconstruction; it has been learned that in the original the arm was bent in near the head.

620 B.C. It might almost be taken for a pillar or a tree trunk with summary indications of a head, arms and a girdle. Another archaic feminine type, the famous Hera of Samos, now in the Louvre, is about thirty or forty years later in date. The general aspect is still that of a column, but the goddess is draped with a shawl in which the folds, though severely conventionalized, show that nature has been consulted. A male statue standing stiffly with his arms against his body and the left foot advancing was developed in the sixth century; it was the type first applied to Apollo and to victorious athletes. Such an archaic Apollo is reproduced on page 222. The protruding eyes, the mouth with upturned corners, apparently the result of the artist's inability to convey the transition between the lips and the cheeks, are typical of Greek archaic statues. Other sixth-century figures, those found on the Acropolis, such as the

LIFE-LIKE ROMAN HEAD

This head of a lady, a typical Roman portrait from the first century A.D., is vital and probably also an excellent likeness of the subject.

one shown on page 50, are draped, and though the pose is rigid, they have an air of sophistication lacking in the nudes, due to the elaborate decorative treatment of the hair and garments. Some traces yet remain of the vivid colouring which once adorned these statues.

In the Hellenic period the sculptor began to temper these archaic forms by approaching nature more closely. His aim was, however, not the imitation of nature but the refinement of proportions; Pheidias' contemporary Polycleitus even worked out an ideal set of proportions for the human figure. The celebrated Charioteer of Delphi (page 221), a bronze statue which once belonged to a group with chariot and horses, retains the austerity and formal beauty of archaic work combined with naturalism in the detail. Pheidias' Athena Lemnia (page 222) has more freedom of pose than the charioteer especially in the placing of the head, which is turned to the right and slightly lowered. This head, like the sculptures from the Parthenon, which may also be the work of Pheidias, is generalized in character; it expresses only the essential aspects of the structure and is scarcely more naturalistic than archaic statuary. Fifth-century sculpture in Greece does indeed maintain a rare balance between the reproduction of appearances and the preservation of the quality of the material in which the artist is working.

This impersonal attitude soon gave way to greater individuality. In Praxiteles' Hermes (page 221) the delicate charm of the facial expression, the languid, dreamy impression of the whole are more strongly felt than the exquisite texture of the marble. The artist's feeling for the stone is less than his ambition to make stone resemble flesh; the balance between material and subject is no longer quite even. In the familiar draped seated figure known as Demeter of Cnidus in the British Museum, the folds of the garments are not all necessary to the design, but are introduced merely for the sake of imitating nature.

During the Hellenistic period of Greek sculpture the tendency towards naturalism became ever more marked, and was allied to a feeling of restlessness. In the Victory

ACCURATE REPRESENTATION IN ROMAN PORTRAITURE

This detail, from a full-length statue of the Emperor Augustus addressing his army, is typical of Roman portraiture in its accurate treatment; it is of marble and originally was painted. It was found at Prima Porta in the villa of Livia, wife of Augustus, and is now in the Vatican.

oi Samothrace (page 40) the centre of interest is in the restless curves and minute folds of the wind-swept drapery. Realism reaches a climax in the famous Laocoon group (page 225) not only in the modelling of the bodies but in the tortured expressions of the faces. In later Greek sculpture, subject matter became more varied and included trivial and even frivolous themes. But the same period produced the charming Tanagra figurines, thousands of which, both isolated and forming part of the decoration of pots and other objects, have been found, chiefly on burial sites. Their purpose is unknown. They are distinguished by a natural grace and spontaneity entirely suited to the clay technique.

Clay was the favourite medium of the Etruscans who were culturally closely allied to the Greeks. The strange Apollo of Veii of about 500 B.C., among the best-known Etruscan statues, is clearly influenced by the archaic Greek type of Apollo, but compared with early Greek sculpture there is a startling vigour and robustness in the forward movement of the pose.

ETRUSCAN MODELLING OF TERRA-COTTA SARCOPHAGUS

The detail reproduced here shows the upper portion of two recumbent figures on a sarcophagus from Caere of about 500 B.C. The figures are of terra-cotta, the material most favoured by the Etruscans, and are conventionally coloured. The gestures of the hands and the alert poise of the heads are expressive of considerable vitality.

HUMAN FEATURES IN THE ROMANESQUE

Now in the Victoria and Albert Museum, this capital shows Christ's entry into Jerusalem. The complete disregard of natural proportions, the treatment of the hair and features—particularly the full, rounded cheeks—are typical of the decorative character of Romanesque sculpture.

The Romans decorated their huge villas and baths with statues brought from Greece or copies of Greek statues, such as the well-known Venus Preparing to Enter the Bath adapted to suit Roman taste. Authentic Roman art is, however, best represented by portraiture, which enabled the Romans to indulge their love of literal fact. Their portraits are outstanding for their vitality and are, for the most part, extremely realistic. The statue of Augustus (page 227) has something of the broad simplicity of Greek work despite the elabor-

ate rendering of the costume, but most Roman sculpture is interesting chiefly as a photographic record of a remarkable people.

In the early Christian era sculpture was produced to a very limited extent only, the statue in the round being considered a pagan graven image. Sculpture is found in the reliefs on the sarcophagi where classical figures are used to express Christian ideas, but the tradition of sculpture was carried on chiefly by ivory carvers, who kept it alive until it emerged hundreds

BYZANTINE AND GOTHIC FIGURES

When in A.D. 330 the Emperor Constantine moved his headquarters from Rome to Byzantium (later Constantinople and now Istanbul) Roman architects working there came under the influence of the Byzantine Greeks. It became the custom for interiors to be richly decorated, particularly with mosaics. Owing to the controversy over the use of images, Byzantine sculptors developed abstract conventional designs and on the rare occasions when figures were introduced they followed a set formula. The stereotyped figure of the small ivory Madonna and Child (c. 1000) on the left is typical of the period, particularly in the treatment of the drapery. Yet there is obvious similarity between this small Byzantine statue and the great rigid stone kings and queens from the western porch of Chartres Cathedral opposite. Begun in the twelfth century, Chartres Cathedral is regarded as one of the finest examples in France of Gothic architecture and contains many excellent examples of typical medieval figure sculpture, it being possible to trace, among those in the south transept, the rapid technical advance which took place toward the middle of that century. The sculptor of the kings and queens illustrated, not inhibited as were the Byzantines by religious controversy, decided to adorn his pillars with human figures and still to preserve the impression of columns. He therefore made the lines of the figures and garments resemble flutings.

BRONZE EFFIGY OF A QUEEN

This effigy of Queen Eleanor on her tomb in Westminster Abbey, was ordered by Henry III in 1291 and cast by William Torel, a noted goldsmith and citizen of London, as described in contemporary records.

COMPANION PIECE

Like that of Queen Eleanor, the effigy of Henry III shown above is by William Torel. It is on the king's tomb in Westminster Abbey.

THIRTEENTH-CENTURY ARCH

The magnificent Virgin's Portal from the Cathedral of Notre Dame, Paris, so richly adorned, should be compared with the sculpture from Chartres of the previous century (page 231). The treatment of the figures here is much more natural and there is more individuality and variety in their pose. At the same time the result is decorative and the design is made to fill the shape of the pointed arch so that its main features are not obscured.

of years later to adorn the Gothic cathedrals. The ivory carvings followed the idiom of the Hellenic style, naturalism gradually giving way to a formal beauty based on convention and symbol.

When sculpture began to revive again on a large scale, it took the forms of the Byzantine craftsmen. Romanesque sculpture is always architectural, spirited, varied and highly decorative. The tympanum in the porch of the abbey church, Moisac, is an oft-quoted and typical example of Romanesque fantasy. Creatures of the imagination here keep company with kings and saints, and scrolls, twists and conventional ornament create an almost Eastern atmosphere. The carving is an integral part of the stone masonry. In the Gothic period also, from about A.D. 1150-1550, sculpture was almost entirely associated with architecture, its purpose being the enrichment of the cathedral. The rows of kings and queens on either side of the celebrated western portal of Chartres (c. 1145) (page 231) are rigid elongated figures, their arms close to their bodies, the lines of their draperies like flutings, so that they give the impression of columns. The conventionalization of the figure so that it harmonized perfectly with the place it was to occupy was frequently combined in Gothic sculpture with an intense liveliness and a marked feeling for individuality.

This led to a similar development already recorded in the outline of Greek art, an ever-increasing naturalism. The celebrated Smiling Angel of Reims of the thirteenth century is much more realistic than the

ENGLISH ALABASTER

Alabaster was generally used in England for religious and monumental sculpture from about 1350. The chief interest of alabaster effigies is that they faithfully render every change of fashion. In that reproduced Sir Richard Redman wears the Tudor collar combining the Lancastrian with the Yorkist roses; Lady Redman is dressed in widow's weeds of the time. The effigies were executed about 1490 and show the technique widely favoured by sculptors during the Tudor period.

kings and queens of Chartres; this is shown in the tilt of the head and the swing of the body, though the sense of decorative fitness has not been lost. In such carvings as the foliage-clustered columns from Southwell the native English oak, blackberry, wild rose, strawberry and other plants are reproduced with complete adherence to nature. Whatever the liveliness and keen perception of the medieval sculptor it is clear that his skilful imitation of appearances has destroyed the essential character of the stone.

From the late thirteenth century onwards memorial statues for tombs were made which gradually became portraits, such as those of Sir Richard and Lady Redman at Harewood (page 235). The likeness of effigies to the persons whom they commemorated was frequently heightened by the practice of taking casts from the actual heads. Thus portraiture was another road which led to naturalism.

Gothic art flourished most in the north. In Italy the revival of interest in Greek and Roman culture began about 1300. Renaissance sculpture was not a repetition of the past; it was animated by a very different spirit from antiquity, a spirit modified by all that had been achieved during the Middle Ages. And although to Renaissance sculptors classical art meant a return to nature, naturalism in the greatest of them was not mere description but a means of conveying spiritual significance. Donatello (1386-1466) accented individual traits as in his celebrated Zuccone (pumpkinhead) in order to express inner meaning, while with him realism is always controlled, as in Greek Hellenic work, by great formal power. There is a wealth of detail in the bronze equestrian statue known as Gattemelata (page 243), but it is subordinated to the massive character of the whole and related as a design to its architectural site in the square of Sant' Antonio, Padua. Verrocchio's dramatic Colleoni statue in Venice, makes an interesting comparison with the Gattemelata. The forceful, impetuous nature of the military leader is suggested by the violent twist of the body, the grim expression and the piercing eye, but the

formality of the design again controls the realism of the conception.

This uncompromising realism, combined with the attempt to express formally what was most significant in character, reached a climax in the work of Michelangelo (1475-1564). All his sculptures were designed as a definite part of an architectural setting. In his work formal value and representational content are perfectly balanced; he has absolute control over the human figure as an organic structure, but he never loses his feeling for the nature of his material. Parts of the figure of Day, for example, in the New Sacristy of San Lorenzo, Florence, are highly finished, the back and shoulder being most scrupulously modelled, while other parts, the head and the left hand are still in the rough, giving all the innate quality of the marble and arousing the feeling that the figure is struggling to free itself. There is a restless, tortuous element in much of Michelangelo's work, but the interlocking movements of which he was fond are always resolved into a perfect harmony, as in the Madonna of the New Sacristy. In the restless rhythms of his sculpture Michelangelo heralded the baroque art of the succeeding century, but in baroque sculpture as in late Greek work there is complete loss of feeling for the stone. The dominating personality of the period was Bernini (1598-1680), architect as well as sculptor; he shows astonishing technical virtuosity in the handling of materials with no regard for their true nature or limitations. In Spain, where the baroque spirit found fruitful soil, realism was developed to such an extreme that actual hair and garments and glass tears were used. In France during the seventeenth and eighteenth centuries the exaggerated emotionalism and realism of southern baroque art was modified by a native grace and suavity especially in portraiture.

In the nineteenth century sculpture was more and more restricted to the imitation of natural appearances. Before tracing its further development some mention must be made of the great cultures of the East, of India and China, where sculpture had followed a different line of development,

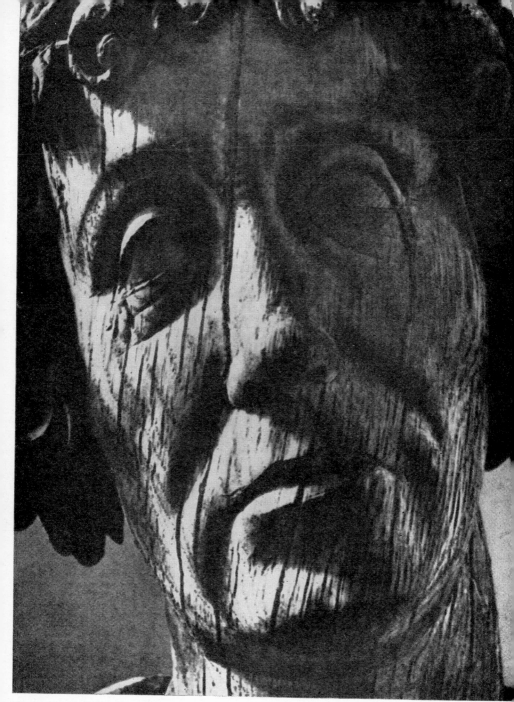

FOURTEENTH-CENTURY WOODCARVING

Medieval German sculptors excelled in woodcarving. In this fourteenth-century head of St. John the exposure of the pronounced grain of the wood, which originally was hidden by paint, enhances the expression of piety.

237

PROFILE PORTRAIT

*Desiderio da Settignano, who is noted for his delicately carved busts of
women and children, worked in Florence and was for a short time a pupil
of Donatello. He has carved this portrait almost as though it were incised
rather than in bas-relief, so carried away is he by the design made by the
striking profile and waving hair, the long neck and full bust, of his subject.*

FLORENTINE WOODCARVING

Of roughly the same date as the relief on the opposite page, this Florentine bust of coloured and gilded wood renders a similar subject in a strikingly different manner. Whereas Desiderio makes ample use of line, here the emphasis is on mass and every unnecessary detail is eliminated. Florence became the chief centre of artistic activity early in the fifteenth century.

IMPRESSION OF MOVEMENT

*Michelangelo's statue of Moses was designed between 1513 and 1516 ; it
was intended originally to decorate the tomb of Pope Julius II, which, however, was never completed. The statue is now in the church of San Pietro
in Vincoli, Rome. Although the figure is compact the pose suggests alertness.*

of the primitive carvings of the African and Oceanic peoples and of the sculpture of the ancient Mexican civilization which were to have great influence on European art.

Negro carving has nothing to do with the representation of natural appearances; it is symbolic and connected with ancestor worship and religious rites. Usually a cylindrical mass, sometimes starkly geometric, sometimes with a richly carved surface, it reveals an intense feeling for three-dimensional organization and is full of vitality. Most African sculptures are relatively small and most of them are made in wood. The Oceanic peoples often represent ancestors by a rough cylindrical column surmounted by an elliptical shield carved in the semblance of a human shape, boldly designed and coloured red or black. Towering above the natives, they produce a startling effect in their tropical surroundings.

Mexican sculpture, chiefly stone carving, which is exceptionally well represented in the British Museum, is remarkable for its truth to material. In its exuberance of detail it recalls Indian sculpture, and like Indian art it was the product of a people obsessed with the spiritual world. It reached its climax during the first five or six centuries A.D. and some of the finest examples come from the great Mayan city of Copan in the east of Central America. The variety and fertility of invention exhibited in the work from this one area are illustrated by the two examples on pages 247-8, the almost classical figure of the maize goddess, conceived entirely in the round, and the huge sandstone monument, made as nearly rectangular in shape as possible, with its complicated, carved designs and hieroglyphic inscriptions.

Indian sculpture shows in its development a trend towards florid elegance and the over-emphasis of decorative detail, but it never becomes subservient to nature. It is concerned with all the sensuous aspects of nature, the human figure and all the teeming animal and vegetable life of the tropics. It is, like Gothic art, exclusively religious and has none of the defects of

GOLDSMITH OR SCULPTOR?
The bronze Perseus with the head of Medusa in the Piazza della Signoria, Florence, is the work of Benvenuto Cellini (1500-71), a goldsmith as well as a sculptor of great merit.

EQUESTRIAN STATUES

     Hubert le Sueur studied in Italy and his Charles I (top left) done in 1633, now to be seen in Whitehall, London, has something in common with Donatello's Gattemelata (1446) at Padua (bottom left). Both statues are in bronze—as is Verrochio's Colleoni (1486) shown above—and in both the detail is deliberately subordinated in order to emphasize the general form. In the Charles I the large, simplified proportions of the horse and the some-what passive figure of the rider suggest gentleness as well as dignity, as does the Gattemelata who sits relaxed in the saddle. In marked contrast to both these statues, Colleoni appears almost to rise in the stirrups. Energy and determination are expressed by the twist of the figure and the alert turn of the horse's head. Realism is here offset by the decoration on mane, tail and saddle, which is quite out of keeping with the treatment of the figure as a whole.

TECHNICAL SKILL IN THE USE OF MARBLE

The melodramatic grouping and intensity of facial expression, together with the impression of intense agitation conveyed by voluminous folds of the drapery beautifully depicted in marble make this detail from Bernini's Ecstasy of Santa Teresa, executed in 1646 for the Church of Santa Maria della Vittoria, Rome, overwhelmingly theatrical.

official art. The influence of Greece penetrated to north-western India through the conquests of Alexander the Great and modified the characteristics of Indian art during the first centuries of the Christian era, but it did not bring about, as in the West, a superficial imitation of natural appearances: the native Indian spirit reasserted itself and gradually threw off the foreign influence. This spirit is manifested in monumental figures of the Buddha seated with legs crossed, his hands folded in his lap and eyes downcast; the forms are simply treated with only the essential planes represented and with no individual lines in the face. But Indian sculpture has another aspect; it is often characterized by an intense and literal realism, always controlled, however, by extraordinary feeling for plastic relations and rhythm.

The Indian sculptor loves to reproduce the actual surface and texture of the flesh, but he is interested above all in making a design from the undulating and yielding movements of the body. He can twist the torso to any angle and relate the limbs to the trunk in any possible pose and in his eagerness to express movement he often gives the figure four or more arms. Feeling for material is never lacking. The Avolo-kita (page 250) is made in bronze, the only material which would have suited its small size, fine detail, grace and suavity.

REALISM IN SPANISH WORK

This eighteenth-century wooden figure of Christ bearing His Cross, by the Spanish sculptor Alexandra Carnicerno of Salamanca, has real rope round the waist and neck, dried grass is stuck to the rock and the tears which fall from the eyes are of glass. These are probably additions to the original.

AFRICAN WOODCARVING
In this seventeenth-century portrait of a tribal king (above) in polished wood from the Congo, the emphasis is on the head. No attempt has been made at accurate portraiture.

In Chinese sculpture, nature is always subordinated to an ideal of conventions and abstract form. Buddhist subjects showed at first strong Indian influence, but during the Wei dynasty archaic figures were produced in a definitely Chinese style. The features are conventionally treated and, except for the head and the arms, the figure is so flat that it seems more like a relief than sculpture in the round. The drapery is formed into a sweeping linear design. In the T'ang dynasty the forms become fuller and more rounded, the poses elegant and relaxed. Later on there was more delight in decorative detail for its own sake, a more naturalistic approach, and instead of stone, wood was often used covered with a special preparation of plaster of Paris, known as gesso, and painted. The Chinese genius was perhaps most characteristically expressed in smaller works, in clay figurines and in bronzes. The Chinese had exceptional feeling for clay, particularly in the modelling of animals which, when finished, were painted or glazed not naturalistically but according to conventions. Bronze was used from the earliest times by the Chinese for the making of sacrificial vessels many of which are decorated by monstrous and terrifying animals, dragons and strange birds handled with great sensibility in spite of the stylization. The sacrificial vessel in the form of an owl, reproduced on page 255, shows the Chinese power of retaining all the essential character and vitality of the bird.

In later nineteenth-century European sculpture the outstanding figure was Auguste Rodin (1840-1917), who tried to free sculpture from representational aims just as his contemporaries had attempted to free painting. "I find the cubic factor

MAYAN STONE CARVING

The elaborately carved figure of a Mayan priest (right) although in relief on a squared pillar, has almost the appearance of a statue, so deep is the carving.

247

CENTRAL AMERICAN STONE CARVING
Now in the British Museum, the statue (left) from Copan, in Central America, dated A.D. 300, is an example of the early work of the Mayas, an Indian race.

and clay figures of horses and dancers, reveals a gift, rare in European art, of conveying in a momentary pose all the essence and vitality of his subject. Aristide Maillol (1861-1945), imbued with the spirit of classical antiquity, worked in terracotta, stone and bronze and achieved a balance between art and nature.

The works produced today reflect all the confusion of a rapidly changing age where there is no unifying philosophy or tradition. Frank Dobson (b. 1887) reveals an attitude similar to that of Maillol; Eric Gill (1882-1940), a highly decorative artist, attempted once more to relate sculpture to architecture; Jacob Epstein (b. 1880) has also produced architectural sculpture and is a fine portraitist in bronze.

Another group of sculptors, concentrating on their material and determined at all costs to escape from the representational, have experimented in purely abstract or geometric forms carried out in various mediums. Among these are Brancusi, Lipshitz, Ossip Zadkine, Barbara Hepworth and, in some of his work, Henry Moore (b. 1898). They derived something from Negro art. But great sculpture can never be purely abstract: it must always be related to life and seek to create a balance between art and nature.

everywhere," he said, "so that plane and volume seem to me to be all the laws of life and beauty." This statement shows that Rodin's understanding of sculpture was comprehensive enough to include all the developments that have taken place since his time, but he did not completely realize his ideals, and feeling for form is often with him overweighted by his psychological interest. Degas, in his bronze

Test Yourself

1. What is the difference in motive behind the rigidity of an archaic Greek Apollo and the formality of typical Egyptian sculpture?
2. Can you point to resemblances between the Greek Charioteer of Delphi and the Gothic Kings and Queens of Chartres?
3. What are the characteristics of Roman sculpture?

Answers will be found at the end of the book

CHAPTER XVII

THE SCULPTOR'S TECHNIQUE

SCULPTURE is an art wrought by men's hands in a variety of materials and by many processes. We learn to appreciate sculpture, more perhaps than any other of the arts, through a knowledge of the methods of execution.

To get a general idea of the many stages through which a work passes from its inception to completion we will, first of all, summarize them. Later each process will be described in greater detail.

We will suppose that the sculptor intends to carry out his idea by means of a life-size figure, or group of figures, carved in stone. There are different methods by which this is done. The one most frequently used is the following: the sculptor first expresses his idea in several small sketch models in clay (the same clay as that used by the potter); in these models he tries out the design of the silhouettes from every angle and the true relation of the principal and subordinate masses to one another. The final sketch model is of vital importance for on this effort to express the idea with arresting silhouettes depends the success or failure of the finished work. No armature, i.e. a support inside the clay, is used, as this would restrict freedom in making quick alterations.

Having satisfied himself that he has obtained the most striking and impressive interpretation, the sculptor will proceed to make a working model, using this sketch model as a guide; this will be to scale, probably one-third full size. That is large enough to work out every problem of proportion, treatment and detail, and yet small enough to allow experiments and alterations to be made easily and quickly, so saving much time and labour on the full-sized statue.

For this model an armature or framework must be made to support the clay. When finished, this armature will be covered with clay about half an inch thick. The nude model is now posed on the throne according to the previously made sketch, and, with the use of proportional callipers for measuring, the figure is modelled. Even if the statue is to be draped it will first be modelled nude to ensure the proper construction of the figure. This will not be a photographic representation of the nude, for liberties will be taken with the forms of nature according to the require-

CHINESE BUDDHIST SCULPTURE

This painted dark-stone head of a Buddha is of the Northern Wei Dynasty (early sixth century A.D.) and comes from the cave temples of Lung Men. The sharply cut features give the impression of great majesty and austere character.

ments of the subject and the sculptor's preferences. To exaggerate or to modify these forms is the prerogative of the artist.

The working model should be a finished miniature of the full-sized statue, every problem of composition and treatment being worked out; when completed, this will be cast in plaster and painted with white shellac. The full-sized armature of iron, wood, and lead piping is made and covered with clay, with the help of a pointing instrument for enlarging, the full-sized statue is built up from the working model. When this large model is completed and cast in plaster an exact replica will be carved in stone. For this work another form of pointing instrument, illustrated on page 269, is used.

Now as to other methods. The sculptor may prefer to give himself a freer hand in the stone, carving his statue or group with only a small-scale model as guide. Or again he may prefer from the outset to have the expression of his idea influenced only by the material in which the work is to be executed. Then with no preliminary clay model and with but a drawing or two, he will carve his idea direct into the block of stone. It should be realized that this method demands a long sustained and clear perception of the effect which the sculptor seeks to produce, the power to visualize the relationship of forms from every point of view and an unerring control of his material.

When the work is to be in bronze a full-size model must be made. Work treated with almost unlimited freedom can be cast in metal. Therefore, the modelling in this case, calls for and allows of a treatment entirely different from that for stone. A

DISTORTION TO CREATE RHYTHM

The purpose of this graceful Avolokita (Lord of Pity) is to create a rhythmical design and the human body is distorted to that end; the waist is impossibly narrow, the arms are elongated and the swaying pose is echoed by the undulating forms of the vines.

Gestures of the hands are effectively used in this Indian bronze from Tanjore
to convey the impression of rhythmic movement.

STATELY FIGURE OF A CHINESE GOD
The posture of royal ease exemplified in this Kuan Yin (Goddess of Mercy) of the Chinese T'ang Dynasty was inherited from India. As the worship of the Bodhisattva Avalokitesahvara spread into China the god assumed first a sexless and then gradually the feminine form seen here.

rough surface reproduces better in bronze than a smooth one; for a greater variety of colour in the metal results and breaks up what would otherwise become a polished surface reflecting a number of distorting highlights. It will be seen from this summary how many and varied are the stages of a work. These processes will now be described in more detail.

First, a framework or armature must be made on which the clay is built and supported. This armature must be strong. It consists of a peg of wood about fourteen inches long and two inches square fixed firmly into a board about eighteen inches square and two inches thick, made so that it will not warp with the wet clay; at the top of the peg two lengths of lead or composition piping are nailed, and two small pieces of wood, joined together by wire in the shape of a Latin cross and known as butterflies, are attached to these to carry the weight of clay.

This framework is placed on a modelling stand with a revolving top. The model or sitter is seated on a model's throne, also with a revolving top, the head of the sitter being on a level with the clay model. Clay is then quickly built up round the framework to the general mass of the head, the model's throne and the clay model being constantly turned to ensure that work on all the views is kept at the same state of progress. At this stage many careful measurements must be taken with callipers from the sitter and transferred to the clay. It may not be possible for the sculptor to determine the final pose of his figure for several sittings, until he has had time to study the most characteristic position. The easy and safe movement of the head to the desired position is made possible by the armature.

CASTING THE BUST

The portrait bust has now been modelled in clay. If left exposed to the air, clay will soon dry and shrink, so the bust is cast in plaster. There are three methods of casting: (1) waste moulding, so-called because the mould is, in this method, destroyed; (2) piece moulding, so-called because the mould is made in as many

small pieces as is necessary to avoid any undercuts (a term used to describe modelling and carving of projections behind and beyond what is visible to the spectator) enabling the mould to be pulled easily off the cast and to be used again for further casts; (3) gelatine moulding. This method is used to make a mould from works in plaster, marble or other materials should copies be required. The gelatine is melted and a mould made in two parts; when the gelatine has set, the plaster is poured in and when that has set the mould is removed.

It will be seen that the danger of a mould in such a material is that it is apt to bend and so cause defective casts unless extremely carefully handled. Waste moulding is the process most generally used.

PREPARING THE MOULD

In casting a bust by waste moulding, a thin clay or zinc band about one and a half to two inches wide is first made. This little band is lightly fixed on the bust, passing completely from top to bottom round it about half an inch behind the ears, dividing the bust into two parts. A little ochre is now mixed with water to which the dry powdery plaster of Paris is added until it is of a creamy consistency. This mixture sets hard very rapidly and consequently must be quickly thrown on to the front of the bust, completing a thin covering over the whole surface. This having set, a little clay water is brushed over it. More plaster is now mixed, this time without any ochre, and is thrown on as before until the mould attains a thickness of about an inch. When this has set, the clay band is removed and the back of the bust is moulded in similar fashion. The mould of the back of the head is now removed from the clay by tapping wedges between the two portions of the mould; this leaves the front part of the mould with the clay inside it. This clay is removed and we have the mould or negative, a reverse of our model. This is now washed, soaped and oiled so that the plaster to be poured into the mould will not adhere to it. The two moulds are now fitted and firmly tied together. For

REALISM IN CHINESE STONEWORK

This over-life-size figure of a man-darin with a casket, now in the Victoria and Albert Museum, is of the Ming Dynasty (1368-1644). It copies contemporary dress in minute detail without regard for the stone.

the casting, a thin mixing of plaster of the consistency of milk is poured inside, and the mould turned in all directions so that the plaster reaches every part of the mould. This process is repeated until the cast is sufficiently thick. When the plaster has set hard, the cast has been formed inside the mould. The mould is chipped away with a blunt chisel and mallet, the ochre, used in the first mixing, acting as a warning as the actual cast is approached. The mould cracks away from the cast revealing an exact reproduction in plaster of the clay bust. Exact it may be, but as a material for sculpture, plaster is so life-less that it has been said that the clay model is the birth, the plaster cast the death and the translation of the work into marble, stone or bronze the resurrection of a piece of sculpture.

Plaster is essentially a transition stage in a work, though when coloured by various means it can be given an interesting quality.

To carve a bust in marble, a good, sound block of statuary marble as near as possible to the size required must be chosen, preferably of Serravezza, green from the quarry. Vents or faults in marble are not infrequent. Often these can be detected by the ring of the block when hit by a hammer. Dark coloration and sand holes are difficult to detect and that chance must be taken, but by washing the block of marble streaks of colour may often be seen. To rough out the bust a well-balanced steel hammer of about two and a half or three pounds weight is used, and highly tempered steel tools called points. It will be clear that many measurements will have to be taken. For these a pointing instrument is used by which, when fixed to three points on the plaster, a sliding needle held on an arrangement of arms fitted on ball-and-socket joints will give three-dimensional measurements. This instrument is transferred to three similarly related points on the marble and the needle will give the same position on the marble. When most of the waste marble is punched away from the block, smaller tools are used thus avoiding the risk of bruising the marble in the process.

work in bronze: the *cire perdue* (lost-wax) and the sand process. The first is the older and better of the two methods. Cellini, in his autobiography, gives a lively account of the casting of his Perseus by this process.

To cast a work using the *cire perdue* method a plaster cast is first made, a clay model will serve but the risk of damage is great. The plaster cast is given a coat of shellac and a gelatine mould is made over it. The flexibility of the gelatine enables it to be pulled away from even the undercut portions of the model. This mould takes an impression in reverse of every detail. A wax casting is made from

CHINESE BIRD AND ANIMAL FORMS

Animal and bird forms are a favourite subject in Chinese sculpture, particularly that of the Chou period. The jar in the form of an owl (left) belongs to that period and is now in the Victoria and Albert Museum, while the camel (below) is in the British Museum. The figures illustrate the Chinese gift for reducing such forms to conventional pattern without losing anything of the essential characteristics of the creatures.

The tools are kept constantly sharp by rubbing them on a piece of smooth York stone wetted lest the heat of friction should take the temper from the tools. Then with the help of measurements taken by the pointing instruments, the forms are laid in with big claw tools in a broad manner. Undercutting is avoided at this stage so that, should a blemish or vent in the marble make it desirable slightly to adjust the position of the bust in the rough block, it is still possible to do so.

The main shapes of the head are roughed out with the claw tool. Bit by bit the forms are more closely carved with small claw tools, chisels and rifflers till at last all the smaller planes and subtleties of shape are reproduced and improved upon from the forms of the plaster cast.

Some sculptors consider that the beauty of marble is best shown by a smooth, almost polished finish. But, of late, there is a tendency to obtain a crisply carved and faceted surface. Thus, it is thought, the beautiful quality of the materials is shown to the greatest advantage.

There are two methods of casting a

this mould of the same thickness as the bronze cast is intended to be; this varies according to the size of the work, but for a life-size figure it needs to be no more than one-quarter of an inch thick. This hollow wax cast is filled with a composition of brick dust and plaster of a paste consistency which is called the core. When this has set, it serves to support the wax and to prevent twisting in hot weather. The outside mould is taken away and the wax cast can then be worked on by the sculptor. Some sculptors leave a finger-print impression on the base which, being reproduced in bronze, is a proof that it is that particular artist's work. The founders' wax is hard and brittle but by holding a steel tool over the flame of a candle it can be made sufficiently warm to melt the wax or soften the surface and so a considerable amount of touching-up can be done.

Ducts and air jets are provided inside the core to allow the gases to come away when the molten bronze is poured in. Runners and pins are arranged to hold the inside and outside compositions in their proper relative positions when the wax is melted out, and an outside composition mould is made round the wax. When this has set it is placed in a kiln and baked until the wax is melted out of it and runs out through the ducts. The mould is packed round with sand to hold it firmly when the metal is poured in. The molten metal is now poured in through

FRENCH DECORATIVE SCULPTURE

In Jean Goujon's Diana and the Stag (c. 1550), the elegant, formal detail and grace of the figures reveal a master of the art of decorative sculpture.

EMOTION AND ELEGANCE

It is interesting to compare Pierre Puget's seventeenth-century Milon de Crotone (above) with the Laocoon group (illustrated on page 225). Both are characterized by great technical virtuosity.

VIGOUR IN PORTRAITURE
The original of Houdon's portrait statue of George Washington is in Richmond, Virginia, but there is a replica of it in Trafalgar Square, London. The statue was made in 1796; although it is restrained there is vigour in the resolute pose, a feature lacking in much eighteenth-century sculpture.

the runners, filling the spaces where the wax was formerly. When the metal has cooled the mould is removed, and then the pins, ducts and runners are removed by saws and chisels, leaving no trace. The cast is then cleaned in a bath of weak sulphuric acid, and touching up may again be done by the sculptor with chasing tools.

The materials used for sculpture are as numerous as the methods of treatment. Marble, sandstone, limestone, granite, terra-cotta, wood, bronze, ivory and gold are but a few of those which have been used. As previously stated, the problem of sculpture is the translation of form into the language dictated by each material.

The stones employed are limestone, sandstone and granite. Of the limestones, marble is a popular and beautiful material of which there are many varieties. With the Greeks their own Parian and Pentelican were favourites. The Italian Carrara marble has grey veins running through it, but Serravezza has a beautiful creamy tone with less granular sparkle than the Greek marbles. All marbles when freshly quarried, or "green" as it is called, are more easily carved than when they have been exposed to the air for a considerable time. The great variety of coloured marbles, including some of the British, are but rarely used for carving. Apart from its use for architectural sculpture, Portland stone has often been found suitable for large sculptural work.

Other stones now frequently used are the mottled brown Hopton Wood stone quarried at Wirksworth, in Derbyshire; Ancaster which, when polished, has granitely patterned rich red markings, and Bath stone. Some of the sandstones are of a hard, non-porous quality, and are of great durability as is well proved by some of the ancient buildings on the banks of the Rhine.

The hardness and mottled appearance of granite necessitates a broader, stronger treatment than for other stones. The superb works of ancient Egypt and Assyria are lasting examples of the severe, monumental repose inherent in this rigid substance.

Alabaster is a form of gypsum, soft and beautifully translucent. It is either white or delicately tinted and veined.

Concrete and artificial stone have been more frequently used for sculpture since the adoption of reinforced concrete for buildings. Portland cement mixed with sand and aggregates of powdered granite and other stones is either modelled or cast from a plaster mould. The mixture can be kept moist enough to be worked on for two or three days. With a careful component, a mixture can be obtained in which small detail can be reproduced.

Bronze is an alloy of copper and tin, the proportion generally used is of eighty-seven per cent copper, four per cent zinc, two per cent lead and seven per cent tin.

Wood with its beauty of colour and interesting grain markings is a favourite material for sculpture. A very large num-

IMAGINATIVE PORTRAIT

Pieter Scheemaker (1691-1770) who lived in Amsterdam, executed eleven monuments in Westminster Abbey of which this imaginative portrait of Shakespeare, made about a century after his death, is one.

ARCHITECTURAL SCULPTURE

*The artist of this plaster model of a marble mantelpiece, Alfred Stevens
(1818-75), is clearly inspired by those Renaissance models in which sculpture
and architecture are successfully united.*

FORMAL DESIGN

The *Vierge d'Alsace* (below) by Antoine Bourdelle (*1861-1929*) shows a return to the method of formal design followed by the earlier masters of sculpture, the ancient Greek and Romanesque.

DETAIL OMITTED

Auguste Rodin (1840-1917) was the most outstanding of nineteenth-century sculptors. In his bronze known as The Thinker the aim is not mere representation but the expression of a mental state; the strong element of realism is directed to this end, unnecessary detail being omitted. Rodin challenged the classic tradition, developing an impressionist style which, by encouraging individualistic development, exerted considerable influence on contemporary work before and for some time after the First World War.

CONTEMPORARY SCULPTURE

*Aristide Maillol (1861-1944), con-
cerned himself wholly with the subtleties of the human figure. The Lady
with a Necklace (left) is a good
example of the type of female form
which he developed and which has had
considerable influence on many of
his contemporaries both in France and
England. The bronze fountain group
(above) shows the influence of the
baroque style. It was designed by
William McMillan (b. 1897), who
also designed the statue of Earl
Beatty for Trafalgar Square, London.
Prospero and Ariel (right) on the
façade of Broadcasting House, London,
is one of the few examples of sculpture
in the round by Eric Gill (1882-1940),
who specialized in relief carvings
and who did so much for the improvement of the carved stone inscription.
He designed the type face in which
the captions in this book are set.*

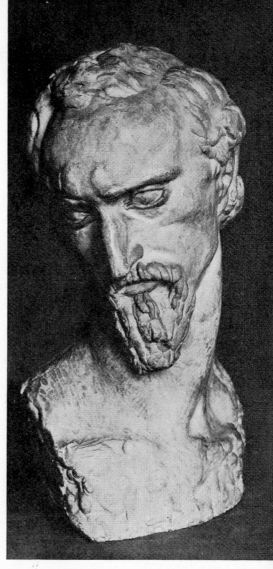

YUGOSLAV SCULPTURE

Ivan Mestrovic (b. 1883), whose self-portrait is shown above, was a pupil of Rodin and has the same tendency as his master to ignore the texture of the material in which he works. Together with Rosandic he helped to create in Yugoslavia a vigorous school of sculpture which had a quality influenced by local art as well as by Byzantine traditions.

TWENTIETH-CENTURY ARCHITECTURAL SCULPTURE

Night is one of a pair on the façade of St. James's Park Station on the London Underground Railway. It is the work of Jacob Epstein (b. 1880). The building is austere in appearance and the simplified character of the carved reliefs harmonizes with the character of the architecture. The subjects typify the day and night service rendered to the public in the building they adorn.

ber of varieties have been used. Whatever the wood, it is essential that it should be well seasoned, otherwise with the change of temperature cracks appear. In such woods as box and lime with their strength and closeness of grain, it is possible to give a representation of the most delicate forms of nature.

Terra-cotta, which is baked clay, has been, and indeed is, much used by sculptors. It is a cheaper and simpler method of producing works than is the use of stone or bronze, the statues and statuettes discovered at Tanagra in the nineteenth century being perhaps the finest examples for this medium. Donatello and other Florentine sculptors also produced some beautiful work. After the sixteenth century its use declined, but was revived in the nineteenth century. The Natural History Museum, London, is one of several buildings where its use may be seen. In modelling for this medium the clay must be pressed together

CONTEMPORARY PORTRAIT SCULPTURE
By contrast with his treatment of Night (shown on the page opposite) the bronze casting of a portrait bust of the scientist Einstein by Jacob Epstein (above) has a vitality characteristic of the artist's bold treatment and the rough texture in the original clay. Charles Wheeler (b. 1892), in his portrait of Montagu Norman (Governor of the Bank of England from 1920 till 1944) (left), unites a forceful interpretation of character with a conventional use of pattern which has something in common with the style of Bourdelle an example of whose work, The Vierge d'Alsace, is shown on page 261.

CONTEMPORARY MEMORIAL

An impression of the grimness of war is conveyed successfully by the determined pose and expression, the large, emphatic hands and harsh, rigid lines of the soldier from the memorial at Hoylake by Charles Sargeant Jagger (1885-1934) to those killed in the First World War. Jagger designed many war memorials, the best known being the Royal Artillery Memorial at Hyde Park Corner, London.

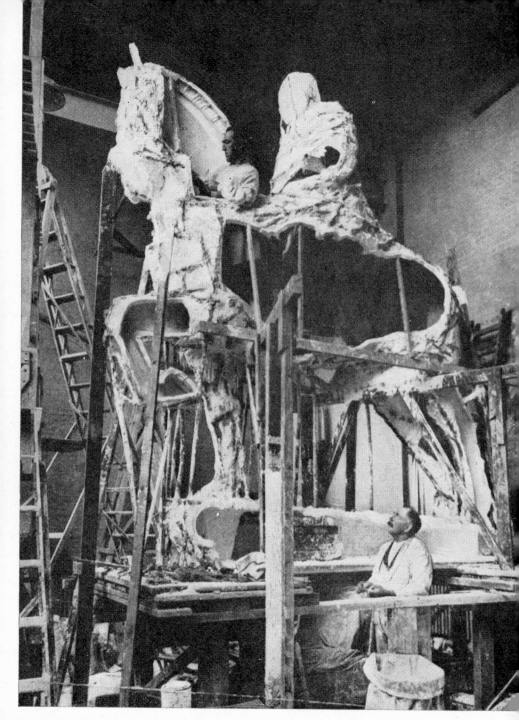

PREPARING A MOULD FOR CASTING
Above is shown a plaster mould made from the original clay model for an equestrian bronze. For work so large as this the mould is made in sections.

INCOMPLETED CARVING

The photograph reproduced above left shows a stage in the carving in Honiton stone of the Madonna and Child by Henry Moore (b. 1898). The head is already partially defined but the rest of the figure and the child are only beginning to emerge from the stone. Alongside is a view of the finished work which is now in the Church of St. Matthew, Northampton.

very tightly to avoid air being left inside, otherwise in the baking, the clay will burst open and ruin the work. When the model is finished it is cut up into parts and the clay scraped from the inside leaving a uniform thickness. Slow and soft firing, just enough to change the colour and consistency from soft clay to terra-cotta, is best for works of art as then there is less fear of twisting and less contraction which occurs in the burning. If the work is for out of doors a harder firing is necessary.

The clay used by the sculptor is pottery clay. If kept clean and free from bits of

plaster it lasts indefinitely and improves with use. It must be kept moist in a clay bin either in the form of a concrete pit under the floor of the studio or in galvanized tanks, one for clay in good condition, the other for clay which has been used and requires beating up to get it to the required consistency, sufficiently soft to be easy to manipulate but not so soft that in handling it adheres to the fingers.

Plaster of Paris is a fine powder which is obtained from gypsum after this has been burned in kilns and afterwards ground to powder. It must be kept in a dry place as it becomes lumpy if damp. In mixing for casting, the plaster is sifted through the fingers into a bowl of water until a little "island" of plaster arises just above the water in the centre of the bowl, it is then beaten up with a spoon much as one would whip an egg, after that it must be used immediately as it quickly sets. What is called the "life" of the plaster is the interval between the actual mixing and the "going off" or setting. This is important, for when it is going off it is no longer of use.

Test Yourself

1. Describe one method of making a plaster cast.
2. Name some of the materials used in carving and state what part the nature of that material should play in the finished work.
3. What is the *cire perdue* process of casting a bronze?
4. What are the possibilities of terra-cotta as a medium of artistic expression?

Answers will be found at the end of the book

PROPORTIONAL POINTING INSTRUMENT

Before work begins on the marble block, a detailed small scale model of the statue is prepared. For enlarging from the scale model to the marble many exact measurements are needed and with a proportional pointing instrument such as that in the photograph below, these can be made quickly and accurately.

CHAPTER XVIII

WHAT IS ARCHITECTURE?

ALTHOUGH we think we know instinc-tively when a building is worthy of the term architecture and when it is not, it is very difficult to define the content of the word. All building is not architecture, but could it be? Yes, if by the shape and texture of its masses it appeals to the imagination, if it serves its purpose as well and has character and significance and, most of all, harmonious unity. One can imagine a Greek designer of ancient times able to give such harmony and significance to any object, however unimportant in daily life, and make any building architecture. Then we think of the slums of our own big cities as seen from the train or the rows of little villa residences in our suburbs and we see at once how much and how far away building can be from architec-ture. What then is the essential factor? We can get a hint of it in the word imagina-tion. Which building is it which moves our imagination, which stirs us to the pits of our stomachs? Which makes us happy and smiling, or which leaves us cold?

If we have seen but a few great buildings of the world and analysed very shortly their content our imagination will do the rest. The simple appeal to the imagination by itself is not enough. If we know nothing, a vulgar cinema or garish hotel may seem to be architecture, but if we have seen, say, the ruins of the Parthenon at Athens, the twin domes of Greenwich Naval College, Durham Cathedral or the nave of West-minster Abbey, a terrace of Georgian or Regency houses, a Cotswold farm-house or an old Welsh cottage, a modern building by Gropius or Mendelsohn, and felt for a moment or two the beauty of one or other of them, then we may know that any other building which similarly stirs our imagina-tion has about it the quality of architecture. We can go on in safety from one such building to another and from the harmony of a single building to the harmony of a group; from village to country town and

great metropolis; and feel we have within us a standard by which we can safely appraise its architecture, and even to some extent its town planning as well. We may sometimes be wrong about the latter socio-logically, but we shall not err æsthetically.

To reach this happy state, however, with conviction our knowledge of the pur-poses of the buildings must all the while be growing. We may admire the soaring beauty of a cathedral but if we know nothing of the ritual and the meaning of its services much of its significance is lost. This applies to secular forms of building also, for example the special services which a modern house or block of flats provides, the special purpose of a theatre or great store. The function of a building, the practical service it is to render, is the pro-gramme. Has that been fulfilled, not only with success but with imagination?

The buildings and towns of the world which will most strongly appeal to the imagination will vary from time to time. Ruskin talks, for instance, about the base Renaissance architects of Venice, yet to the designers of the beautiful later Venetian palaces all Gothic buildings were no doubt barbarous. Nevertheless no one can gain a proper appreciation of architecture with-out some knowledge of what has appealed to the imagination of past ages and races. Architecture, however, has or should have little to do with fashion. Le Corbusier, the well-known modern French architect and critic, rightly says in his book *Towards a New Architecture*: "Architecture has nothing to do with the variations of style. The styles of Louis XIV, XV and XVI, or even of Gothic, are to architects what a feather is to a woman's head. It is some-thing pretty, though not always, and never anything more. Architecture has graver ends, capable of the sublime it impresses the most brutal instinct by its objectivity, it calls into play the highest faculties by its very abstraction.... Mass and surface are

270

the elements by which architecture manifests itself. Mass and surface are determined by plan. The plan is the generator." All this is very valuable, especially the last two sentences. It is by mass that the imagination is chiefly affected, and it is the relation of the masses one to another that the plan determines. How different from the Ruskinian attitude of only half a century ago! Architecture was then looked on primarily as decoration. In the preface to the second edition of his *Seven Lamps of Architecture*, Ruskin says : "The fact is there are only two fine arts possible to the human race, sculpture and painting. What we call architecture is only the association of these in noble masses, or the placing of them in fit places. All architecture other than this is mere building. . . .

All high art consists in carving or painting natural objects, chiefly figures."

To go back farther, to that old Roman whom the architects of the Italian Renaissance were wont to think inspired, Vitruvius Pollio, we find him claiming in proper professional fashion all the arts and sciences for the architect, about which of course, we cannot complain, but it does not help very much in determining the content of architecture. If the writings of a Greek architect had been discovered instead we might have had something more philosophical. Vitruvius, for instance, says: "An architect should be ingenious and apt in the acquisition of knowledge. Deficient in either of these qualities he cannot be a perfect master. He should be a good writer, skilful draughtsman, versed in geometry

RENAISSANCE ARCHITECTURE

Formerly Greenwich Royal Naval Hospital and now the Royal Naval College, this is one of the buildings for which Sir Christopher Wren was responsible. Here is seen the gaiety and grandeur which are the essence of Renaissance architecture in England. The picture shows the pair of domes and the columns, features which may be compared with Wren's masterpiece, St. Paul's Cathedral, shown on page 353.

GRANDEUR OF EGYPTIAN ARCHITECTURE

Some of the columns of the great Hypostyle Hall of the temple at Karnak erected about 1200 B.C. Apart from the magnificence of its conception, the hall, considerably larger than Westminster Abbey, is famed for the beauty and complexity of the highly finished carvings on the pillars, of which the height and girth are illustrated by contrast with the figure of the man.

NEW STONE AGE IN BRITAIN

Ruined Stonehenge is a tribute to the skill and vigour of the people who built this great temple about 1750 B.C. But for the fact that many of the stones were used in the Middle Ages to build roads, it might well have survived to the present day in a still more intact form. Its great interest architecturally lies in the trilithons, of which the horizontals are attached to the uprights by simple toggle joints. This use of a formal joint marked the first serious attempt at " architecture " in primitive Britain as opposed to the mere laying of one stone upon another. The big stones (megaliths) composing the outer circle and those of the great trilithons of the centre (clearly seen in the picture) are local in origin and are part of the covering of sandstone which in earlier geologic times was laid over the greater part of Wiltshire. The stones of the inner circle, however, occur no nearer than the Prescelly Hills in Pembrokeshire. It remains one of the great wonders of the world how these primitive architects who lived nearly two thousand years before recorded history began in Britain, contrived either to raise the great stones which form the trilithons or to transport from so great a distance the smaller " blue stones " which were, no doubt, thought to be important because of any sacred properties they might possess.

ROMAN MONUMENTAL ARCHES

The Arch of Trajan (left) and the Arch of Constantine (below), illustrate the pre-eminence of Roman monumental architecture during the early centuries of the Empire, when the power of Rome was at its height. Triumphal arches such as these set a style which was followed all over the western world and formed the basis of the more formal examples of classical architecture in Britain, as witnessed by the work of Inigo Jones and Sir Christopher Wren in the seventeenth century. They bear at least a superficial resemblance to the façades of some of the finest Renaissance churches and still later public buildings erected in the tradition and spirit of architecture of the Renaissance.

ROMANESQUE STYLE

Iffley Church, Oxford (right) and the Galilee Chapel of Durham Cathedral (below), are illustrative of the Norman style of architecture in England. This style was directly descended from the art of the Romans, by contrast with the later Renaissance buildings, for which the inspiration came indirectly through medieval Italy. The west front of Iffley Church, in which the rose window and the ornamentation of the doorway are remarkable, dates from about 1100, and the moulding round the doorway is some of the most elaborate to be found in the smaller parish churches. A different kind of moulding, but one equally characteristic, is seen in the Galilee Chapel of Durham Cathedral.

and optics, expert in figures, acquainted with history, informed on the principles of natural and moral philosophy, somewhat of a musician, not ignorant of the sciences both of law and physic, nor of the motions, laws and relations to each other of the heavenly bodies." The only thing this Roman paragon is not said to have is the only necessary quality—that of being an artist and using his imagination.

Remembering then, chiefly, what Le Corbusier said, let us take a tour past some of the chief buildings of the world of various epochs, including the present age, and see how they impress us, remembering the reasons for which they were built and the materials used. We shall find certain qualities of mass and texture in them all, and we shall see how naturally their shape is related both to their programme and to their construction. We shall find in each a definite appeal to the imagination, often of a power and scale the other arts cannot approach. Sculpture, limited in size and range of materials, is perhaps the nearest to architecture and though it can express more lively human emotions it can rarely lift up the human spirit to another plane and hold it there as can a great building. Certain works of music in their combined simplicity of form and elaboration of detail seem to be nearer. Such comparisons, though, are only useful by analogy. Each art, in spite of what Ruskin says, is supreme in the quality of its appeal when the way for that appeal lies open.

In order to understand the living quality of the buildings which we shall look at and consider, we must view them as structures enclosing space and not as dead, inert masses of stone, brick or concrete. Each of these main building materials has its own special forms of structure in which it excels, forms which are natural to its qualities. Let us briefly consider these qualities before we turn to the buildings.

Stone can clearly be used in two ways according mainly to its size. Large stones can be used in post and lintel construction as at Stonehenge in single blocks or, as in an Egyptian or Greek temple, with one

stone on another making the uprights. Others can be used as bridging stones between uprights. The distance apart of these uprights may well be determined by the distance it is safe to bridge with a single piece of the particular stone. This arrangement of the stones is called trabeated construction, and people, like the Egyptians and Greeks, who used it, never used any other, though no doubt they knew of the arch. Trabeated construction is monumental and restful, relying for its strength

ITALIAN GOTHIC AND RENAISSANCE STYLES

Above is the Palazzo Strozzi at Florence, on the left the Palazzo della Cà d'Oro at Venice. The Gothic features of the latter are typical of the fifteenth century and bear some relation to the Decorated style current in England at that period and a little earlier. But the general effect is of a flamboyance and individual beauty which is entirely Italian. The Palazzo Strozzi by contrast is built throughout in the Italian Renaissance style and this, too, shows marked individuality and difference from the Renaissance styles both of France and of Britain. The main contribution of the Italian Renaissance architects has been aptly described as " the development of the big house and its relation to the street."

and, largely, too, for its effect, on dead weight.

The other form of stone construction is one of small stones, and is consequently one shared with bricks. One cannot obviously use small stones or bricks to bridge from pier to pier or wall to wall except by the invention of the arch where all the stones are trying to push through and fall to the ground, but are held in their place by the pressure of their neighbours against their sides, brought about by the weight above and the resistance of external buttresses. The stones themselves in an arch are generally of a wedge shape making it more difficult for them to slip through, and ensuring that the pressure against their sides is at right-angles to those sides. In brickwork, where specially shaped bricks are not used, the wedge shape is generally secured by tapering the mortar so that it is thicker between the bricks at the top of a ring of bricks forming an arch than at the bottom. Once the arch was discovered it was an obvious step to extend it horizontally from wall to wall into a barrel- or tunnel-vault or to rotate it into a dome. All these forms are used in Assyrian, Etruscan, Roman, Byzantine, Romanesque and Gothic architecture, not to mention Oriental styles.

Lastly, we have concrete made of sand and an aggregate of small stones or broken brick with sufficient cementing material to hold it together even under water. It was the discovery by the Romans that by mixing a clay, first found at Pozzuoli in Italy, with lime mortar they could achieve a sort of Portland cement which made concrete possible and led them to use it in masses, not only for the interior of their walls and piers, but also for vaulting. As, however, they could use it only in compression, they could not use it even for short straight lintels bridging a few feet. The underside would be in tension

IRON-AND-STEEL CONSTRUCTION

Built in the years 1887-89, the Eiffel Tower is an example of one of the great inventions of modern architecture, the use of iron and steel for large structures in the open.

GEORGIAN DESIGN

The Regency tradition, culmination of Georgian architecture in Britain, is exemplified by this view of Park Crescent, London, erected to the design of John Nash at the beginning of the nineteenth century. It is part of an early town-planning scheme which produced the old Regent Street and aimed at bringing spaciousness and grace into the heart of London, a grace that would be unified by an architecture which was at once consistent and magnificent. In the same tradition are the squares and crescents of Bath created by the Woods, and the new town of Edinburgh planned by Craig.

and would crack under the pressure.

The great inventions of modern times were first, the use of iron and steel in the open, dictating the forms, as in the Crystal Palace and the Eiffel Tower, and second placing steel bars within the lower part of a concrete lintel to take up the tension. Once that was done—and the fact that steel and concrete expand and contract to changes of temperature very much at the same rate made it possible—a lintel so formed could bridge almost any distance, say forty feet instead of four feet for the same size and weight per foot. Clearly this made a new architecture possible and even

inevitable. The change is as great, if frankly faced, as from the lintel to the arch, that is as from Greek architecture to Gothic. With ferro-concrete the builder has at his disposal a material as strong as stone in compression and as tough as steel in tension. All kinds of shapes become possible if not all are desirable. Ships can now be built in ferro-concrete, though this is mentioned only to show the versatility of the material and the stresses it can take. Clearly with such a material a new conquest of space, with new forms of enclosure, is possible to the architect and engineer.

Modern architecture, therefore, with

TEMPLE OF HATHOR AT DENDERA

Carved reliefs on the walls of the Temple of Hathor at Dendera, which is of the Ptolemaic period and was built in the first century B.C. These reliefs are typical of later Egyptian work. They show Cleopatra and Julius Cæsar sacrificing to the gods of victory, and commemorate the famous visit of the Roman Cæsar to the Court of Egypt. In the centre is their son, Cæsarion.

ferro-concrete, steel, glass, plywood and plastics at its disposal, as well as modern methods of heating, would be wasteful and wrong if it kept to the old forms whether of Greek or Gothic architecture when none of these things existed. Like modern methods and standards in the other arts, however, the new architecture calls forth new standards of judgment. Nevertheless to have an informed taste and understanding in architecture we must see what the main forms of the past reveal as well as the modern ones, for even the slight deviation of a wall may, by association of ideas, by recalling, say, Egyptian buildings, imply a great deal. Nevertheless a great work in architecture, as in other arts, always makes its own great and direct appeal to the imagination. One need have no previous knowledge to feel that, yet a little helps the average person to a better appreciation.

ARCHITECTURE OF THE EGYPTIANS

Let us then first consider Egypt. What is it that so impresses us in an Egyptian temple or even in a great pyramid? It is chiefly its sense of permanence combined with mystery. That the great pyramid has lasted for thousands of years and will go on defying time with its simple shape, so grand when seen against the flat lines of the desert, is in itself a highly impressive fact. Why were such things built? Clearly because life after death was more important than this life. At all costs the physical form had to be preserved. The mummy must be kept in safety. This everlastingness of life seems, too, a reflection of Egypt and the Nile, and especially of the latter, the long, slow-moving river passing for hundreds of miles through similar country dependent on it, a country whose architecture to judge from its temples hardly changed for hundreds, nay thousands, of years. These temples in their ruins remain today when all else of great cities has disappeared. Clearly, like the tombs, they had some spiritual value. What did they aim to express?

One approached them through long avenues of sphinxes and saw in the distance a high wall with two great slightly tapering pylons guarding a small entrance between them. Inside was the surprise of a great sunlit, rectangular court, perhaps with columns or statues or both against the same high wall. Opposite was a similar pair of pylons leading to another but smaller court also surrounded by the same high wall and then perhaps to another. At last, through another impressive gateway, one entered the temple proper, a forest of great columns close together carrying stone beams and making the human being seem minute. The central avenue was maintained and the columns on either side of it were higher to let in light through comparatively small clerestory windows. This forest of columns shaded off into darkness on either side, but the columns themselves were nevertheless carved in low relief with strange figures, often of human beings with animal heads.

When a priest walked by with a lamp, patches of light would appear on the nearby columns, and it would be seen that the figures on them were highly coloured. The central avenue went on with more columns, but in complete darkness unless a priest appeared. Clearly everything was done to impress the beholder as he solemnly and silently passed down the avenue through the courts and into the temple, perhaps a mile or more in all. On that axis he could not help being increasingly impressed. He could not help feeling small and insignificant against the enormous columns with their mysterious carvings and capitals carrying heavy beams, and with the darkness and other columns in every direction. If, however, he did not keep to the straight path but walked round the outside of the temple, he merely found a high wall like that of a private park, at intervals turning in to enclose a smaller space. There was not an exterior sense of unity or any effort made to impress the distant beholder as was the case in a Greek or Gothic building.

GREECE

In the buildings of the Greeks we find the same simple post and lintel construction but with elements if originally derived from timber structure, such as short uprights in the Doric frieze with their grooves and guttæ suggesting the ends of ceiling timbers and the way of fixing them carried to such expressiveness and refinement that one is almost justified in saying that they have reached perfection. Under a regime of political freedom, with less slave labour available than in Egypt, the size of the buildings had to be less. That, however, suited the Greek temperament. A smaller task done perfectly was more important than a greater one done imperfectly. This ideal was fostered by the use in their chief buildings, temples once more, of a homogeneous magnificent marble, that from Mount Pentelicon. Again, these temples were monuments to be seen by everyone from every side. Few went inside. They were usually on a low hill overlooking the town and in touch with it, yet raised above it. It is always a surprise to find that the Acropolis at Athens, where the chief temples are, is not the highest hill in the neighbourhood. There was inside, the figure of the god, lit through a window at the side and possibly by an opening in the roof, but it was before an altar in front of the temple that most of the ceremonies took place. The temple was there, like the other monuments on the Acropolis, to be viewed largely as a piece of sculpture. For this reason the greatest care was taken over all optical effects. To ensure, for instance, that the end columns of those surrounding the main temple should look the same size seen against the sky as the rest their diameter was slightly increased.

To prevent any effect of sagging in the long lines of the side of the temple both the steps on which the columns were stood and the entablature connecting them were slightly curved upwards. Just what this meant in the matter of craftsmanship it is difficult to estimate. To have carved the flutes in place on the columns and at the same time to have given these latter its proper entasis, or swelling to give the appearance of strength, to make the whole range of columns slope inwards a little to give a more monumental appearance, must have been difficult enough, but this curving of the horizontal lines must have been more difficult still. The same carved finish was applied everywhere. Wall faces were rubbed and the drums of the columns were rotated till they fitted so well that no joint could be seen, all with the ideal of making a perfect monument as if carved from one gigantic lump of marble. Sculpture was used in the end pediments of the roof and in the panels between the grooved uprights in the external frieze, and in the Parthenon at Athens, in a frieze as well on the wall of the temple itself behind the columns, lit by reflected light from below. The sculpture, however, like every line in the building, was designed and carved to enhance the general effect. The sculpture reinforced the lines of architecture which in itself aimed at a solemn monumental unity, which must have been felt still more strongly when the external paint in bright primary colours reinforced the parts and their functions. When marble was not available limestone was used and the whole covered with a fine stucco to give the same monolithic effect.

The type of Greek temple did not greatly change during the few hundred years in which it rose to perfection, maintaining the while its single rectangular shape. This remained in spite of two different kinds of columns, entablatures and other parts, Doric and Ionic, corresponding to two racial streams each with its special deities. The buildings expressed the ideas and answered very closely, as all good buildings must, to the character of their designers, the Doric, the more stable and monumental, the Ionic more Asiatic and ornate. The two, indeed, came together in the Parthenon which fused the streams for a while. There they reached—the Doric being kept to the exterior and the Ionic to the interior—a perfection of craftsmanship never equalled, either before or after, so that today even the fragments on the ground seem like broken pieces of sculpture or even of porcelain. To attempt to copy the subtleties and finish of these buildings with rougher materials and cruder craftsmanship under northern cloud-filled skies, as was done last century all over England and in the United States for their banks and museums is not only to mistake the religious character of the original but to attempt the impossible. The influence of

TEMPLE OF THE NEW EMPIRE IN EGYPT

So that the architectural forms of the terraced temple at Deir el Bahri,
Thebes, might seem part of the cliff face, a continuous lintel was carried
on piers right across the front. The building is an enlarged edition of an
Eleventh Dynasty temple completed in the Eighteenth Dynasty by Queen
Hatshepset. Under the Eighteenth Dynasty began a renaissance due to
foreign influence, particularly Syrian, resulting from widespread conquests.

In its original form the Parthenon at Athens, top left, illustrated better than any other single edifice how in Greek buildings sculpture is employed as an integral part of the architectural design. The figures from the carving of the frieze are in the British Museum, yet enough remains to recall the perfection of craftsmanship which created it. No break can be seen in the columns, the joins fitting so well that it seems as though each column was fashioned from a single piece of marble. There is restraint in the Doric capitals which reflect the spirit of native Greek culture. The Temple of Wingless Victory, Nike Apteros, bottom left, is also on the Acropolis of Athens, but the columns have the more ornate Ionic capitals. This picture shows the relation between the outer part of the temple and the inner, the latter being subsidiary and comparatively unimportant in the plan as a whole. The temple was designed to be viewed from outside, and comparatively few of those who worshipped at it actually entered the inner sanctum, where the figure of the god to whom the temple was dedicated was situated. Below, by contrast, is one of the famous temples of Rome, the Temple of Fortune, which indicates how much Roman architecture owed to Greek ideals and conception. The same striving after effect; the same graceful fluting of the columns, and the same sense of balance and proportion is evident.

ROMAN ARCHITECTURE OF THE FIRST CENTURY, A.D.

One of the most memorable feats of architecture in the ancient world is the Colosseum, a magnificent amphitheatre. It was begun when Vespasian was Emperor and was completed in the time of Titus. It thus represents the full flowering of Roman architecture towards the end of the first century A.D. The Colosseum was originally the scene of gladiatorial combats but they were abolished in 405 by Honorius as being inconsistent with Christianity.

their refinement however on modern work can and should remain.

ROME

The perfecting of single buildings or types of buildings was very far from the Roman spirit. As conquerors of the world the Romans needed a set of architectural forms which could be used anywhere and of the materials always to be found on the spot. The lintel of a single large stone, carefully carved, was not only difficult to handle, even when the right kind of stone or marble existed, but took too long to make. From the Etruscans, their neighbours in Italy, they took, therefore, the arch of small stones which could spring

from pier to pier or wall to wall, and were quick not only to develop it further with its natural extensions of tunnel-vault and dome, but invented the intersecting vault, of two tunnel-vaults meeting, which can stand on four piers at the corners of a square. When, too, they had invented concrete and cast their piers and vaults in masses of it, they could extend these simple ideas until not only could they vault in a great apartment in a fireproof way, but make one apartment lead to another, alternating their shapes till they built up the great plans of their thermæ (public baths) round two axes at right-angles, ending vistas with apses and semi-domes and making a dome perhaps the central climax. It is from these Roman plans for their great baths that the western world has learnt to plan its public buildings, as it is from their forums—particularly at Rome with one forum surrounded by its colonnade and leading to another, and each containing its temple or basilica—and from the long colonnaded Roman streets and their triumphal arches, that the same world has learnt the more monumental and formal parts of its town planning. Rome, a crowded overgrown city pinched in between its seven hills, had largely to be screened by vast semi-circular walls and colonnades in order to make that formal setting for its public buildings which the Romans felt necessary.

Columns, therefore, with the Romans were used decoratively as well as structurally. To the two Greek kinds they added three others, making in all the Five Orders, the Tuscan, the Doric, the Ionic, the Corinthian, an invention largely of their own, and the Composite, a mixture of the last two which was quite theirs. This standardization, for that is what it amounted to, with the precise rules they gave for setting out each order, meant that they could cover their walls and make decorative screens in marble pilasters and columns wherever they went without much further invention. After the founding of the Empire their usual practice was indeed to build thick brick and concrete walls

COMBINED BRIDGE AND AQUEDUCT

Near Nîmes, France, the Pont du Gard is one of the most elaborate bridges built by the Romans in the provinces. It combines effectively a real aesthetic sense with functional efficiency and demonstrates how well the Romans understood the use of the arch form, first as regards the aesthetic value of its repetition and secondly as a means of saving materials in a structure which would otherwise be solid. It is probably the most famous aqueduct outside Rome, and the designer has taken advantage of the opportunity to symbolize the supreme power of the Roman Empire. Almost all the many aqueducts constructed during the height of prosperity of the Roman Empire were built in this form.

ROMAN DEFENSIVE WALL BUILDING

The Romans were great military architects, and in their outlying province of Britain they carried this art to its fullest development. They excelled particularly in the building of defensive walls round towns, although their greatest single feat was the construction of Hadrian's Wall dividing the Roman province from that part in the north still overrun by the unconquered Picts and Scots. The view below shows a largely undamaged stretch of the wall near Housesteads, Northumberland, a notable monument to the passive strength of construction which has defied the ravages of nearly two thousand years of weather and man. Originally Hadrian's Wall stretched from Bowness on Solway Firth to Wallsend on the Tyne, a distance of seventy-three miles. It varies in thickness from seven to nine feet, and the height was probably fifteen feet or more, although through the ages it has sunk and is now rarely more than six feet high. The stone used was local but even so the construction of the wall was a mighty feat of military engineering. It was probably begun about A.D. 80, but was completed and strengthened when Hadrian was Emperor about A.D. 120. Left, below, is a portion of the wall at Housesteads Fort which shows the methods of dry-stone walling, which the Romans adopted. The portion of wall shown, above left, is of an entirely different kind. It is part of the wall of the Roman city of Verulamium and was built of rubble and cement, faced with stone and strengthened by courses of red Roman tiles or bricks, clearly seen in the photograph. The Romans were the first to use bricks for building in Britain.

BYZANTINE ARCHITECTURE

Above is the Church of Santa Sophia, Istanbul (Byzantium), erected during the reign of Justinian in the sixth century A.D. Opposite is the modern Roman Catholic Cathedral of Westminster, London, built under the direction of the architect J. F. Bentley. These two represent respectively the classical and the modern interpretation of the Byzantine style, which originated when the capital of Rome was moved to Byzantium and the then declining Roman forms were revitalized by the influence of Greek architects. The result was an incorporation of Oriental elaboration of detail with classical forms. In St. Sophia the great dome is carried high in the air and the dome form is also repeated with impressive effect in Westminster Cathedral. But it was in the splendour of the interiors that Byzantine art reached its highest expression, Byzantine churches being designed for large congregations in the church itself, in contrast with the Greek and Roman temples, which were designed to impress congregations which in the main stayed outside.

and vaults, reinforced with brick arches and tiles, and cover the walls so formed with a marble veneer into which they introduced the orders at will. For the vaulting they invented indeed a very suitable form of ornament. By placing boxes of the right shape, depth and contour on to the wooden centering, on which the wet concrete for the vaults was poured, they formed those recesses in the curved surface of the concrete, called coffers, which give such

perspective and relief to their vaults and domes, as in the great dome of the Pantheon at Rome built A.D. 120-124, still the largest in Europe (142 feet in diameter against St. Peter's, Rome, 127 feet, and St. Paul's, London, 105 feet). The use of screens of columns as decoration to the curved recesses sunk in the great circular wall can be studied there, though the large marble panels above are said to have been added by Michelangelo. Whether he, or some other Italian Renaissance architect, added these or not, there is enough that is really Roman in this great domed interior with its alternate rectangular and semi-circular niches, and their ranges of fine monolithic columns, and its tier upon tier of recessed coffers in its great dome to make this interior one of the finest interiors in the world.

The effect of Roman concrete vaulting, apart from the dome, can perhaps be best studied in the remains of one of the great basilicas or in one of the vast baths like the Thermæ of Caracalla. There most of the marble screening and panelling and the stucco work has disappeared, yet the remains of these vaulted structures are as impressive, perhaps even more in their simplicity, than the interior of many a great Gothic cathedral. The parts are larger and the scale everywhere greater, while in the brick strengthening arches hidden in their vaulting may be said to be the germ of things to come. Indeed in the best of the larger work, where the Romans get away from trying to copy the Greeks, as they did in their smaller temples, one gets the same masterful impression of immense size and strength as one does sailing up the Hudson to New York, or better still, when walking between the sky-scrapers. Their great aqueducts, and an occasional vast masonry wall like the back wall to the theatre of Orange in the south of France, suggest a race with an immense labour power and a few grand simple ideas. It is quite easy to see on a visit to Rome why Roman work has had such an effect

TYPICAL NORMAN WORK

Though dismantled after the Civil War, the keep of Castle Hedingham, Essex, has retained most of its original façade. The moulding of the arches of the main entrance and above the window openings in the top floor is typical of Norman work. The masonry in the foreground is the remains of a massive gatehouse protecting the main entrance.

NORMAN CHURCHES

The south porch of Barfreston Church, Kent (below), and the triforium of the south transept of St. Albans Abbey (right), are both characteristic of the finest Norman architecture in Britain. The decoration, more ornate in the case of Barfreston than at St. Albans, and the sub-divisions of the arches at St. Albans are effective inspirations of Norman architecture.

on the western world ever since and why in the first enthusiasm of the Italian Renaissance this work was considered the work of a race of supermen, and why even the very ordinary professional writings of Vitruvius, when found, were taken as gospel not only by Italian architects but by some Englishmen.

BYZANTINE AND EARLY CHRISTIAN ARCHITECTURE

The spiritual qualities that architecture lacked through the Roman desire for grandeur, and their wholesale methods of building were largely regained in the styles which grew out of Roman work. When the capital of the Empire was moved to Byzantium by the first Christian Emperor, Roman architecture with its great vaults and domes came under the influence of the Greek mind. Elsewhere, as in beautiful Maison Carrée at Nîmes, Greeks had only been employed as craftsmen. At Byzantium they were the architects, the designers once more, and applied themselves to the heavy concrete domes of the Roman, solid-like lids, and turned them into living constructions. In Santa Sophia, the great example of the period, they carried high in the air the great dome, which they had lightened very much by the introduction of hollow amphora (wine bottles), each fitting into the neck of the one below, and so adjusting themselves to the curve, and by a series of windows, on great curved corbels called pendentives, springing from the four piers and the four great arches connecting them. Two of these latter they filled with semi-domes on apses, and in the other two they built great walls of windows standing on monolithic columns, and arches, but carrying the latter direct from capital to capital, a big innovation dispensing with the Roman entablature. The artificial screen of columns and pilasters, as well as the similar covering to walls, were also done away with. The walls, the pendentives, the domes and semi-domes were all covered instead with gold mosaics which perfectly followed their curves, and on which floated figure designs of great beauty and solemnity. Indeed mosaic designing may be said to be one of the chief beauties of both Byzantine and early Christian architecture, for in the latter, which was often otherwise decadent Roman, a band of noble figures, as at Ravenna, would make a great frieze above a row of re-used Roman columns.

Byzantine architecture was indeed a rebirth in which the logical Greek mind this time applied itself to the construction of domes instead of to lintels and to the richest possible interiors for large congregations instead of to exteriors where the congregation mainly stayed outside. Not that the Byzantine Greeks neglected the exteriors of their buildings, but they allowed them to take their natural shapes showing the dome and semi-domes together with the great buttresses to the former, indeed emphasizing the weight of these latter by alternate layers of brick and stone.

This rich method of building, freed from the rules for each type of column which the Romans laid down, was left to express the feelings of architect and craftsman and became a mine of wealth in detail by which the West was continuously fed. Through Romanesque, and even into Gothic days, fresh waves of ornament seemed to come from the East, perhaps helped by the Crusades, though it is said the Crusaders did more harm to Santa Sophia when a mosque than ever the Saracens did to it when a church. The late J. F. Bentley's Roman Catholic Cathedral at Westminster, with its grand procession of domes, is an almost complete example of Byzantine architecture in which one wishes, however, that the mosaics were up to the Greek standard. Nevertheless, as a modern cathedral, it has had great influence on many churches which have been founded upon it both here and in America. There is a certain kind of emotional appeal which

TRANSITIONAL STYLES

The ruins of Fountains Abbey from the south-east (opposite), illustrate the contrast between Norman architecture proper and the transitional stage which followed before the Gothic styles were fully established. In the foreground the two styles are seen side by side—a lovely Norman doorway together with the slightly pointed arches characteristic of the transitional style of the end of the twelfth century looking forward to the sharply pointed arches of later forms of Gothic. King's College Chapel (above), was built at the end of the architectural period of which Fountains Abbey represents the beginning. This chapel was one of the latest major buildings to be erected in the Perpendicular style of Gothic when Tudor influences were at work and the transition to the classical forms of the Renaissance was already foreshadowed. The doorway shows evidence of the classical revival while the windows remain in the tradition of late Gothic churches like Thaxted.

great aerial enclosures made by the gracious shapes of domes and semi-domes, and the blueing of the atmosphere which often follows, always bring about. It is an appeal different in kind both from Greek purity and from Roman grandeur and is indeed perhaps all the more valuable as a corrective to the latter.

ARCHITECTURE OF THE MIDDLE AGES

Before the splendid rise of Gothic architecture in the north of France, which was to make the third and perhaps the greatest epoch of western building, till the one we can forsee today with the new and wonderful means already at our disposal, there were attempts all over Europe to emulate the great Roman halls, although the secret of making cement and consequently of concrete was lost. These attempts, which we may call Romanesque like the languages which grew out of Latin, all had local names such as Norman, Lombardic or Provençal, yet the basis of them all was the Roman barrel-vault. If, however, a great deal of early Christian work, except in its decoration and furniture, was decadent

CANTERBURY CATHEDRAL

The Mother Church of the Church of England is architecturally one of the most magnificent ecclesiastical buildings in the world. This aerial view shows some of its most beautiful external features. It shows, too, how the cathedral dominates the town; to a traveller approaching Canterbury from Harbledown or the south the city retains its medieval appearance of a village clustering round the cathedral. In the foreground are some of the narrow streets of medieval Canterbury (grievously damaged by enemy action during the Second World War when the cathedral itself escaped with only superficial damage). The cathedral was founded, according to tradition, soon after St. Augustine came from Rome as a missionary and converted Ethelbert, King of Kent, but no traces of the Saxon cathedral church remain above ground. It was twice burnt to the ground, first by Viking invaders, then in 1067 in a great fire which destroyed most of the town. The new cathedral was consecrated in 1130, and the Norman windows seen in the photograph beyond the central tower belong to this period. After yet another disastrous fire, it was rebuilt and enlarged by William of Sens (who started his work in 1174) and, after his death, by William the Englishman. The south and west sides of the nave, which appear nearest the camera in the photograph, belong to an enlargement carried out at the end of the fourteenth century; the great central tower is a magnificent example of the later style of Perpendicular.

CHURCH AND FORTRESS

Above is a general view of the island and church of Mont St. Michel, below is the Knights' Hall, part of the church. This is one of the most effective buildings in France in the Gothic style. The church appears half church and half fortress, an effect which is given added point by the medieval defensive walls seen in the foreground.

Roman, the reverse is the case with Romanesque. Think of the nave of Durham Cathedral or of the great Romanesque churches in northern Italy and southern France, or our own Norman castles, and it will be seen that, if the finish of Roman work is lacking, a new spirit of adventure has arrived when, with small stones or even with brick, piers, arches and vaults are carried to a greater height than even the Romans reached.

There was indeed no concrete, but instead, it may be said that the Roman system of reinforcing their concrete vaults with brick arches was brought to the surface and these arches were to be found again in the ribs of Romanesque vaulting. To hold great vaults high in the air, however, needed either walls of Roman thickness or the buttress system developed by the Gothic builders, and the Romanesque buildings had neither. The result is most

of their great vaults have fallen and have
been replaced by later and lighter structures. A similar vigour, however, to that
which attempted such great architectural
shapes is to be found in their carvings.

It was probably from an appreciation of
the function of vaulting ribs, buried as in
Roman work, or in the open as in Romanesque, in upholding vaults that Gothic
architecture grew. By making the arched
ribs steeper with pointed arches instead of
semi-circular ones, the thrust on the
thinner walls favoured by the Gothic
builders was lessened and the idea of
resisting it by buttresses and then by flying
ones crossing aisles, must soon have
followed. We know how quickly in the
twelfth and thirteenth centuries a complete
engineering system of balanced arches,
vaults and buttresses was established until
we get the light Gothic stone frame filled
with great stained-glass windows, culminating in an almost Crystal Palace effect, with
a stone ceiling and a wooden roof above.
That of course is the merest outline of
Gothic construction and with that construction grew the whole Gothic art of painted
glass, wood and stone carving, and
tapestries.

The whole world of the Arts changed
with its architecture, as indeed it always
does. Hence no doubt, the name of the
Mistress Art for architecture, which most
people give it without perhaps realizing
its real meaning. How deeply the new
spirit penetrated in its search for truthful
expression may be judged from the fact
that where a Roman builder would cover
his structure with a veneer of another
material and articulate it in a manner
unrelated to what was behind it, a Gothic
builder would delight in the texture and
inherent qualities of the material with
which he was building. Its very in-
equalities and accidental variations would
give him pleasure and be utilized by him
as they are today by a modern sculptor.
When his system of vaults or buttresses
became fully developed, similar accidental
variations in planning, owing, say, to the
site, would be turned to happy account.

At Athens, the top of the Acropolis was
levelled to make a site for the temples. At

ADAPTATION OF GOTHIC IN SPAIN

*Seville Cathedral is an example of
the adaptations of Gothic architecture carried out in European countries. Its forms here are noticeably
different from the Italian Gothic
on the one hand, whence the whole
movement sprang, and the highly
characteristic form of English Gothic
epitomized by the great English
cathedrals. The cathedral of Seville
is one of the most magnificent
churches built in Spain in the style
of the Gothic period. It was begun in
1402 and completed in 1519 so that
one style is preserved throughout.*

The cathedrals of Toledo, Spain (left), and Notre Dame, Rouen, France (below), are two of the most famous ecclesiastical buildings to be erected in the Gothic style in Europe. Just as Britain produced a national individual style, characterized by Canterbury, Wells, Salisbury and Westminster Abbey, so several European countries also developed along individual lines when the new style superseded the Romanesque. Toledo is just as essentially Spanish and Rouen essentially French as Salisbury is English. France and Spain were, in fact, the two countries of the Continent in which Gothic building reached its highest expression, when the new style spread outward from Italy, but Germany and the Low Countries emulated, if they could not quite achieve, a similar excellence.

Mont St. Michel, the church which crowns it, seems to emphasize the hill and extend it upwards. All this means that adventure, romance, mystery and picturesqueness were once again sought and loved. Such architecture could, of course, only come about in a virile race and in lands, too, where the sun was less intense and where Roman rule, with its centralized government and denial of freedom to the individual, was less strong. It flourished as we know in England, where it produced our great cathedrals with their grand groups of towers as at Durham and Canterbury, the great west fronts of Lincoln and Wells, and the nave of Westminster Abbey, to mention only a few of the greatest. It spread over Europe till Spain produced Seville and Toledo cathedrals; France, those of Amiens, Beauvais, Rouen and others. Germany and the Low Countries followed suit, if inferior in quality.

Although Gothic architecture rose with extraordinary rapidity out of Romanesque experiments and though it reached heroic heights of adventure with which there is little to compare in other styles, it lasted in its main manifestations only three centuries. The particular spirit which brought it about died down. Nevertheless, it corresponds to something very deep in human nature which must always be present, and we may, therefore, expect revivals of it from time to time. For church building today, witness the great Anglican Cathedral at Liverpool, it is still the recognized form of expression, though modified there by classical balance, and elsewhere softened by Byzantine forms and influences. In the

CONTRASTS IN BRITISH MILITARY ARCHITECTURE

Nearly two centuries separate the magnificent fortress of Caernarvon, North Wales (above) and the Castle of Bodiam (below). Caernarvon was built in the reign of Edward I, and the photograph shows the Eagle Tower where the first Prince of Wales, afterwards Edward II, was born in 1384. This is one of the later castles to be built for purely military purposes, in this case to hold in check the Welsh people who had never fully accepted English suzerainty. Bodiam, built in the fifteenth century, is more a castellated manor-house than a castle, though it retains the military form of draw-bridge, moat, fortified gatehouse and circular angle-towers.

DEVELOPMENT OF TUDOR ARCHITECTURE

The house in the Old Town, Hastings, Sussex (above), and Moyns Hall, Steeple Bumpstead, Essex (below), represent two distinct phases in later Tudor architecture. The former shows how the small house began to take on a definite character, and this lovely half-timbered building should be compared with the old houses in Chiddingstone, Kent, shown on page 349. In Kent, Surrey and Sussex, in the fifteenth and sixteenth centuries extensive use was made of timber from the remains of the wealden forest. Local stone was used where it was plentiful, as in the Cotswold country and all the great Cotswold Tudor and Elizabethan houses are built of native grey limestone.

RENAISSANCE STYLE IN ITALY

The Palace of the Riccardi in Florence, is in the same tradition as the Strozzi
Palace pictured on page 277. It reflects the complete break-away from
Gothic forms which in Italy came with the Renaissance and a return to the
classical dignity and formal lines of ancient Greece and Rome.

nineteenth century in England, Gothic revival architecture existed, side by side with Greek revival, but that was largely because it was an archæologically minded century. Today, however, with a new outlook, and with reinforced concrete as the new material with which to create wonders as strange and new as was the Gothic arch, buttress and vault when first introduced, we may be led, let us hope, to a new architecture of our own day which is neither an archæological revival nor a sham, but a truthful expression of new powers and new ways of life. Later, some attempt will be made to show how far we have already gone in this direction.

RENAISSANCE AND BAROQUE

The Renaissance was a phenomenon in all the arts in every country in Europe, but more particularly, as was natural, in Italy. There the Roman remains were to be seen in almost every city, and there, too, Gothic building had not the hold it had elsewhere. It was to begin with, however, the sensible function of Italian architects not to bring back the methods of Roman building so much as a sense of Roman

REGENCY ARCHITECTURE IN LONDON

Typifying the spirit of Regency architecture which also gave London the Regent's Park terraces, the Athenæum Club in London, represents the last original work in a well-defined original style before the period of nineteenth-century Gothic revival in Britain commenced.

orderliness after Gothic haphazardness. There was no attempt to copy Roman buildings. It has often been remarked, for instance, that there is more difference between an Italian Renaissance church and a Roman temple, than between the latter and a Greek temple.

The early Renaissance architects, like Brunelleschi in Florence, were indeed no copyists and invented many lovely things, some almost Greek in their purity, like the Pazzi Chapel. They worked, it will be remembered, at a time of great adventure and striking ambitions, the time of

EIGHTEENTH-CENTURY WORKMANSHIP

Blenheim Palace (above), and Somerset House, London (below), together represent some of the finest workmanship of the eighteenth century. It was Vanbrugh who inspired Blenheim Palace in the true tradition of Sir Christopher Wren. Less formal than the Italian Palladio on whose work Inigo Jones himself had modelled, Vanbrugh retained the formality of the classical column and rows of equal-sized windows from one end of the façade to the other. Yet there is freedom in the ingenious corner turrets and varied window heads and the irregular façade. There was an inevitable reaction against this freedom and Sir William Chambers, who was the architect of Somerset House, is most closely associated with it.

Christopher Columbus and Galileo, figures to be equalled or surpassed if possible. It was not till the discovery of the works of Vitruvius and their publication in endless editions that an academic interest in the rigid proportions of columns, cornices and other details came about, and formed a strait-jacket from which it was the function of Michelangelo and his followers in the baroque world to release design. Perhaps the main contribution of these Italian architects was the development of the big house with its courtyards and its relation to the street, like the Strozzi and Riccardi palaces in Florence and the Farnese in Rome, the model for the Reform Club in Pall Mall. For such buildings with the emphatic lines of their cornices and the cliff walls of their façades the ragged medieval street was no suitable approach, but it was the French who made the most of Roman axiality and developed the idea of Roman planning in buildings, towns and gardens. With them the Renaissance in architecture started with the country house rather than the town house, as in Italy, so that roofs which meant nothing in narrow streets became important in the open country, and with the roof the idea of the pavilion became emphasized, too, as a main unit in the masses of the building.

ITALIAN INFLUENCE IN ENGLAND

The chief function of the English in the Renaissance of Roman forms was to give them a domestic character. Inigo Jones, the first to bring Italian architecture to England, visited Italy when the Roman detail had

already been formalized, and it was the architecture of the mature Renaissance he therefore brought back with him. Indeed Palladio, an Italian of the middle period whose chief work is to be seen in the palaces and villas at Vicenza and in a church in Venice, became for a time the same sort of impeccable guide to English architects, and to other Englishmen who had taken the grand tour, that Vitruvius was to the Italians. Sir Christopher Wren, on the other hand, was far more free and even baroque in his methods. His travels did not take him farther than France, but he describes how he there had a glance at the drawings of Bernini the designer of the grand columned piazza to St. Peter's, of his very baroque scheme for the front of the Louvre.

Before, however, we pass on to English work, a word must be said of the baroque, hardly ever properly understood in this country. It was the expression of a new spirit in architecture, that of self-dramatization, almost of a definite swagger perhaps not wholly believed in by its practitioners. Its products must not be confused with the massive grandeur of Roman classical work on the one hand or with the trumpery glitter of the rococo, a small scale degeneration of it, on the other. Although a great deal of Roman architecture was scenic architecture it was not necessarily dramatic. The baroque, however, always is. Its greatness lies in the ideas expressed, rather than in the materials used, which were often poor enough. It came as a reaction to academic Vitruvian architecture and, answering a universal craving, overtook the more sober forms of the Renaissance but particularly, and as was perhaps natural, in Germany and Austria. The baroque architect conceives his building as so much plastic form, just as a sculptor sees his clay. Plaster therefore became, especially in interiors, its natural medium. Though the building has its apartments and staircases like any other building these are all given by sweeping curves a sense of movement in relation to the movement of the whole. Every part is indeed subservient to the dramatic effect. Palaces, monasteries, churches and semi-tropical gardens all naturally fell within its scope, but its chief value today is that in certain buildings its lively spirit could well form a contrast to the harder mechanical spirit of modern steel or ferro-concrete construction. The cinema might well be such a building, yet it is difficult to recall one such at any rate of any merit. While a large baroque town might be a nightmare, an incident in it, with its variety and life, might be an ornament as welcome as are the baroque fountains in Vienna. For a time the baroque swept Europe, outside this country, only of course to meet the inevitable reaction of a pure classicism of long colonnades and buildings like St. George's Hall, Liverpool, and Schinkel's work in Berlin. In Spain and South America, however, the rich all-over modelling though small in scale in the style called Churrigueresque may also be traced to the Baroque movement.

In England the young scientist turned architect, Sir Christopher Wren, who never went farther away than Paris during the plague, but saw there some of the great baroque architects' drawings, came home and not only made a plan for London after the fire but rebuilt St. Paul's in a grand and, for this country, rather baroque manner, and surrounded it with churches

EXPERIMENT IN NEW MATERIALS

Erected in Hyde Park as the Great Exhibition building by Paxton, the Crystal Palace, shown here as it was before being destroyed prior to the Second World War, was re-assembled in 1853 in the locality still bearing its name. It was made of iron and glass, the new materials of the nineteenth century, and was remarkably successful, simple, yet magnificent. It represented the beginning of modern functional architecture.

NINETEENTH-CENTURY CLASSICAL REVIVAL

St. George's Hall, Liverpool, is one of the most magnificent instances of nineteenth-century classical revival. Harvey Lonsdale Elmes was the architect and the conception is purely Greek, of a formality which is as great as that of any of the Renaissance architects.

and their towers of the greatest beauty and originality. In these he seems to have caught the spirit of the Italian Renaissance, using the orders but using them freely, and in a manner neither classical nor baroque. Up to the coming of Inigo Jones and Wren, England had had its great Tudor, Elizabethan and Jacobean buildings, mostly in large houses but, though the plans of these were generally stately, their detail was often second hand from German printed plates, sometimes even used upside down.

Inigo Jones brought to England the pure milk of the word in the fully blown classic of the Banqueting Hall, Whitehall, and the Queen's House, Greenwich, now part of the National Maritime Museum, while Wren brought it life, gaiety and grandeur in such things as the completion of Greenwich Palace with its contrasting vista from the river to the Queen's House, emphasized by his pair of colonnades and domes, and with his great Chelsea Hospital and dignified, noble additions to Hampton Court and its gardens. In these, as at Kensington Palace, the Temple and elsewhere, he used brick in its varieties as well as stone, and may be said to have paved the way for the Georgian brick house which we share with Holland. Indeed Wren, who lived and worked through five reigns, which in itself needed some adroitness, could and did work in as many materials. No wonder therefore that under him craftsmen, like Tijou and Grinling Gibbons in metal and wood, found their opportunities and flourished. Nevertheless, in his great cathedral of St. Paul's and its circle of church towers he produced as well our most imaginative architecture.

To Wren's freedom, and, remembering Blenheim Palace and the interior of the hall of Castle Howard and other fine things, one should add also to Vanbrugh's genius, there was of course a reaction and the Palladian architecture flourished once more. Sir William Chambers, the architect of Somerset House with its great long terrace and front to the river, was perhaps the best of its practitioners. The system of the big order of columns or pilasters raised on a basement, generally of plain grooved stone-work, became the fashion for public buildings. When the Woods, father and son, romanized Bath, as they called it, laying out its fine terraces and squares, its Crescent and Circus, they

MODERN FUNCTIONAL CONSTRUCTION

The interior of the Boots' factory at Beeston (above), and the façade of the theatre of the Champs-Élysées, Paris (right), are in different ways characteristic of modern trends in architecture. The Beeston factory was designed by Sir Owen Williams with avowedly functional intention, yet it demonstrates how successfully architecture, even if it is utilitarian, can with the help of a vivid imagination, be given aesthetic value. The theatre of the Champs-Élysées, built in 1914, by Auguste and Georges Perret, is one of the earliest buildings to make effective use of ferro-concrete, the new material which, in the twentieth century, has widespread application.

used it, too, and used it beautifully, as an easy and ready method of expression. It was an architecture, with its central pavilions often crowned with a pediment and its end ones emphasized, which lent itself very readily to the grouping of houses in terraces or squares, and was similarly adopted by the Adam brothers, as in Portland Place, London, at the end of the eighteenth century and in the beginning of the nineteenth by the Regency architects. The great development of the square of houses in England, with its central communal garden, which is to be found in most of our big towns, no doubt grew in popularity from the universal village green of medieval times, with houses facing one another across the grass, though in the squares the use of such communal gardens was restricted to the inhabitants of the surrounding houses.

This uniting of individual buildings into one close architectural design which was started in Covent Garden and Lincoln's Inn by Inigo Jones and carried on with such noble results in Bath, probably reached its climax in this country in old Regent Street, destroyed in the present century, for its commonplace successor. There John Nash carried out not only a great town planning scheme bringing together the Pall Mall and Piccadilly districts of London with the fields north of the Marylebone Road by forming Regent Street and Regent's Park and their adjuncts —probably the finest addition to London since St. Paul's—but lined his great new street with a series of elaborate buildings

COMBINATION OF STYLES

Part of the city of New Delhi, the Governor-General's House is the work of Sir Edwin Lutyens. It represents a successful attempt to combine the characteristic styles of architecture of the East with the aesthetic taste of the West. The result is a building of dignity in a classic style, which yet retains more than a reminder of architecture characteristic of the Orient.

stretching from side street to side street, yet divided into shops on the ground floors. These designs were not all Nash's own, but by a series of like-minded architects working in the same manner the best way in which to carry out any big scheme was arrived at. The buildings, all of one height and low enough to let plenty of sunlight into the street, which the present buildings do not, were plastered and then painted afresh each spring so that the street always looked bright and gay. The much-bombed

Regent's Park terraces, the Brunswick terraces and Square at Hove, the Athenæum Club, the Mall at Cheltenham, the Carlton House terraces, London, were all of the same Regency architecture, and probably among the last original work in a clearly felt style before the period of the nineteenth-century revivals set in. After that the country was divided into its classicists, leaning to Greek architecture, whose most notable work is the great St. George's Hall, Liverpool, by Harvey Lonsdale

DESIGN IN STEEL AND CONCRETE

Below is the Senate House of the University of London. Opposite is Shell Mex House, facing the Thames near Waterloo Bridge. Each represents a highly successful experiment with the new materials and new style forced on modern architects. Thus construction in concrete demands windows of severely classical shape with square heads. Both buildings exhibit these with something of the regularity and impressiveness of the finest Georgian buildings. They represent a trend in British architecture which is as distinctive in its own way as the architecture of New York's skyscrapers. They represent, in fact, yet one more instance of an international trend being given a strong national flavour and emerging in Britain as a recognizable characteristic of British architecture of today.

Elmes, and the Gothic revival school, encouraged by Ruskin, who copied medieval architecture but were always changing the exact fifty years of Gothic they thought the best to copy. Alas, their leading architects, like Sir George Gilbert Scott, in restoring the cathedrals of Britain sometimes pulled down the fine work of one period, as the Chapter House at Westminster, to make way for their imitation work of another.

England, however, was not the only country where this state of affairs existed. Over most of the Continent the same indecision and futile experimenting in imitations of the past was occurring, till the light broke through in several directions.

An architect in England named Philip Webb saw that Victorian Gothic and Victorian Classic were equally untrue to the facts of construction and function, and designed for the poet and artist, William Morris, the Red House at Bexley Heath in 1859, where he returned to a direct expression of the needs of his client in plan and detail. Other English architects like Norman Shaw and C. F. A. Voysey, and a little later, Sir Edwin Lutyens did the same. No other European architects indeed in the last half of the last century built houses comparable to theirs, and their influence was immense, the former German Embassy even going so far as to appoint an architect attaché

to follow this English domestic work.

It was, however, from the new art of bridge and roof building, first in iron and then in steel, that the new impetus was chiefly to come about. Most architects tried for a long time not only to hide the new material from sight behind stone and brick façades, but failed to let it directly influence their design. Stone columns, for instance, appeared to carry great buildings which were really carried on hidden steel. The first iron bridge was the famous one erected at Coalbrook late in 1779, from designs of T. F. Pritchard executed by Wilkinson's of Bilston, which even then showed the elegance the new material could bring about. Telford, the engineer of the Holyhead Road to Ireland, designed in 1801 a lovely single span for London Bridge but it never was carried out. The new material was soon to spring from bridges to roofs, and in 1843 the Bibliothèque Nationale in Paris not only had two iron roofs but had a colonnade of cast iron columns down the centre of the big reading room. In 1851, followed the Great Exhibition building in Hyde Park by Paxton,

rebuilt as the Crystal Palace in 1853, and destroyed only just before the Second World War. Many people date modern functional architecture from it, and certainly both inside and out it was a remarkably beautiful, simple yet imposing building of cathedral size in glass and iron, and erected quite quickly. The best contrast perhaps between the directness of iron when left to itself and not hidden away under other materials, and those materials in all the complexity of borrowed plumes, is the grand simple roof of St. Pancras Station, London (1887), and the complication of the Gothic hotel Sir George Gilbert Scott stood in front of it. The final roof span of the century in size was 378 feet in the Galerie des Machines in the Paris exhibition of 1889, where the roof arches sprang from the floor. The ferroconcrete parabolic arches of the airshed hangers at Orly (1916), was another form of the same scheme, showing the new and imposing shapes now possible.

Before, however, the simplicity, which steel naturally must lead to, whether alone or embedded in concrete in the form of

County Hall, London, is one of the largest modern buildings carried out strictly in the style of the Greek revival. It is Palladian in conception, with its immensely long vista to the river, the extreme formality of its colonnade and the exact conformity between its two wings. Yet in spite of this adherence to traditional forms it is distinctive, due partly to the magnificence of its conception and its fine proportions. It forms a complete contrast with the Senate House shown on page 314.

ferro-concrete, there was a last attempt to create a modern style out of ornament instead of construction. It is generally called L'Art Nouveau, and probably reached its climax in Belgium. It was an attempt to replace traditional ornament, Classical or Gothic, by naturalistic ornament from leaf and flower forms, but it was ornament applied like wall-paper rather than growing naturally out of the construction. It was, therefore, bound to fail, and become as it were a living proof of the wrongness of Ruskinian and Victorian theory.

After this attempt at smothering buildings with meaningless ornament it was a natural reaction to return to simplicity, and cut out ornament altogether. While indeed, the Cubists in painting were trying to find a cubic basic form for natural objects, architects may be said to have seized on simple rectangular forms with flat roofs and made them the basis of their work. A leader was Adolph Loos in Vienna in the early part of this century who, it is reported, went as far as saying "ornament was a crime," but who nevertheless himself

built some fine interiors as well as his simple cubical exteriors. Like our own English Lethaby he preferred in his reaction against all traditional detail to think of architecture not as an art but as the craft of plain building, which it must be fundamentally, but it becomes something more directly the imagination plays upon it.

Le Corbusier, as he likes to be called, belongs to the same school of thought, but he clearly sees and proves by his work that all great architecture, though governed by geometric laws, belongs also to the world of the imagination, and that it is only by that indeed that it becomes great. The interior of the Boots' factory at Beeston, though claimed by its author, Sir Owen Williams, the engineer, to be purely functional, nevertheless achieves this quality, whereas the far bigger one for the Fiat Automobile Company at Lingotto, near Turin (1919-20) by Matte Truco, with its banked race-course on the roof for testing the cars, fails as architecture because the function of a hollow static building in which the cars are made conflicts with the idea of a race-course above for moving ones. The main function of a building must be clear and obvious. It cannot successfully possess two pulling in different directions.

While Germany built churches in heavy mass concrete and got some mysterious and impressive effects of vaulting, it was in the use of ferro-concrete in church construction, principally by Auguste and Georges Perret of Paris, and in their theatre of the Champs-Élysées, that elegance was first given to the material in a complete building (1914). Maillart's bridges in the same material over gorges in Switzerland achieved in their more limited conditions something even more lovely. The fine Penguin Pool at the Zoological Gardens, London, with its crossing pair of light elegant spiral slopes by B. Lubetkin, shows another graceful use of a material which to begin with was thought to be clumsy, and suited only to foundations, beams and piers which were not to be seen. The Second World War interrupted its growth, as that of so many other things, but it may safely be said that even yet all the elegance of its forms has not been discovered. It is already producing a new architecture, and where that may lead in the future no one can say. It should be noted, too, it is an architecture when, as in the best periods of the past, architect and engineer are one.

All this time steel was being used everywhere in beams and stanchions behind or imbedded in stone, brick or concrete, and not therefore allowed freely to express itself. Protection from fire was the excuse, but the forms of covering were those of the old architecture. All through this century there has been in England a school of traditional architects, who, forced to use steel for economy of space, yet failed to let it influence their buildings openly. Even the late Sir Edwin Lutyens, the last perhaps of the great English traditional architects, but with many real inventions to his name, like his great palace for the Viceroy at New Delhi, where he attempted with considerable success to marry the architecture of the East with that of the West, failed to give steel its due as the chief constructional material of bigger buildings. It was left to German architects like Gropius and Mendelsohn and the younger English architects like Maxwell Fry and William Crabtree to do this. They emphasized the fact that the steel or ferroconcrete frame underneath a modern building is finally bolted or cast together in one piece, and therefore, large parts of it can be cantilevered out from the rest. This at once solved the problem of the appearance of the big building above shop windows with their sheets of glass. If the rest of the building was clearly cantilevered the shops' fronts could nestle underneath the mass without seeming crushed. Erich Mendelsohn's great stores, as in his Chemnitz one with its layers of cantilevered solid building over layers of windows at each floor level, seems a perfectly satisfactory construction, and being on the convex curve of a street the long horizontal lines emphasize the curve. It would appear, therefore, with steel and ferro-concrete at his disposal, both of which can be designed to take any direction of thrust, witness ships built in ferro-concrete in war-time, the modern architect is largely free from both the balancing of one thrust by another, as in Gothic or the dead loads and masses of classical architecture. It is difficult, indeed, to see what shapes he will not be able to build in the future when the human eye and mind are trained to read their meaning and understand the construction used. This though is for the future. For the present, and perhaps for ever if its life is limited, steel is still ruled out in new monumental buildings. Charles Holden, who built so many imaginative structures for London Passenger Transport Board stations, when he came to build the great tower to store books for his London University building close to the Ionic façade which Sir John Burnet and his partners added to the British Museum, purposely left out all vertical steel because the length of its life is not yet known and he was building for posterity. It is indeed interesting to contrast these two buildings both built this century, one a Greek revival building with low colonnades, and the other, though with the vertical classical windows, which stone construction dictates, yet following the modern movement for

FRENCH-CANADIAN ARCHITECTURE

Exemplifying a startling compromise between the more strictly functional architecture of the New World and the traditional forms of medieval French architecture, the Château Frontenac in Quebec forms a natural part of a city of Canada which is still predominantly French in outlook and in which French is still a widely spoken language.

simplicity and reliance on contrasting masses of plain building. It is in this latter way, say by contrasting the sloping lines of cooling towers with the rectangular masses of the other buildings making up the modern big factory group, that Erich Mendelsohn was able to get his good effects in that field of work, such as on his great textile factory at Leningrad. Indeed, the large factory building such as the splendid Van Nelle cigarette one at Rotterdam, with its fine curved glass wings, of which J. H. Bruinhinn and L. C. Van der Vlugt were

the architects, is perhaps the typical building of this present age.

Though the factory in its finest form, clean and electrically driven as so many are today, with the dwellings of the workers close at hand yet with plenty of open space and communal facilities, and not tucked into the dirty slums of the Victorian era, may be the typical building, the most monumental is still and is likely to remain the big church or cathedral. Of the latter, the Anglican one at Liverpool by Sir Giles Gilbert Scott, grandson of the Sir Gilbert

of the Foreign Office and St. Pancras Station, is the outstanding example. Though Gothic in its detail and vaulting and in its great height and generally aspiring character, towering up as it does above the town from the edge of the quarry out of which the older buildings of Liverpool were built, it nevertheless has the balanced character—with its four transepts at the base of its single great tower and its short balancing nave and chancel—of a symmetrical monument.

The architect of this supposedly Gothic building and one of the biggest in the world, has gone still farther from thirteenth-century models, and has eschewed the flying buttress, keeping instead to the ordinary one and to walls of almost Roman thickness. This means that he is able in his interior to have sheer plain walls rising straight from the floor, enormous piers and a general solidity and strength, as well as a vitality which an archæologically correct building would not have. St. George's Hall, Liverpool, may be the finest existing classical building in Europe, but even its most ardent admirer must admit it has not the life of this still unfinished, so-called Gothic cathedral. The new Guildford Cathedral by Edward Maufe, half built, too, will have something of the same character as it stands alone, a pilgrimage church on the downs outside the town, a character emphasized in this case by large-scale sculpture.

The extraordinary thing is that Liverpool is to have another and still larger cathedral, a Roman Catholic one, on the same range of low hills overlooking the Mersey, by the late Sir Edwin Lutyens. This, in the

FRENCH RENAISSANCE INTERIOR

Rebuilt during the reign of Louis XIV and completed in 1679, the Hall of Mirrors (Galerie des Glaces), one of the largest parts of the Palace of Versailles, is a very successful example of the highly decorated form of Renaissance style, and makes full use of the repetition of the arch form. The paintings on the ceiling are among the most elaborate of their kind in France.

LARGE-SCALE DECORATION

Castle Howard, Yorkshire, English contemporary of the Palace at Versailles, was built to the design of John Vanbrugh (1664-1726). Dramatist as well as architect, Vanbrugh made considerable use of details on an unusually large scale. In 1695 he was made a commissioner for completing the work on Greenwich Hospital which had been designed by Sir Christopher Wren.

TWENTIETH-CENTURY CHURCH

Isolated on the downs outside the town, an isolation accentuated by its large-scale sculpture, the new cathedral at Guildford, by Edward Maufe, was started between the two wars, construction being suspended at the beginning of the Second World War. The building is destined to have something of the strength and majesty of Liverpool Anglican Cathedral as well as an individual grace of its own.

baroque manner crowned with a great dome, bigger than that of St. Peter's at Rome, is a five-aisled church, and with the four great piers carrying the dome so big that two of the aisles, one on either side, pierce them, and all the difficulties are avoided that Sir Christopher Wren encountered in adapting his dome to the Latin Cross plan forced upon him. Of this great Roman building, Roman in both senses of the word, only the fine vaulted crypt, rather like a Roman thermæ, is yet built, but Sir Edwin completed most of the drawings and made a large scale model of the finished building before he died. When these two great cathedrals of Liverpool are finished, one with the loftiest tower in the country and the other with the biggest dome, the appearance of

Liverpool from the Mersey, already enlivened with the fine series of square-topped towers (by Herbert Rowse) ventilating the tunnel under the river, will present one of the finest silhouettes in the world.

It may be thought, with some truth perhaps, that the age of monumental buildings on the scale of cathedrals, in spite of the ones building today, is passing, and that the future of architecture will lie on the one hand with the great factory and the communal buildings of our towns, and on the other, with the new grouping of little houses and flats which have grown up with the town planning movement of the present century. Let us consider for a moment this town planning point in relation to architecture.

The idea of a planned town is not a new

one. What is new today is the object for which the planning is done. From Roman times till this century one may say the emphasis in planning was to provide as fine a setting as possible for the few chief buildings of the town. In medieval times the great church or cathedral had pride of place. It dominated the town and did still during the Renaissance—in the case of St. Peter's at Rome. On the whole though, in the Renaissance days it was the power of the prince that the plan expressed. In our own more democratic country, the palaces of the great being mostly outside the towns, the plan begins to express the power of wealth and of the great middle class. It was for them that the squares and terraces of the eighteenth and nineteenth century were built. The houses for the increasing flood of workers which industrialism brought in were crammed as many as possible to the acre, often fifty to fifty-five, both to get them close to the places of employment and to make as much money out of them as possible. Hence the slums of our big cities and the deadly monotony of our prosperous manufacturing towns, like Preston in Lancashire, with street after street of little houses in little streets all alike. Then came the Garden City movement early in the century with the idea of the town controlling, if not owning, itself with the buildings grouped and designed to make the life of everyone better and happier. From fifty houses to the acre a drop to twenty, or even to ten was common even if few completely planned towns sprang up. We have at present only two in this country, Letchworth and Welwyn Garden City, though some twenty more are now contemplated, but the idea of the planned community became common and with the damage by bombing in the late war has now become universal. The result to the happiness and convenience of the community cannot yet

LONDON UNDERGROUND STATION

Chiswick Park Station, just outside the County of London, is typical of the many pleasant and often imaginative structures which were built for the London Passenger Transport Board, now the London Transport Executive.

325

be measured. For the architect, however, it may well be that in the future, instead of thinking and designing individual buildings he will think of and design each building in relation to others, in groups, some small, some as big as the town itself. It will in many cases be a return to the eighteenth-century system of combined buildings, but the terraces will not generally be so close together. The new church, the new library, art gallery, community centre, the clinic and shops will, it is to be hoped, and it seems likely that it may happen, be designed, if not as a whole by one person, at any rate in definite relation one to another, and to the community as a whole.

Some would go further and say the residential parts of the town, whether of a new one or of an extended old one, must be built up of more or less self-contained communities of five hundred to a thousand persons all using the same community centre which is to be as real a centre as was once the village inn and from which, as the petals of a flower, a series of greens surrounded by houses, can radiate. This form, which is being adopted in several places, may indeed in time replace the criss-cross of streets with their houses where neighbours hardly know one another and more clearly express the new communal life, the desire for which the late war, among other things, seems to have fostered. It will, if persisted in, take away a great deal of the ill-odour of the suburb with its Victorian ideal of keeping oneself to oneself.

We shall in future therefore look for three things from architecture: (1) A new enlarged expression of communities; (2) the occasional monumental building to express our age and add to the accumulation of such buildings from past ages as when the Liverpool cathedrals take their place among the cathedrals of the country, and, (3) industrial buildings, large and small, but as functional as the aeroplane, and like it taking as novel shapes but like it, too, with a definitely limited life. In all these, in the completely planned community as seen from the air, in the cathedral or church or other monumental building expressing deep and permanent need or aspiration, and in the engineering structure for a definite purpose, architecture will find its scope, and it will not be less but far greater than it has been in the past, for its aim will in the main be an expression of the hopes, the ambitions of the community as a whole rather than of the idiosyncrasies of the individual. With new materials at hand and methods of construction, and with wider purposes to aim at, the imagination, which can turn any structure into a work of art, which can make architecture of any building, will have a field to play upon wider and greater and more full of possibilities than it has ever had before.

Test Yourself

1. How far does taste in architecture vary from time to time? Give some examples to support your answer.
2. What are the greatest inventions of the last hundred years as applied to architecture?
3. Name some of the characteristics of Ancient Greek temples.
4. What effect did the Renaissance have on the development of architecture?
5. In what way can John Nash be regarded as the father of town planning? Estimate the lasting value of his work.
6. (a) Name the architect of the Anglican Liverpool Cathedral; (b) in what style is it built?

Answers will be found at the end of the book.

CHAPTER XIX

ARCHITECTURE IN BRITAIN

WE have seen in the previous chapter that the story of architecture is international. The same trends can be discerned in many different countries, not always occurring at the same time in each, but following each other in orderly succession as each style in turn spreads outward from its country of origin.

Within this international pattern every country shows also a national interpretation and a national development which deviates from the general trends. The individual deviations are due to local needs, to the character of such building materials as are easily accessible, to the emergence of some great architect whose work revolutionizes the style of his own times, or, it may seem, to some mere caprice of fashion. Britain is no exception to this rule, for from the eleventh century onwards there is a distinct national style and local variations on that style are also noticeable.

In no other of the arts is Britain so rich as in its wealth of architectural beauty, a great deal of which is truly original in conception as well as admirably competent in execution. Up and down the country there are many examples, both in the Romanesque and in the Gothic style some of which are comparable with any of the masterpieces of Europe.

It is perhaps true that, after the Renaissance, the works of the Italian and French masters of classicism are without peer, but until then architecture in Britain was considered to be second to none. A great deal of the priceless heritage of the twelfth, thirteenth, fourteenth and fifteenth centuries has been handed down intact to the modern age, so that everyone who travels about Britain has the opportunity of seeing at first hand the miracles which the medieval masons wrought in stone, flint and brick.

In order to appreciate the development of architecture in Britain, it is essential to be familiar with the various styles and their order of appearance. It is helpful also to attach approximate dates to each of the principal types of building, although these dates are by no means fixed even within the narrow confines of England. When a style was well developed in the south, it was often only just beginning to make its appearance in the north.

The Romanesque style is seen both in Saxon and Norman work. The Saxon is roughly co-extensive with the first half of the eleventh century. It is possible that some existing Saxon work is earlier, but until the influence of the Norman master masons was felt about the beginning of the eleventh century, it is doubtful whether the Saxons built extensively in stone. Previously there were many fine structures of wood, and some of these were rebuilt after the original plan in stone.

The Norman style was current in the last decades of the eleventh century and the first half of the twelfth. Thereafter the Gothic style began to make its appearance, although there was first a stage generally known as Transitional, which lasted nearly until the end of the twelfth century.

In the Gothic style proper the student will note three principal types; the Early English, covering approximately the first half of the thirteenth century; the Decorated, extending from about 1250 to 1350; and the Perpendicular, from 1350 to very near the end of the fifteenth century, when the characteristic Tudor styles were current and the great era of church building had come to an end. The full flowering of the British classical designs of the Renaissance did not take place until the beginning of the seventeenth century.

The earliest permanent buildings in Britain which have been preserved in recognizable form are Roman; these were erected during the four hundred years of occupation, when Britain was a flourishing part of the Roman Empire and its civilization reached a peak which it took nearly a thousand years to match.

SAXON CHURCH ARCHITECTURE

The Church of St. Laurence, Bradford-on-Avon, Wiltshire, is one of the most perfect examples of Saxon architecture in Britain and shows most of the leading characteristics of the style.

Roman Britain in the fourth century reflected the highly developed culture of the Romans themselves. But there is evidence to show that even at this early stage the British people superimposed on the Roman models something of their own spirit and something of their own individuality. Towns such as Bath, London and St.

Albans (Verulamium), were full of notable buildings in stone and the characteristic thin red Roman bricks, but unfortunately the ravages of time and man have swept most of them away. The Saxon invaders who swept the country with fire and sword when the strong arm of Roman protection was removed regarded large buildings as only the lurking places of possible enemies and deliberately razed them to the ground.

The walls of the Romano-British cities are some of the most significant tributes to the skill of the builders of those times and there are fragments of these in many modern towns including London, but none finer than that surrounding Verulamium, where one long stretch has been left almost unimpaired. It is made of rubble faced with flints, with parallel lines, or courses, of red bricks. Just how extensively these bricks were used can be inferred from the appearance of the older parts of the abbey of St. Albans, and in particular the tower, for the medieval city was largely built from the ruins of the Roman town, with the result that, in certain lights when the sun lies to the west the Norman tower of the abbey church gleams red.

Indeed, the presence of these thin red bricks in medieval buildings is nearly always a proof that they are on or near the site of a Roman town, as for instance the Norman castle of Colchester, which was built from the ruins of the Roman city of Camulodunum and has the same quality as the tower of St. Albans Abbey.

In addition to the great buildings in the cities, the Roman architects built a number of villas in many parts of southern England. These were self-contained farm-houses and country workshops, housing a number of workers as well as the master and his family. None of these has remained intact, but a few retain sufficient of their original shape to allow an exact reconstruction. Notable among them is the villa of Ched-

SAXON NAVE OF TIMBER

The parish church at Greenstead-juxta-Ongar in Essex is the only building in the country to retain a substantial part of the original Saxon wooden nave, which was composed of the trunks of oak trees split in two. Most early Saxon churches were of timber but in every other case the original structure has been replaced by one of stone. The windows shown in the photograph are comparatively recent additions to the original structure.

worth in Gloucestershire, which was buried by a landslide soon after the Roman occupation and consequently survived better than most the ravages of the Saxon invaders.

Here the dominating influence of the native Italian builders can be seen, for it was a courtyard house, with long ranges of low buildings facing the court on three sides. There were beautifully decorated living-rooms, with paintings on the walls and elaborate mosaics on the floors and there was a central heating system, known as a hypocaust, primarily intended for the elaborate series of baths which were a feature of every Roman house, but which also had the effect of warming the main living-rooms.

The system was essentially the same as that used at Bath in the great baths, which

NORMAN CATHEDRAL OF DURHAM

Durham Cathedral is one of the most magnificent examples of Norman architecture in England. The massive building stands on a rock almost surrounded by the River Wear, a position impregnable in medieval times. The many round-headed arches in the façade are evidence of its Norman origin, though the photograph also shows several later features, including the fine Gothic window between the twin towers.

NORMAN TOWER OF ST. ALBANS ABBEY

In this photograph of St. Albans Abbey from the south-west the Norman tower is seen at its best. The sub-division of the round-headed openings gives lightness to the massive square building. The Norman windows of the south transept and of the nave clerestory can also be seen, together with the courses of thin red bricks (often called tiles), which were taken from the ruins of the Roman city of Verulamium when the abbey was being built.

NORMAN NAVE OF CHICHESTER CATHEDRAL

Almost every feature of this beautiful nave is Norman. Its supreme artistry has been retained through repeated restorations. Its appearance today differs little from that of the original nave which was built in the early part of the twelfth century. The breaking up of the main columns and the subdivision of the round-headed arches are typical of the period.

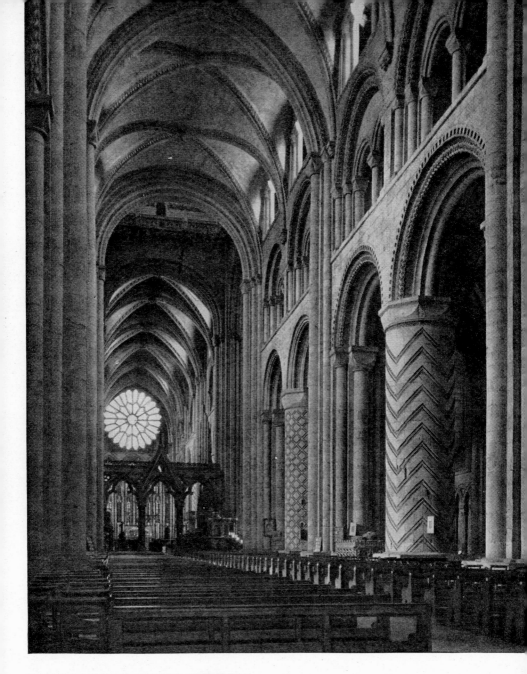

NORMAN NAVE OF DURHAM CATHEDRAL

*This makes an interesting contrast with the nave of Chichester opposite.
There is the same general plan, but the impression is of a heavier and
more austere architecture, chiefly because of the weight of the columns,
which, like those of St. Albans, are really piers and can claim the name of
column only because they have the traditional capital and base.*

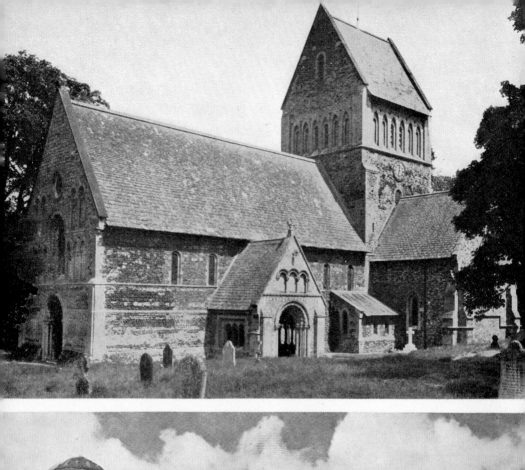

EXAMPLES OF ROMANESQUE STYLE

The essential unity of the Norman style of English Romanesque is well seen in these three contrasting examples of its application. The parish church of Castle Rising in Norfolk (top left) is one of the finest and most perfect of the smaller Norman churches and dates from the early part of the twelfth century. Here are many of the features which are illustrated on a grand scale in the photographs of Chichester and Durham on the preceding pages. There is ornamental moulding round the arches of the west front of the porch reminiscent of the moulding at Durham, but here it is repetition of the arch form rather than its sub-division which gives an air of lightness and grace. By contrast the castle at Colchester (left below), is almost unrelieved in its massiveness and passive strength. Colchester Castle Is the largest Norman keep in the country and, as early as the year 1100, it is described as one of the royal castles. As in the abbey church at St. Albans, the thin red Roman bricks can be discerned, taken in this case from the ruins of Camulodunum, which was on the site of Norman Colchester. The Jew's House at Lincoln (above), is one of the few surviving examples of Norman domestic architecture. Its age is evidenced by the masonry, the round-headed porch and the round-headed windows. Houses such as this with shops opening on the street were typical of the residence of the townsman of the period, and it was here he worked and sold his goods; behind the shop are the kitchen and the stairs leading to the bedrooms above.

335

were modelled after the fashion of those of Caracalla in Rome. There was a central furnace fed with wood or peat, or any other suitable material, and the hot air was carried from it along flues built under the floors of adjoining chambers, in much the same way as hot water flows along the pipes of a modern central-heating plant.

There is evidence, too, of the massiveness of Roman architecture in Britain in the ruins of the line of forts built round the south-east coast towards the end of the Roman occupation under the direction of the Count of the Saxon Shore. These extended from Burgh Castle, near Yarmouth in Norfolk, round the coast to Porchester Castle, near Portsmouth. The finest of them all is the great castle of Anderida near Pevensey, which demonstrates that these castles must have been as imposing and as durable as any which the medieval masters built nearly a thousand years later.

From the end of the Roman period until the eleventh century there is necessarily a gap in the story of English architecture, for none of the wooden buildings of the Saxon period was durable enough to withstand the lapse of time. Probably the oldest surviving work of the Saxons is the nave of the church of Greenstead-juxta-Ongar, which is composed of the split trunks of oak trees and was probably similar to many hundreds of the village churches which the Saxons built. But once the use of stone had been introduced great numbers of churches were rebuilt in the new style.

The Saxon style of architecture, along with the Norman, is called Romanesque because it is based on the classic buildings of ancient Rome. Now, one of the most distinctive features of the classic style is the round arch, reproduced in the bigger buildings as a barrel-vault, and the round arch is one of the most important features

EARLY GOTHIC ABBEY—RIEVAULX, YORKSHIRE

This is one of the loveliest of the many Yorkshire abbeys which have escaped total destruction and have been sympathetically preserved. The style is early Gothic, dating from the first part of the thirteenth century, but in spite of the pointed arches characteristic of that period, Rievaulx shows its debt to the Norman styles of the preceding century.

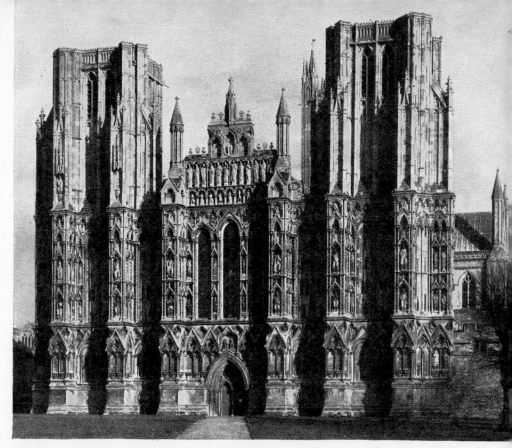

DECORATED GOTHIC WEST FRONT OF WELLS CATHEDRAL

*This is an outstanding example of the Decorated style of Gothic architecture.
Lavish and exuberant in its ornament, it makes a surprising contrast with
the quiet beauty of the Transitional and Early English styles. Many of the
large number of carved stone figures in the niches of the façade were
mutilated at the time of the Reformation, as was the case in so many of the
noblest churches in every part of England.*

of Saxon work. The Saxon round arch
is distinguished from its Norman counterpart by being ruder and rougher, and
composed of larger and generally less-
well-hewn stones. There is little ornament
round the arch, which is plain and severe
in the extreme, austere by modern standards,
as well as by the standards of later medieval
art.

Another distinguishing feature of the
Saxon period is "long and short" work,
particularly at the corners of buildings.
By this is meant stone slabs set alternately
horizontally and perpendicularly, and it
used to be an axiom that wherever this

type of corner was found the building
must be of Saxon origin. There is reason
to think in the light of later criticism that
the manner persisted into Norman times,
but certainly the vast majority of the
instances are definitely Saxon.

Among the churches which retain most
of their Saxon form are Holy Trinity,
Colchester; St. Benet's, Cambridge; and
the parish churches at Earls Barton in
Northamptonshire and Bradford-on-Avon
in Wiltshire. The most complete of them
all is probably Bradford-on-Avon, where
the nave and chancel are covered with
arcading in low relief, which imitates the

effect gained by a wooden structure and is obviously a carry-over from the previous styles current in the timber age. One or two Saxon towers, such as Earls Barton, give the same effect, the place of the timber beams being taken by raised stone strips, which from a distance look very much like a timber frame.

The transition from the Saxon to the Norman was a gradual one and the Norman churches, whether the great cathedrals or the little village churches, were still strictly in the Romanesque tradition. In fact the only difference in appearance was brought about by a gradual refinement, a greater delicacy, and by the introduction of classical columns into the framework of the building. The window openings were still small and round-headed, the chancel and porch arches being similarly rounded. The towers are square and solid, and broken up by round-headed openings. In some of the earlier of the great churches such as Chichester Cathedral, the columns which support the roof of the nave can be called columns only because they have the traditional capital and base. Rather these columns are great circular piers of enormous massive strength and solidity.

In a few Norman cathedrals the infinite beauty and grace of Norman work is seen at its best, and in spite of the continuing solidity of the building there is an impression of airy grace, the origin of which is not clear at a casual glance. It arises particularly from the superb artistry with which the Normans sub-divided their arches, as seen, for instance, in the triforium of Chichester, where the monotony of a long row of semi-circular arches is given new grace and variety by the sub-division of each into two or more separate smaller arches. In place of the unrelieved massive piers of St. Albans the columns are flanked by additional slender columns and the main arches (for instance of the lord or chancel arch) are stepped back into what are termed orders and are, in effect small recesses.

Some of the loveliest of early twelfth-century work appears in the ruins of abbeys and priories founded later in the Norman period. To take one example at random, the west front of the priory church at Castle Acre in Norfolk is a triumph of the restraint and beauty of the period's finest workmanship. Here there is nothing in the way of ornate decoration and the whole effect is obtained by the use of interlacing arches or arcading.

Apart from the genius of this device of sub-division and arcading, the Normans made use of some sculptural decoration which, though in character with all their work, was restrained, nevertheless contributes immeasurably to the total effect. Sometimes the recessed orders of important arches, as mentioned above, are set off by moulding which continues through the whole of the semicircle. Sometimes, as in the unique "wheel" window in Barfreston Church, the whole is embellished with pictorial carving, either representing the figures of human beings or of incidents of mythology.

The simple zigzag moulding is typical of many a small village Norman church, so are richly carved capitals such as those of St. Peter's Church, Northampton, or of the prior's door of Ely. The arcading of Durham Cathedral proves, however, that richness of ornament or elaboration are utterly unnecessary to produce the supreme artistry which distinguishes the period in general.

From Norman times onwards churches are not the only vehicles for the expression of the builder's art, although they remained throughout the Middle Ages the principal medium of architectural beauty. But just

LATE GOTHIC ARCHITECTURE

Bath Abbey is one of the latest of the great Gothic churches in the Perpendicular style. It was begun in 1500, but was not completed until the end of the century. The great number and size of the windows, the profusion of flying buttresses and the elaborate ornament of the tower are all features characteristic of the Perpendicular style and combine to make this one of the most impressive churches in the west of England.

PERPENDICULAR GOTHIC CHURCHES

Long Melford Church, Suffolk, provides a fine example of the Perpendicular style of Gothic architecture. Many of the features displayed on such a grand scale in Bath Abbey—see page 338—such as the square ornamented tower, the profusion of windows with straight " up and down " tracery, a feature which is suggested by the very name Perpendicular as opposed to the delicate curvilinear tracery of the Decorated style and the buttresses, are reproduced here on a smaller scale. In the case of Northleach (opposite) the lofty square tower is in the same tradition as Long Melford and Bath Abbey. This is another of the fine Perpendicular Gothic churches built during the fifteenth century. Northleach was at that time an important centre of the Cotswold woollen industry in England.

as life in the Middle Ages, at least for the upper classes, was either religious or military, so military buildings began to take their place side by side with ecclesiastical. The lord of the manor, and later medieval guilds, contributed to build "to the greater glory of God" (and there was often extreme rivalry between neighbouring parishes to secure the finest church), yet the home of the "baron" began to have lavished on it almost unlimited time and expense.

This fact arose partly from military necessity, for when Saxon Britain recognized Norman suzerainty there were still many in the land who would have nothing to do with the Normans and regarded them as conquering bandits to be impeded and attacked at every opportunity. So William

of Normandy laid it on his barons as a bounden duty to build themselves castles which would act as a rallying ground for loyal forces and at the same time hold the lawless elements of the countryside in check. Later, when the need for the passive strength and battlements of the Norman fortresses had ceased to exist, the tradition was maintained in castellated mansions whose battlements were for show rather than defence, and whose ramparts and gatehouses were no more than a sham display.

To the early Norman period belong some of the strongest and most magnificent of the castles, including the White Tower of the Tower of London, Rochester, Colchester, Norwich and Castle Hedingham.

There are two kinds of Norman castle, the square keep type, of which these five are typical examples, and the shell keep type. The latter were generally built on the site of earlier Saxon fortresses, whereas the square keeps were characteristically on new sites and were designed to protect some place of great strategic importance, as London guarded the point where the main road from the port of Dover to the Midlands crossed the Thames, and Rochester the point where it forded the Medway.

The Saxon castle had consisted of a "motte and bailey," that is to say, of a sizable enclosure (the bailey), protected by palisades with an artificial mound capped by a wooden building, itself further protected by palisades. The main part of the enclosure, that is to say, the bailey, contained the normal dwelling-place of the chieftain and his retainers, while the mound buildings were only a last refuge in case of assault.

In the shell keep type of castle the Normans maintained this tradition, replacing the wooden palisades of the main enclosure with a strong wall and building a roughly circular fortress upon the mound. In this type, as in Saxon times, the fortress was intended only as a last place of refuge.

In the square keep type, however, the keep itself was the dwelling place of the Norman baron and his family, as well as a fortress proper. Norwich Castle has been restored in accordance with the style of the period, but perhaps the finest castle of all for studying the work of the period is Rochester, which though in a ruined state, is very largely complete. We can see here the same dominance of the rounded arch as in the architecture of the churches, the same massive solidity of the walls and of the structure as a whole. Naturally, the masonry is not so highly finished, the moulding that enriches the architecture of the churches being almost entirely absent. Yet, even so, the Norman keep must have been a thing of beauty as well as of utility.

The window openings on the lower floors are very small, in order to reduce the risk of the arrows of attacking forces penetrating. But on the second floor, which was the main hall of the castle, the windows are larger and the chambers loftier, and there are recesses in the walls to which the baron and the closest members of his family were able to retire to rest in a measure of seclusion, which was novel in an age in which the usual practice was for even a noble, together with his personal servants

to live and eat and sleep together in the same room. After meals the rough wooden tables were pulled aside and the floor strewn with fresh straw, and the whole household lay down to sleep upon it, warmed by the heat of a wood fire burning in a central hearth from which the smoke escaped only through a small hole in the roof.

The principle of the hall home survived into the thirteenth and fourteenth centuries, the modern idea of separate bedrooms and sitting-rooms only emerging fully in the conception of the great Tudor and Elizabethan manor-houses.

In addition to the building of the great castles the Norman period witnessed the beginning of the smaller domestic buildings, the direct forerunners of the Englishman's home. These were often erected within the precincts of the abbey for the benefit of the abbot and, towards the end of the period, within a few of the growing towns for the use of the richest of the merchants, who were beginning to be an important element in the population. The Jew's House at Bury St. Edmunds is an example of this innovation, though its only distinguishing feature today is the round-headed windows which are so obviously of Norman workmanship.

THE GOTHIC STYLE

Though it revolutionized the character of English architecture, the Gothic style was not really new in the sense in which the classical styles of the Renaissance emerged from a different tradition, but was a logical development from the Norman. The term Gothic itself was not current at the time, but is said to have been invented by Sir Christopher Wren, who referred to it as Gothic or barbarian, in contrast with the pure classicism of the Romanesque and of his own Renaissance architecture. Some modern critics incline to agree with the implied judgment of Wren, but the truth is that the Norman in its highest expression approaches perfection and so does the Gothic.

The pointed arch, as opposed to the round arch of the Romanesque, is typical of the Gothic style. This type of arch is indeed the one feature which persists from the earliest Gothic to the latest. Its use facilitated a complete revolution in the principles of construction affecting in particular the character of the vault. When a semi-circular arch form is used the height of the structure is limited by the arch form whether it is the chancel arch dividing the nave from the chancel of the parish church, or the vaulted roof of one of the great cathedrals, in which the height of the "roof" in Norman times was strictly limited by the height of the walls. Perhaps the twelfth-century builders yearned for a form which would enable the height of the building to be independent of the height of the walls, and in this perception may lie in part the reason for the introduction of the new style. Certainly in the latter part of the twelfth century there are many cases where typical Norman forms of building and decoration persist while the arches are definitely pointed. This is the style known as Transitional, although it must be remembered that every style of architecture is in a sense transitional and this represents only the special transition from the Romanesque to the Gothic.

The question of supporting the roof has been the main problem confronting mankind ever since he began to build, and it is this problem of keeping a roof in position which (turning to our immediate subject) explains the whole development of Romanesque and Gothic architecture.

The Norman builders failed to find the satisfactory answer, although they were making a groping advance towards a solution. To the Gothic builders fell the distinction of a complete and brilliant answer—"the application of equilibrium to construction in strong contrast to that of inert stability," as Banister Fletcher calls it. And until the significance of what they discovered has been grasped and until the evolution of the practical application of their discovery has been traced, the meaning of the changing form of the architecture of our cathedrals and abbey churches will in all probability be missed.

It is perhaps true that the Normans had little theoretical knowledge of building construction; they were pioneers, on whose methods later builders improved. Their method of tackling the problem of keeping a roof in position—perhaps the main purpose in building—was not altogether satisfactory. But the Normans had made some advance towards a solution of the problem of keeping a roof in position.

The Norman roof took the form of what is called the barrel- or tunnel-vault: it consisted literally of a succession of semi-circular arches supported by a similar succession of piers, giving the appearance of a tunnel. The downward and outward thrust of the rounded arches was exerted uniformly along the whole range of the supporting wall, or succession of piers, as described. Perhaps when playing with children's bricks you have done rather what the Normans did—erected two

BARONIAL HALL

The hall of Penshurst Place (below) is a fine example of a Gothic baronial residence. The photograph shows the central hearth which was usual in all medieval buildings, the smoke making its escape through a small hole in the roof.

FIFTEENTH-CENTURY BANQUETING ROOM

The minstrels' gallery is another common feature of medieval halls. The Stranger's Hall, Norwich, of which the banqueting room is shown above, is part of one of the great East Anglian merchants' houses of the fifteenth century.

rectangular columns and bridged them with a semi-circular arch. Behind that put two more columns and an arch; do it again and again until you have a tunnel-like construction, and you have a passable imitation of the Norman barrel-vault. Although the supporting columns had the appearance of a continuous wall, any interference with them usually resulted in part of your arch (or roof) toppling down. The Normans found that any piercing of the wall by insertion of space for door or window resulted in dangerous weakening of the structure and, being practical, they restricted windows and doorways as much as possible with the result that their buildings tended to be dark and gloomy.

Without quite realizing the importance of their discovery they developed the groined vault—two barrel-vaults crossing

MASTERPIECE OF MILITARY ARCHITECTURE

A fine example of castle building at a time when the strength of the defences lay in the complexity of the outer fortifications rather than in a central keep is Harlech Castle, Merionethshire. On a site impregnable on three sides the castle dominates the fertile valley and proved an effective threat to the activities of Welsh insurgents. From the angle-towers cross-fire covering any of the approaches is possible. With Caernarvon, Harlech ranks as a masterpiece of the military architecture of Edward I, of the type usually known as concentric. The massive gatehouse can be seen in the background.

each other at right-angles. From this it was an easy step to the ribbed vault where in place of the intersecting barrel-vault there is a simple framework of ribs supporting slabs of stone; the ribs transmitted the thrust of the vault to the points on the wall from which they sprang. So long as these points were made sufficiently strong by thickening the wall into buttresses the intervening wall-spaces had no functional purpose in supporting the roof and so could be removed, thrown open to admit light. Buttresses, after all, can be looked upon as the wall-space intervening between roof-supporting pillars turned outwards at right-angles from the line of the wall. At this point the Normans were baffled by the fact that a semi-circular

arch has its height conditioned by its span; being a half-circle the height is half the diameter of the circle, in fact, half the width of the arch. The Normans never got over this limitation. The Gothic builders solved the difficulty by introducing the pointed arch. With it, instead of the height of the roof being governed by the distance between the walls it became possible to construct a roof of almost any desired height.

The solution of the vaulting problem by the use of the pointed arch allowed a full development of the principles of guiding and controlling the thrusts of the roof. The problem of keeping a roof over your head had been solved.

Hitherto, the vault had been a ponderous,

inert weight requiring proportionately thick and uninterrupted walls to support it, and in the absence of any real scientific principles, the tendency was always to take no risks and to thicken and strengthen the wall too much. Now the vault was carried on a light framework of ribs and shafts, which, it is true, required accurate and delicate balancing and control, but which allowed the display of skill and artistry denied to the cruder construction. The thrust of the vault was concentrated along the lines of the ribs, and, like the veins of a leaf converging on its stem, the ribs were gathered together into the vaulting shafts, which sometimes were carried right down to the firm ground and at others terminated in a bracket (called a "corbel") fixed into the wall. There you had the vital spot. If that was effectively secured, stability was achieved. The normal practice was to carry the thrust from the base of the shaft and throw it across to the aisle wall by means of an arch, concealed in the cavity between the aisle roof and vault, and by thickening the wall of the aisle at the point of contact by an abutment (or buttress).

If it was required to carry the thrust of the vault clear of an aisle or other obstruction such as a cloister walk or chapel, a flying buttress was employed which was comprised of an arch spanning the interval to be crossed to an isolated buttress.

It will be seen from the foregoing

DEFENSIVE BUILDING

Bamburgh Castle is one of the strongest and most massive of the many castles in Northumberland. Like others which played a major part in the Border wars, it was built for military strength alone, although the photograph includes a number of later additions. The larger windows and the graceful lines of the buildings to the right of the keep show that they were added when the needs of defence were no longer paramount. The abrupt cliff on which the castle is built provides a natural defence which here takes the place of a moat which usually surrounds a castle.

explanation that the fundamental character-istics of the Norman and Gothic styles were due not to whims of fancy or changes in fashion and taste. Once the "application of equilibrium to construction" was sub-stituted for that of "inert stability," development inevitably followed the lines of lighter and loftier structures, with less and less wall-space and more and more fenestration (or window-spacing). The history of the next three hundred years is simply the tracing of this development. At first the new technique was applied cautiously and hesitatingly (Early English). Then it grew bolder with experience and more confident with success (Decorated). Finally it threw caution to the winds and created the towering gossamer-like struc-tures we know as Perpendicular, in which the inert wall-spaces had been almost eliminated by vast windows that were literally walls of glass, and the lowering

MANOR-HOUSE AND FORTRESS

This aerial photograph of Arundel Castle shows how a medieval manor-house and modern residence grew up around a Norman fortress. The remains of the original Norman shell keep can be seen near the centre, together with parts of the original " curtain," or surrounding wall, which was the protecting bulwark of the keep, which is built mostly of flint faced with Caen stone. The rest of the medieval castle was reduced to ruins in the Civil War after the siege in 1644. It was entirely rebuilt in the nine-teenth century by Charles, Eleventh Duke of Norfolk.

CASTELLATED MANOR-HOUSE

Hurstmonceux Castle, Sussex, makes an interesting contrast with Arundel opposite. Whereas Arundel was developed from an original Norman keep but is now predominantly a modern castle, Hurstmonceux, so far as its exterior is concerned, has changed very little since it was built in 1440. It is not a castle in the sense of being a fortress; military defence was sacrificed to the comfort and grace of the buildings. It is in fact a castellated manor-house, the form of defence being retained more as a decoration than as a necessity. Although the external façade has changed little, the interior was dismantled in the eighteenth century, being restored and largely rebuilt in 1911. It is now the home of the Royal Greenwich Observatory.

barrel-vault had been transformed into the web-like tracery of the fan-vault.

It may be asked, at this point, why not (if it is such a troublesome problem to support a stone vault) construct it of some lighter and more manageable material such as wood.

There are several answers. One is that in many cases it was done, but if the original intention had been to construct the building of a durable material such as stone it was an admission of failure to substitute a less-durable material in any substantial part of the structure. Further, a work of art should be homogeneous. That is the aesthetic aspect.

But the practical objections to wood are just as cogent. Wood is highly susceptible to destruction by fire and decay. The former risk was especially heavy during the period under review, when fire-fighting

apparatus was unknown and lighting was obtained by crude wax candles and torches, and floors were covered with straw and rushes. Medieval people had an unholy horror of fire—and with good reason. Practically every abbey or cathedral church suffered terrible damage from it at one time or another, and it was the ambition of everyone to possess a stone vault.

By the time the Early English style was fully matured the average church gave an impression of a lightness of touch in marked contrast with the massiveness which was the keynote of early Norman churches. Some of the most magnificent buildings were those of the Benedictine and Cistercian abbeys. The lovely ruins of Rievaulx Abbey in Yorkshire, which are typically Early English in conception, have no superior in the whole world, whilst in the

TRADITIONAL DOMESTIC ARCHITECTURE

Magdalen College Hall, Oxford, has in large measure retained its medieval appearance. The carved-timber roof is very fine and though the exact date of the Jacobean woodwork of the screen behind the high table is uncertain, it was probably introduced at the beginning of the reign of James I.

TRANSITION TO TUDOR STYLE

Chiddingstone village (below), is notable since it retains several cottages built during the reign of Henry VII, and gives a fine impression of the general appearance of an early Tudor village. Moreton Old Hall, Cheshire (above), is more strictly transitional between Gothic and Tudor, although the classical square-headed doorways and oriel windows and the arrangement of the gables are all characteristic of Tudor craftsmanship.

south, Salisbury Cathedral is a still-present memorial to the grace and pure lines of the period.

The roofs of the Early English churches are lofty, the arches over the porch and between chancel and nave finely pointed and tapering, whilst the main columns of the church were disguised by the presence of encircling miniature columns, which contributed to the general effect of ethereal lightness. The Norman fashion of the sub-division of arches is maintained, as in Southwark Cathedral, but the heads of the windows remain rounded, the difference from the Norman being represented by greater length and consequently more light, as befitted churches of the new order. At the east end of the chancel, for instance, these long slender windows, known as lancets, are frequently grouped together three or five in a row, forming essentially a single window. Though there is no confining arch, they anticipate the rich windows of the Decorated style of Gothic.

The two subsequent styles the Decorated and Perpendicular, are easily recognized by the windows and by decorations, both internal and external. Carving and elaborate sculpture came into their own. The rood screens and the choir stalls, the pulpits and the fonts all took on fresh beauties and constantly developing forms. But, above all, the artists of the period expressed themselves in the manifold designs and intricate patterns of the windows. Perhaps it was a developing consciousness that religion was no longer a secret thing, or perhaps it was just an instinct for artistic expression that led to the greater size of church windows in general, and to their far greater elaboration.

The windows of a Decorated church are nearly always executed in perfect taste and with consummate skill. Where in the Early English the lancets were ranged side by side, in the Decorated and Perpendicular styles the lights are enclosed in a pointed arch and stone carving, or tracery as it is

TUDOR MANOR-HOUSE

Compton Wynyates, Warwickshire, is one of the largest and most perfectly preserved of all the great Tudor manor-houses which are a remarkable feature of the Cotswold country. In this photograph a great deal of the original work can be seen. The fine oriel window and the curiously fashioned and moulded chimneys are worthy of note. The gatehouse here is well marked, but by this period its purpose was for ornament rather than defence.

EAST ANGLIAN PARGE WORK

Parge work, or pargeting, of which the Sparrowe's House, Ipswich, is one of the most famous examples, is an art which flourished particularly in East Anglia. It ranges from insignificant designs in the plaster covering of small houses and cottages to the elaborate moulding of figures and scenes of everyday life. The parge-work designs of the Sparrowe's House were probably executed in the early part of the seventeenth century.

generally called, is inserted to fill the whole space within the arch. Typical Decorated designs range from the simple trefoil to most complicated flights of a vivid imagination. The west front of Wells Cathedral is the classic example of the style. The parish church at Berkhamsted is typical of many of the smaller churches of the period, but there are literally hundreds in which either one window or all the early windows of the church are good examples of the style.

At the beginning of the fifteenth century the Orders of preaching Friars had enormous influence on the religious life of Britain. In their doctrine, religion became something

that the common man could understand and for them the more light that could be thrown upon it the better. The Friars were austere in their own lives and simplicity was their watchword. It is due to their influence also that the many noble parish churches of the fifteenth century are comparatively free of sculptural ornament as a reaction against the elaboration of some of the later Decorated structures. Wide and lofty windows light up the interior of the church in contrast to the "dim religious light" in the traditional sacred building. The fifteenth century was an era of great prosperity in the wool-producing districts, particularly East

Anglia, the Cotswold country and Kent. Consequently it is in these areas that the fifteenth-century church is seen at its finest —Thaxted and Saffron Walden in Essex, Lavenham and Mildenhall in Suffolk, Tenterden in Kent, Cirencester and Northleach in the Cotswolds, for example.

In place of the curvilinear tracery of the later Decorated windows there are lofty straight divisions between the lights and the building as a whole depends for its effect on its loftiness and on the lines of its structure. Though stone carving is comparatively rarely found, the age of craftsmen in wood was at hand and the characteristic hammer-beam roofs of the Perpendicular church are often embellished with elaborate carving and sometimes also with painting. The loftiness of the church as a whole is enhanced by the loftiness of the tower. Weirdly fashioned gargoyles are often a feature of the exterior, as at Thaxted. But over all is an impression of an almost geometrical regularity.

While English church architecture was thus developing, there was a parallel development in the building of castles and manor-houses. The predominant note of the castles in the thirteenth century, as of the churches, became the pointed arch. Towards the end of the Norman period the rectangular plan was abandoned and an octagonal form, as at Orford, superseded it in the interest of easier defence. Later the typical form of the castle became more complex and its military strength depended on the fortifications of the outer ramparts, which were sometimes reinforced by one

EXAMPLES OF THE CLASSICAL STYLE

The classical style of architecture returned to Britain with the work of Inigo Jones and Sir Christopher Wren. The cloisters of the quadrangle of St. John's College, Oxford (below), were built in 1631, and are said to have been modelled on a building in Milan. The classical revival is well marked but features are apparent which make it an interesting blend of the traditional Gothic of Oxford with the Italian Renaissance style.

MASTERPIECE OF THE CLASSICAL RENAISSANCE STYLE

St. Paul's Cathedral is recognized as the masterpiece of Sir Christopher Wren. It represents the full flowering of the classical Renaissance in Britain. Almost every feature of the mighty façade, not shown in the photograph, is in the new style and owes nothing to the Gothic master builders.

or more strongly built concentric walls.

Pembroke Castle is typical of the first half of the thirteenth century; and Conway, with its several towers defending the outer wall, of the fourteenth century. Towards the end of the fourteenth century the last of the medieval castles were being built, with the domestic buildings ranged around the walls, as in the moated castle of Bodiam.

While Bodiam was being raised, one of the first of the great brick-built manor-houses was being built only a few miles away at Hurstmonceux, but here the defences are more for show than for protection. The same is true of Layer Marney Towers in Essex, which is in the same tradition, and of Penshurst Place in Kent, which retains to the present day its great central hall complete with minstrels' gallery.

From now on it was the manor-house rather than the castle that concerned the architect, and some uncommonly beautiful courtyard houses with elaborate gatehouses were built in the fifteenth century. Ightham Mote in Kent is one of the finest of these and makes a wonderful contrast with the slightly later Tudor manor of Boxon in the same county.

After the end of the fifteenth century few new churches were built, but the art and practice of architecture was by no means stagnant. It was only that thereafter the accent was on the secular building rather than the ecclesiastical.

Gothic architecture only gradually died out and there are a number of admirable buildings in the Gothic style which yet show clearly the coming of the Tudor manner. King's College Chapel at Cambridge was one of the last of the strictly Gothic buildings to be erected in Britain. Some of its features are over-emphasized,

CLASSICAL DESIGN

Chatsworth House, Derbyshire, ancestral home of the dukes of Devonshire, shows two contrasting styles of architecture. The main block with its fine classical design, rather reminiscent of the garden front of Hampton Court, was begun in 1687 and completed in 1706. The north wing was added between 1820 and 1840 by the sixth Duke of Devonshire.

GEORGIAN STYLES IN ENGLAND

Brent Eleigh Hall, Suffolk (above), and the handsome façade of the house from the High Street of Dedham in Essex, shown below, are good examples of two distinct phases of Georgian architecture. The classical columns of Brent Eleigh Hall, modelled on the porticos of Greek temples, are appropriate to the larger manor-house, in contrast with the plain and severe doorway of the other which has been added to an Elizabethan interior.

yet it is a magnificent example of the Perpendicular style, though some of its flattened arches look forward to the classicism of the succeeding centuries.

The period between the close of the fifteenth century and the first half of the seventeenth century is one of extraordinary development but one also which is confusing in the complexity of its styles. This complexity arises partly from the fact that a native English style, represented by what we call Tudor, Elizabethan and Jacobean, was marching side by side with the introduction of classical forms inspired by the Renaissance.

The hall-mark of the Tudor manor-houses is the flattening of the pointed arch of the Gothic style and the introduction of dormer windows, which give houses of this period an altogether distinctive and attractive appearance. Another feature is that the medieval gatehouse now for the first time ceases to be a gatehouse as such but becomes instead a porch and an integral part of the house itself. The idea of the hall home, which was the keystone of

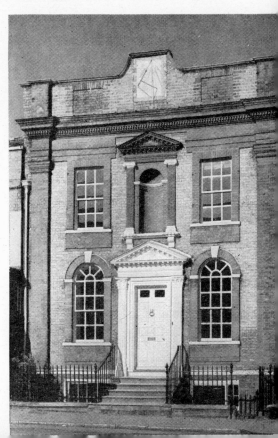

medieval work, tends to be superseded by a division of the house into a much larger number of apartments, though one room continues to be architecturally much more important than any of the others.

A number of Tudor manor-houses have survived almost intact, such as Brede Place in Sussex, and numerous smaller manor-houses all over the Midlands and the south-east. In the more grandiose style there are also many fine examples of the period, such as the early part of the palace of Hampton Court, which incidentally presents an interesting contrast to the classical lines of the later parts added in the typical Wren style. Part of Christ Church, Oxford—the staircase up to the hall, for instance—is another admirable example of the best workmanship of the period, which is reproduced in lesser

degree in a number of the other colleges of Oxford and Cambridge.

In Elizabethan building the best features of the Tudor style persisted, but in many of the most magnificent Elizabethan mansions there is apparent a greater leaning to classical principles. Classical columns sometimes set off a flat-topped porch, which comes very near to the severity of Georgian architecture. There is now a definite porch as opposed to a gatehouse, and there is a movement away from the courtyard house towards a more strictly rectangular design. In many of the larger mansions of the kind which in an earlier age would have been built round a court there are still two wings at right-angles to the main structure and these, together with a prominent porch, gave the E-shape which is a characteristic feature of

TOWN PLANNING IN THE CLASSICAL STYLE
Planned between 1811 and 1825, John Nash's terraces round Regent's Park, London, face a landscape park and form part of a brilliant town planning scheme. The photograph shows Cumberland Terrace as it appeared before suffering bomb damage in the Second World War.

Elizabethan manor-houses and mansions.

A very large number of houses of varying size were built during the reign of Queen Elizabeth and in them we may note to a greater degree than previously the whim of the owner and of the individual architect. In fact, architecture was ceasing to be a strictly stylized art and the common man was beginning to take an interest in it, as in the other arts, and to give expression to his feelings in the kind of building which he was to make his home.

Nor are the Elizabethan mansions confined to the countryside. The era of the town house was beginning, and finely preserved Elizabethan houses still stand proudly, especially in the towns of the Midland stone belt, like Oundle. Overhanging gables and bay windows are a feature of these and fantastically shaped chimneys are an integral part of the design. More and more attention was paid to the interior, and fine panelling was a feature of almost every large Elizabethan house.

The first half of the seventeenth century is of particular interest, for this was the period in which the Jacobean development of the Elizabethan style produced a wealth of ornament which sometimes defeated its own object, whilst it also witnessed the work of one of the greatest of British architects, Inigo Jones, who was the apostle of the severest form of classicism.

In the Jacobean house or public building there are stepped, or shaped, gables and still more fantastically shaped chimneys than in the Elizabethan. Other ornament ranges from the magnificent parge-work designs of the eastern counties to the gargoyles and carved figures which decorated the fronts of many of the larger houses.

Yet at the very same time that the Jacobean mansion of Blickling Hall was being built, Inigo Jones was building the Queen's House at Greenwich, the Banqueting Hall in Whitehall and Wilton House near Salisbury. In these last three there is no superfluous ornament; the house and every feature of it is rectangular, the porch square-headed and the windows rectangular and evenly spaced along the whole of the façade, one set above the other; the sole decoration is the classical ornament of the columns and the open porticos, which take their inspiration from the temples of ancient Greece.

So the story of medieval architecture in Britain is completed by the full turn of the circle, from the directly inherited classical tradition of the Romanesque churches to the indirectly bequeathed ideals of the classical Renaissance which swept across the whole of Europe and established itself in Britain almost last among the nations of the civilized world.

After the middle of the seventeenth century the era of modern architecture began with the classical masterpieces of Sir Christopher Wren, and of the many architects who imitated him and who rather slavishly followed classical models, only slowly evolving the modified British form of classicism known as Georgian.

Test Yourself

1. State the principal styles of church architecture in England between the eleventh and seventeenth centuries and name one example of each.
2. What are the principal remains of Roman military architecture in Britain?
3. Look at the photographs of Chichester nave and Long Melford Church (pages 332 and 340). What is the most significant difference of architectural form?
4. What is the relationship between St. Paul's Cathedral and Durham Cathedral (photographs on pages 353 and 333)? How do you explain the chief points of similarity and difference?
5. It has been said "The manor-house evolved from the castle." How far is this true?

Answers will be found at the end of the book.

357

GUIDE TO MORE EXTENDED STUDY

Painting, Sculpture and
the Graphic Arts

THE ideal way to appreciate works of art is to see them in their original settings. Egyptian sculpture, for example, gains significance from the surrounding expanses of desert which prompted its colossal size. Hellenic and Hindu art are profoundly influenced by natural features and strong light in Greece and India, respectively. In Italy many paintings and statues still adorn the churches and palaces for which they were made. But, however desirable, extensive foreign travel seldom is possible; moreover, very many works of art have been moved far from their places of origin. Perhaps it is as well that this is so—else opportunities for appreciating the works of great masters would be limited indeed.

However restricted one may be in the matter of travel, illustrated books—of which a selection of the important ones is listed on later pages—provide some idea of the beauties of objects one cannot reach, but they can never adequately convey the full glories of the actual masterpiece. Usually many beautiful works are to be found within reach of but a short journey. The nearest cathedral town will in all probability have fine examples of carving, sculpture and stained glass as well as the architectural features of the cathedral itself. In streets, squares and parks there will be statues and buildings worth examination. Painting and the graphic arts, since they are unsuited to exhibition in the open air, are naturally enough less widely distributed. The only practicable means for their study is to visit the national, municipal and private collections which in addition include a great variety of other works of art. Each art gallery or museum has as a rule its own character, specializing in some particular aspect of the subject.

The student will find invaluable the indications in the following pages of the principal contents and character of the British, European and American art galleries and museums. Before embarking on this necessarily brief survey, however, it is pertinent to give some idea of how these remarkable institutions came into being. The word museum is, of course, far older than its present meaning. The Greeks used it to describe a place where literature and the arts could be discussed and practised. Such was the famous Museum of Alexandria, founded and endowed by Alexander the Great as a home for scholars.

The present application of the word to a collection of works of art is quite modern and the museums of today are essentially products of the modern world. The prototypes of present-day institutions are to be sought in Renaissance times, when the revival of interest in the relics of classical antiquity stimulated the instinct for collecting, and kings, princes, nobles and humanists vied with each other in accumulating objects of classical art. These collections existed for the pleasure of the owners and their friends and the foundation of public as distinct from private galleries was the result of the point of view of which the French Revolution was the most striking expression. Yet the great museums of Europe for the most part owe their origin to the royal and princely collections which were made during the sixteenth, seventeenth and eighteenth centuries, and which, surviving political changes, persisted as state museums. Cosimo de Medici's collections, for instance, are now in the Florentine galleries; the pictures at Hampton Court were largely acquired by Charles I, and Francis I was responsible for forming the nucleus of what is now the Louvre. In modern times public museums and galleries are maintained and enlarged by the State or by local authorities, and by private gift and bequest. Museums offer important services to the community of which all art students should avail themselves. They provide free lectures, loan lantern slides and publish and sell inexpensive reproductions, books and photographs.

Museums and Art Galleries of Great Britain

With the exception of the National Museum of Wales at Cardiff and the Scottish National Collections at Edinburgh, the great national art collections are all in London.

The *National Gallery* was founded in 1824 with the Government purchase of thirty-eight pictures from the collection of J. Angerstein, and has since been built up by gift and bequest until it has become the most representative gallery in the world of European painting. Nowhere outside Italy is the Italian school so well represented, or outside Holland, the Dutch school. Some masters can even be studied better here than in their own country. The great Demidoff altarpiece and eight other panels by Crivelli provide a unique opportunity for becoming acquainted with this rare and eccentric master. Among other important works are the Madonna and Child Enthroned, by Masaccio, his most notable picture apart from the frescoes in Florence; three superb tempera paintings by the rare Piero della Francesca, Leonardo's Virgin of the Rocks, the only two authentic paintings by Michelangelo which exist outside Italy, seven pictures by Raphael including the Ansidei Madonna, Correggio's Venus, Cupid and Mercury, works by Mantegna and Giovanni Bellini, Titian's Bacchus and Ariadne and eight other pictures covering the whole course of his development, and representative works by Tintoretto and Veronese, among whose canvases is the famous Darius before Alexander.

Flemish paintings include Jan van Eyck's Arnolfini and his Wife (reproduced in colour facing page 65), and a remarkable series of Rubens's large figure compositions, landscapes and portraits. Celebrated works by Vermeer, de Hooch, Ruisdael and Hobbema (with some of which the reader of this book will already be familiar) enrich the Dutch school while the Rembrandts range from an early painting of Philips Lucasz to one of his latest self-portraits and embrace every aspect of his work except landscape. The Spanish collection is small, but contains magnificent pictures by El Greco and Velasquez and two portraits by Goya. There are renowned pictures by Holbein, and among French paintings, Claude's Marriage of Isaac and Rebecca, Poussin's Bacchanalian Dance, Fragonard's Fête at Rambouillet, Chardin's Lesson and Madame Moitessier by Ingres are outstanding. There is an unequalled group of English pictures; Hogarth, Richard Wilson, Gainsborough, Crome, Reynolds and Romney, Constable and Turner are here seen at their best.

The National Gallery of British Painting and Modern Foreign Art, now known as the *Tate Gallery*, was founded in 1897 for the " encouragement and development of British art." It was the gift of Sir Henry Tate, whose collection of contemporary British painting formed the nucleus of the present gallery at Millbank. The most notable collections of British painting there are pictures by Turner and Blake; the pre-Raphaelites are also well represented. The Gallery for Modern Foreign Art, a subsequent addition, houses fine examples of the Impressionists, and of Corot, Courbet, Daumier, Van Gogh, Degas, Renoir, Cézanne, Utrillo, Bonnard, Vuillard, Rouault, Picasso, Matisse and Braque, and sculptures by Maillol. A few representative works by a number of important twentieth-century English artists are also to be found there, among them being Augustus John, Stanley Spencer, Paul Nash, Graham Sutherland and Henry Moore. Stimulating temporary exhibitions are held from time to time.

Founded in 1753, the *British Museum* is the greatest repository of art in this country, and houses some of the most important collections in the world. Outstanding treasures of medieval illumination are to be found in the Department of Manuscripts, such as the Lindisfarne Gospels of about A.D. 700 and Queen Mary's Psalter of the fourteenth century. The Department of Prints and Drawings contains the finest collection of prints, drawings and water colours in the country. The Chinese paintings in the British

Museum are without rival in Europe. There are also important collections of ceramics and medieval antiquities and world-famous examples of Greek and Egyptian sculpture, conspicuous among which are the Elgin Marbles acquired from the seventh Earl of Elgin in 1816 and comprising fifth-century B.C. sculptures from the Parthenon at Athens, fragments of the pediment groups, the metopes, and substantial portions of the frieze. Among the groups one of the best known is the Three Fates. Other Greek works include the Demeter of Cnidus, the Nereid monument and the remains of the Mausoleum and the temples of Ephesus and Phigalia. The museum contains also the specimens of Sumerian art of the fourth millennium B.C. brought to light by Sir Leonard Woolley.

The *Victoria and Albert Museum* originated in 1837 when the National School of Design was founded with a collection of objects illustrating decorative art. In 1852 the collection was separated from the school and was opened to the public. The museum was intended to fulfil a more creative function than the other national art collections by exhibiting fine examples of industrial art for the benefit of students and manufacturers as well as for the general public. In the belief that public taste would improve with knowledge of the achievements of the past, the museum came to possess one of the greatest fine-art collections in the world. The collections are classified by material and are arranged in eight departments: Architecture and Sculpture; Ceramics; Engraving, Illustration and Design; Library and Book Production; Metalwork; Painting; Textiles and Woodwork. Amid a vast variety, the examples of Renaissance sculpture, Indian sculpture, medieval antiquities, ivories of all periods, miniatures and water colours may perhaps be singled out for special notice. The Raphael cartoons, among the great classics of European painting, are on permanent loan to the museum from the Royal Collection. The museum was the only national institution intended to circulate works of art for exhibition in provincial art schools and galleries and that still

ranks among its most valuable activities.

The outstanding interest and character of the *Wallace Collection* lie in its representation of French art of the eighteenth century. It was bequeathed to the nation by Lady Wallace in 1897 as a private collection formed by the third and fourth Marquesses of Hertford (1777-1842 and 1800-70) and by Sir Richard Wallace (1818-90). All three were for long periods resident in France where the series of political upheavals provided them with unique opportunities for acquiring treasures from the chateaux and palaces of a ruined and vanishing nobility. The charm of Hertford House is its private character. Here pictures by Watteau, Pater, Lancret and Fragonard can be seen in conjunction with the French sculpture, furniture, ceramics and goldsmiths' work which formed the daily setting of the artists and their patrons. There is also a catholic collection of pictures from the maturer periods of all schools, including a miniature self-portrait by Holbein and works by Rubens, Velasquez, Guardi and Canaletto, and by Dutch and English masters.

The *Soane Museum* in Lincoln's Inn Fields is another delightful collection arranged as a decorative whole in its original setting. It was presented to the nation in 1835 by Sir John Soane and is full of the atmosphere of his personality and period. The house contains his own drawings and Hogarth's famous series of pictures The Rake's Progress and the Election canvases.

Museums Outside London

There are many municipal art collections in England, but for the most part they contain little of interest. At Birmingham, however, there is a large collection of pre-Raphaelite paintings and drawings, and the *Barber Institute of Fine Arts*, opened only in 1939, has already built up a notable collection of European paintings and works of art. The *Manchester City Art Gallery* houses a collection of English nineteenth-century painting together with some modern English paintings, water colours, engravings and sculptures. The *Walker Art Gallery, Liverpool*, incorporates the celebrated Roscoe Collection which illustrates in outline almost every aspect of European art from the thirteenth to the sixteenth century.

The University towns of both Oxford and Cambridge possess important art collections in the Ashmolean and Fitzwilliam Museums, respectively. The *Ashmolean Collection*, founded in 1683 and the first of its kind to be called a museum, is renowned for the Arundel Marbles, Greek sculptures collected by Thomas Howard, Earl of Arundel (1586-1646), a varied collection of European paintings and a remarkable collection of drawings, some by Leonardo. The *Fitzwilliam Museum* was founded in 1816 by Richard, Viscount Fitzwilliam of Trinity Hall. It has fine collections, especially of European painting and of pottery and porcelain of all periods.

Continental Galleries

Most of the great art collections of the Continent were deposited in places of safety during the Second World War, and though they have survived with few casualties they have not all been re-assembled. In some cases the buildings in which they were formerly exhibited have suffered severe damage and new homes must be found for them. It will be long before the magnificent collections of Germany and Austria, those from the Kaiser Friedrich and Schloss Museums in Berlin and those from Dresden, Munich and Vienna can again be seen in their entirety. Only those galleries and museums therefore are mentioned here which have once more assumed a permanent character.

France

The *Louvre, Paris*, is the largest and one of the most important museums in the world. It has already been pointed out that the beginnings of this huge collection were made by Francis I (died 1547) who had developed a taste for art during his sojourn in Italy. His example was followed by Henri II and Catherine de Medici. Louis XIV lavished patronage on living artists and made additions to the two hundred old masters in his possession by the purchase of one hundred paintings and well over five thousand drawings. Louis XVI acquired prominent Dutch and Spanish pictures. In 1793 the Louvre was opened to the public as the Musée de la Republique, but on Napoleon's defeat the collection was returned to its former owners. It became the permanent property of the State only in 1848. The museum is especially distinguished for its galleries of European painting and sculpture, Greek and Roman sculpture, and medieval, Egyptian and Assyrian antiquities.

Among renowned Greek works of art are the Venus de Milo, the Victory of Samothrace and the Hera of Samos, perhaps the most interesting example of Greek archaic sculpture. The Italian Renaissance is represented by carvings from the hands of Donatello, Michelangelo and Mino da Fiesole among many others, and by some celebrated pictures, among them Titian's Entombment, and Man with a Glove, Veronese's Marriage at Cana, Correggio's Jupiter and Antiope, frescoes by Botticelli from a villa of the Tornabuoni near Florence, a large Crucifixion by Fra Angelico, Mantegna's Parnassus, Leonardo's Mona Lisa, Annunciation and another version of the National Gallery picture of the Virgin of the Rocks, La belle Jardinière by Raphael, Giorgione's Fête Champêtre and Ghirlandaio's moving picture An Old Man and his Grandson. The collection of Flemish pictures includes J. van Eyck's Virgin and Child Adored by the Chancellor Nicholas Rolin, formerly in the cathedral at Autun in Burgundy, whence it was taken by Napoleon I, Brueghel's Blind Leading the Blind and a large selection of works by Rubens amongst which may be mentioned The Rainbow, the Kermesse and eighteen huge allegorical paintings depicting the life of Marie de Medici, designed 1621-25 for the decoration of the Luxembourg Palace, and Van Dyck's Charles I.

There are many fine Dutch seventeenth-century pictures numbering among them Rembrandt's Christ at Emmaus and Vermeer's Lacemaker. The French School, as one would expect, can be seen at the Louvre as nowhere else. Among countless fine examples the following are a few:

sculptures by Houdon, Puget and Pigalle; Gilles and Le faux Pas by Watteau; Le Nain's Peasants at a Meal; Poussin's L'Inspiration du Poete and Shepherds in Arcadia; exquisite works by Chardin; David's Madame Recamier; The Turkish Bath and La Source by Ingres; The Raft of the Medusa by Géricault; Delacroix's Liberty Guiding the People and the Massacre at Scio; The Print Collectors by Daumier; Manet's Picnic and Olympia; Degas' Women Droning, Foyer de Danse and Café Concert, among others, and fine works by Cézanne and the post-Impressionists.

Other collections in France have not yet been permanently reassembled.

Holland and Belgium

The *Royal Museum of Fine Arts, Brussels,* is particularly rich in its collection of early French and Flemish painting, while the late Flemish School is fully represented with works by Rubens, Van Dyck and Jordaens.

The State Museum of Holland, the *Rijksmuseum* at Amsterdam, is the great repository of Dutch art; it was founded in 1808 by Louis Napoleon. All the Dutch masters are here to be seen at their best, especially Rembrandt—whose famous Nightwatch is here—Vermeer, de Hooch, Hals, Hobbema and Ruisdael. Pictures from other schools include works by Fra Angelico, Tintoretto, Veronese, Bassano, Brueghel, Cranach, Daumier, El Greco, Goya, Rubens, the Impressionists and Van Gogh. Considerable collections of Dutch art are also housed at the Hague and at Rotterdam.

Italy

Despite severe damage sustained during the Second World War Italian Renaissance art can still be studied in almost every town and village. Actual museums are less important in a country where so much remains in its original setting. Among a few of the more celebrated of such immovable works, which every visitor to Italy will seek out, are Giotto's frescoes at Assisi and Padua, Fra Angelico's great series of paintings on the walls of the monastery of San Marco in Florence, Donatello's sculptures on Or San Michele, Florence, and his great Gattemelata outside the Church of San Antonio, Padua; Michelangelo's statues of Night and Day, Dawn and Evening, the Virgin and Child and of Lorenzo and Guilio de' Medici in the Medici Chapel of San Lorenzo, Florence; the celebrated frescoes by Michelangelo and Raphael in the Vatican, Rome; Verrocchio's Colleoni Statue in Venice; Titian's Assumption and Giovanni Bellini's Virgin and Child with Saints, both in the Church of the Frari, Venice, and Tintoretto's Paradiso in the Ducal Palace, Venice, the largest picture in the world.

There are nevertheless several great art galleries in Italy where some of the finest examples of Renaissance painting and sculpture can be seen. The chief centres are Florence, Rome and Venice. The principal museums of Rome are all in the *Vatican,* where there is also a renowned collection of Greek and Roman sculpture, including the Apollo Belvedere. The *Uffizi, Florence,* founded by the Medici, is filled with masterpieces by Raphael, Filippo and Filippino Lippi, Uccello, Pollaiuolo, Ghirlandaio, Andrea del Sarto and Titian; and includes Botticelli's Birth of Venus and Primavera and Leonardo's unfinished Adoration. The *Bargello,* the ancient palace of the Podesta contains sculptures by Donatello, Ghiberti, Verrocchio and Michelangelo; and the Etruscan Museum nearby is the finest in the world.

The *Accademia, Venice,* contains a notable collection of Venetian pictures supplementing the works which are to be found in the churches and palaces of the city. Among world-famous pictures in the collection are Giorgione's Tempest, Titian's Pieta, Veronese's Feast in the House of Levi, Carpaccio's St. Ursula and St. George series, Gentile Bellini's pageant paintings, A Procession in the Piazza of St. Mark's and The Miracle of the True Cross and Giovanni Bellini's San Giobbe altarpiece.

Spain

The principal gallery in Spain is the Prado, Madrid, which contains the collections made by Charles V, Philip II and Philip IV. The paintings include magnificent examples by Titian, Raphael, Tintoretto, El Greco, Velasquez, Goya, Murillo, Bosch and Brueghel, Rubens and Van Dyck.

American Museums and Galleries

The leading art gallery on the American Continent is the *Metropolitan Museum, New York*, incorporated in 1870. It is famous for an unusual assemblage of Egyptian, Babylonian, Assyrian and Etruscan antiquities, and contains the largest collection of Cypriot antiquities in the world. One of the most striking exhibits is the Egyptian tomb of Perneb from Memphis which, with its accompanying sculptures and murals, occupies a huge gallery. Among the Etruscan bronzes is a chariot from Monteleone of 600 B.C., the only complete ancient bronze chariot in existence. There is also a rich collection of Roman glass, and some fine Roman frescoes from a villa near Boscoreale on the slopes of Mount Vesuvius. The galleries of Renaissance sculpture, furniture, textiles and metalwork and of medieval ivories, enamels and tapestries are also notable. The large collection of European paintings of all periods includes Brueghel's Harvesters, Hals' Hile Bobbe, Constable's Bridge on the Stour and Glebe Farm, a version of Géricault's Raft of the Medusa, works by R. Veronese, Rubens, Rembrandt, Fragonard and Bouche, and some remarkable Impressionist paintings, among them Monet's Rouen Cathedral, and some of the most splendid examples of the art of Van Gogh, Degas, Renoir and Cézanne.

Another valuable collection in New York of European paintings is the *Frick Art Gallery*, housed in the residence of Henry C. Frick and bequeathed to the City in 1931. Among its treasures are Titian's Portrait of Aretino, Rembrandt's Polish Horseman and works by Van Dyck, Corot, Manet and Renoir.

The *Museum of Modern Art, New York*, performs an invaluable function in providing frequent exhibitions of any art which has aroused contemporary interest, from that of primitive peoples to the work of living artists. It also shows various types of art together: ethnological, industrial, ancient and modern. Its main concern is to provide a continuous series of new exhibitions.

American Museums Outside New York

There are important museums at Washington, where the *Freer Gallery* contains collections of early Chinese bronzes, ceramics, jades and stone sculptures, Japanese pottery and painting, and Indian sculpture and painting as well as a selection of Whistler's work—paintings, drawings, etchings and lithographs. The *National Gallery, Washington*, contains old master paintings and Renaissance sculpture. The *Walters Art Gallery, Baltimore*, is celebrated for some choice examples of European painting and of Byzantine, medieval, Near Eastern, Egyptian and Greek art. The finest collection of Oriental art in America is to be found at the *Museum of Fine Art, Boston*. There is a small but interesting group of European paintings and drawings at the *Fogg Art Museum, Cambridge, Mass.*

Books To Study

In this list preference is given to books which are copiously illustrated. Many of them may today be out of print but most can be obtained second-hand or from public libraries. The list is divided into sections following as nearly as possible the arrangement of the chapters in the book. Architecture is dealt with separately on later pages.

Histories of Art

An account of the development of the visual arts from the remote days of the glacial age in Europe through the successive civilizations of the Near East, Europe, America and the Orient to the present time is given in *Art Through the Ages*, by Helen Gardner. This book provides a sound introduction to the study of art, whilst a more detailed account, fully illustrated, is given by J. Pijoan in *History of Art*.

Probably one of the most representative collections of illustrations is to be found in the sixteen Propylaen-Kunstgeschicht volumes which include examples from pre-historic and primitive times right down to the twentieth century. In *Apollo*, by Solomon Reinach, a concise illustrated account is given of the history of art, excluding that of the Far East, from the earliest times to the end of the nineteenth century.

Painting

Professor Thomas Bodkin in *The Approach to Painting* gives an admirable introduction to gallery-going. Clive Bell, in *Enjoying Pictures*, places on record his reactions to certain pictures and the pleasure he has derived from them. This is a book calculated to stimulate much additional enjoyment in the ardent gallery-goer. Sir Kenneth Clark's *One Hundred Details From Pictures in the National Gallery* includes provocative notes together with an authoritative introduction and a number of full-page plates. There is also a companion volume, *More Details*.

Graphic Arts

Two books giving a general historical survey of what are known as the graphic arts together with accounts of the processes and materials used, are *A History of Engraving and Etching from the Fifteenth Century to the Year 1914* and *An Introduction to a History of Woodcut*, both by A. M. Hind. One of the best short histories of the subject is *A History of Wood Engraving* by D. P. Bliss.

Sculpture

In the field of sculpture, *A History of Sculpture* by G. H. Chase and C. R. Post gives an exhaustive and lucid account with illustrations, whereas *Wood Sculpture*, by Alfred Maskell, as its title implies, specializes in a particular branch of the subject. M. H. Longhurst's illustrated two-volume *Catalogue of Carvings in Ivory in the Victoria and Albert Museum* is also invaluable to the student of this branch of art.

Methods and Materials

In order fully to understand the subject the student of art must inevitably turn to those books which specialize in particular branches. A valuable account of fresco and tempera painting is given by Cennino Cennini, that eminent Renaissance artist, in *The Book of the Art of Cennino Cennini* and on the technique and materials of painting Max Doerner, who has written *The Materials of the Artist*, is an accepted authority. *Notes on the Science of Picture Making*, by Sir Charles Holmes, gives an instructive account of the elements of painting and *The Painter's Methods and Materials* by Professor A. P. Laurie, deals with the handling of pigments in oil, tempera, water-colour and mural painting, the preparation of grounds and canvas and the prevention of discoloration, together with the theories of light and colour applied to picture-making. For those studying etchings and engravings David Strang's *The Printing of Etchings and Engravings* will be found a useful and practical handbook. Some of the methods of reproduction—engraving, lithography, mezzotint and so on—are dealt with by Harold Curwen in his *Processes of Graphic Reproduction in Printing*. More than one hundred and eighty-five illustrations are included. For a concise account of the technique of modelling, carving and casting the student should read *Sculpture Inside and Out*, by Malvina Hoffman and *Modelling and Sculpture*, by A. Toft, which deals more specifically with the various methods and processes employed in these arts.

Periods and Countries

Having acquired some knowledge of the scope and possibilities of the different materials and techniques the serious student will naturally wish to devote attention to the art of various periods and countries.

Books on the art of Egypt and the Ancient Near East include *Egyptian Art*, by J. Capart, which is excellent as an introduction; *The Art of Egypt through the Ages*, edited by Sir E. Denison Ross; *Babylonian Art*, by S. Harcourt Smith; *Babylonian and Assyrian Sculpture in the British Museum*, by H. R. H. Hall, and *Digging up the Past*, by Leonard C. Woolley.

Aegean, Greek, Etruscan, Roman

An account of the life and civilization of the Cretans as reflected in their monuments and works of art is given in *The Art of Ancient Crete*, by H. T. Bossert. The book has over five hundred illustrations. The daily life, religious ceremonies, temples and houses, feasts and games, costumes, trades and professions of the Ancient Greeks and Romans are dealt with, accompanied by nearly six hundred plates, by the same author in *Hellas and Rome*. J. D. Beazley and B. Ashmole combine in *Greek Painting and Sculpture to the End of the Hellenistic Period*, whilst R. W. Livingstone, in *The Greek Genius and its Meaning to Us* deals with the importance of Greek art and thought to the modern world.

The Phaidon Press has produced two useful works, *Etruscan Sculpture* and *Roman Portraits*, with full-page illustrations in photogravure, each with an introduction by L. Goldscheider. Another fully illustrated account is to be found in *Greek, Etruscan and Roman Bronzes* by G. M. A. Richter.

Early Christian and Medieval Art

The methods and conditions of the medieval sculptor are fully dealt with by M. D. Anderson in *The Medieval Carver* and a short account of Early Christian, Anglo-Saxon and Carolingian art, illustrated by examples from the British Museum, is contained in *Early Medieval Art in the British Museum*, by E. Kitzinger. One of the most authoritative works of its kind is *Byzantine Art*, by D. Talbot Rice. For a straight-forward account of the history of tapestry particularly of medieval times the student is advised to read W. G. Thomson's *A History of Tapestry*.

Renaissance Art

Turning to Renaissance art there is *The Italian Painters of the Renaissance*, by B. Berenson, which deals with the Florentine, Central Italian, Sienese and Venetian schools of painting. Essential as a background to the study of Renaissance art is *The Civilization of the Renaissance in Italy*, by Jacob Burckhardt.

Seventeenth Century

Of those books which deal with baroque art the following may be mentioned:

German Baroque Sculpture, by A. Aycough, S. Sitwell and N. Pevsner ; *The Baroque Painters of Italy*, by A. K. McComb and *El Greco*, and *The Paintings and Drawings of Rubens*, both from the Phaidon Press.

Dutch Art

A useful survey of the Dutch masters, with short biographies of the more important artists, is given in R. H. Wilenski's *An Introduction to Dutch Art*, whilst A. M. Hind in *Rembrandt* gives a critical biographical study with illustrations.

The Eighteenth Century

English Art and English Society, by T. Ashcroft, is an admirable survey of the whole period and, turning to more specific aspects, Laurence Binyon in *English Water Colours* provides stimulating essays on the art of water-colour painting and on individual artists. An excellent introduction to Georgian art is provided by R. R. Tatlock in *Georgian Art, 1760-1820*.

The Nineteenth Century

Outstanding in the world of art during the nineteenth century was the pre-Raphaelite movement on which an authoritative work is *Pre-Raphaelitism and the Pre-Raphaelite Brotherhood*, in two volumes by W. Holman Hunt, himself a member of the Brotherhood. *The Autobiography and Memoirs of B. R. Haydon, 1786-1846*, gives a comprehensive account of the life and art of his day. Similarly Van Gogh's *Letters to His Brother, 1827-86*, is of interest not only from the autobiographical viewpoint, but because it describes in detail many of the pictures Van Gogh was proposing to paint.

Persia, Far East, Africa and America

One of the best surveys of the whole field of Persian art is contained in *History of Art in Persia*, 1892, by G. Perrot and C. Chipiez whilst *Persian Painting* by Mulk Raj Anand, written for the 1931 exhibition of Persian Art at Burlington House, gives a clear and understandable interpretation of the subject.

Indian art is well dealt with in *A History of Indian and Indonesian Art*, by A. K.

Coomaraswamy and E. B. Havell's *A Handbook of Indian Art* which latter gives a concise survey of architecture, sculpture and painting.

A readable illustrated history of Chinese art is given in Leigh Ashton's *Chinese Art*, and in his *An Introduction to the Study of Chinese Painting*, Arthur Waley deals with the characteristics of Chinese painting. Turning to the field of Japanese art, there is E. F. Strange's *Japanese Colour Prints* which is illustrated with prints from the Victoria and Albert Museum, and N. Tsuda's *Handbook of Japanese Art*.

Under the title *African Negro Art*, J. J. Sweeney edits a series of essays with numerous full-page plates from examples in an exhibition held in the Museum of Modern Art, New York.

Illustrations of architecture and sculpture, together with short text, are contained in *Maya and Mexican Art*, by T. A. Joyce, whilst *The Art of Old Peru*, by W. Lehmann and H. V. Goering, provides a fully illustrated introduction to the subject.

Twentieth-century Art

An aspect of art vital to the student is that revealed by the work of modern exponents. In any list such as this, works dealing specifically with that section, must therefore be included. In *Since Cézanne*, Clive Bell gives an account of post-Impressionist painting, whilst the work of those known as the Cubists is dealt with in *Cubism and Abstract Art*, by A. H. Barr. *Modern Sculpture, Its Methods and Ideals*, is the title of Herbert Maryon's review of the progress and science of the art. The whole field of twentieth-century art is surveyed from a philosophical viewpoint by Herbert Read in *Art Now*, and in addition there is *The Modern Movement in Art*, by R. H. Wilenski.

Architecture

The raw material for studying architecture is near at hand for every one of us. A groundwork of theoretical knowledge is essential, but the real study of architecture begins with the study of actual buildings. The two chapters of this book which are devoted to the subject give an adequate first summary of knowledge for the purpose of recognition and comparison; the student who has read and re-read them and who, above all, has studied every photograph carefully and in detail, should be able to recognize and compare the main features of any buildings that he comes upon. But it is necessary to stress the words "studied every photograph in detail," for it is only by the most careful comparison of one detail with another that the niceties of distinction in architectural styles begin to emerge.

Much later in the study of architecture the student will require to read a number of specialized books to enable him to appreciate the imaginative expression of ideas which is represented perhaps by a single sculptured figure or a single item of window tracery. But that is definitely a third stage in study. Before that comes the cultivation of æsthetic appreciation which is inseparable from field work, i.e. from visiting and learning to appreciate buildings rather than pictures of them.

The best advice to the beginner is to start from the simple and proceed to the more complex. Make a start with your own village or town. If you are fortunate enough to live in one of the old towns of England, Wales or Scotland, you have a rich treasure house of architecture at your very door. If you live in one of the new towns, you will have to go farther afield, but there will almost certainly be an historic town within a bus ride or short train journey of your home. If you live in the country, the chances are that your own village has a few houses worth careful study, with perhaps nearby some old farmhouses or manor-houses, and, of course, your own village church and the churches in nearby villages.

When you study a building, think of it in two ways, first as a thing of beauty, secondly as a building with a purpose. The æsthetic and functional qualities of all buildings, whether the smallest cottage or the mightiest cathedral, are the two first and perhaps the only two counts on which you will judge their architectural value. Appreciation of the beauty of buildings comes slower to most than the æsthetic satisfaction which arises from looking at a beautiful painting or piece of sculpture, more slowly even perhaps than that which derives from listening to good music; but once the æsthetic faculty is attuned to the medium which architecture provides, the response is no less emphatic. There is as great a thrill in looking for the first time on one of the great works of man as there is for the wayfarer who climbs up through rough and rugged country and, coming suddenly to the crest of a hill, sees spread before him the fertile loveliness of some rich valley. This is an emotional experience which is open to everyone who has the power to look at fine buildings and has learned to appreciate them.

Great though this æsthetic quality of buildings may be, the student must remember that historically beauty has never been the prime purpose of buildings. Building is a functional thing. A church is a place in which man can worship God. Its whole structure is bound up with the ritual of the Church. A public building is designed for a specific purpose, whether to act as a meeting place or to provide offices; a house is a place in which a man and his family can live most comfortably and conveniently. And this is as true of the oldest buildings as of the newest if we bear in mind that fashions in living, as in everything else, change.

So we come to the next rule to be observed in looking at buildings, that a building must not be judged only in relation to its functional purpose, but in relation to the particular functional purposes which it was designed to fulfil at the time when it was constructed. The only comparison between the medieval hall at Penshurst Place and the newest council house on the local estate is that they were both built for the habitation of man; but the one must be judged in relation to the needs of a medieval lord of the manor, the latter to the needs of the twentieth-century working-class family. It is bad architectural criticism to judge how much more beautiful the hall

of Penshurst Place is than the new council house and to condemn the latter on that account solely, but it is good architectural criticism to relate the beauty or lack of beauty in each to its functional purpose. We may well judge that there is not the slightest need for the council house to be ugly and that it fails architecturally because it is less beautiful than it need be.

The great thing is to remember that we must not expect or look for the same beauty in one as in the other. If the new is made in imitation of the old, the result is nearly always a failure. New needs demand new styles of architecture. The criterion is whether the need of the moment has been served and whether that need has been served in as æsthetically satisfying and imaginative a way as possible.

With this point of view in mind the student will go out into town or countryside with an open mind and a determination to judge and appreciate each and every building from these two inter-related stand-points. Of course, there is a great deal more pleasure in seeking old buildings in out of the way corners than there is in viewing some of the hundreds of thousands of very new buildings which straggle all over the British Isles. And the student will be excused if he does not pay overmuch attention to the very new, because the judgment of critics is fairly unanimous in regarding the present level of architectural quality as low, with certain notable exceptions, some of which are noted in the relevant chapter of this book. And this implied criticism applies to almost everything built since about 1820. The student, however, must remember that there are fashions in criticism and it is quite possible that critics in future ages will praise Victorian and later conceptions as much as they now belittle them.

When you have analysed the buildings in your own locality, when you have separated in your own mind the interesting ones from the less interesting and have made as full a study as possible of some of them, you will be ready to go farther afield to study selected buildings and groups of buildings of recognized historical and æsthetic importance. If you are going to make a really detailed study (and it is not worth doing anything unless you do it well), you will be well advised to make a list of all the places you want to see and then work out which can be visited on a Saturday afternoon, which will need a whole day excursion for a visit, and which you will be able to see only on a longer holiday. By careful grouping and the choice of good centres you will find you will be able to cover the outstanding villages and old towns of England, Wales and Scotland from a relatively small number of centres by utilizing the local bus and train services unless, of course, you have the use of a car.

The point is bound to arise how long you ought to allow to view any specific building or explore any particular town. There is no definite answer. A really detailed survey of the city of Canterbury will take a week at the least, yet it is possible to see a tremendous amount and carry away an imperishable impression of its loveliness in a single day.

A choice must always be made between a very detailed knowledge of a very small district and a much more general and superficial knowledge of the whole country or a large part of it. For the student the best method is probably to combine the two.

The student must remember, too, that although the architectural heritage of the British Isles is an unusually rich one and covers every period of architecture from the Roman to the present day, the heritage of some European countries is also outstanding. In particular, France, Italy, Germany, and Austria and, to a lesser extent, Spain, are storehouses of buildings ranging through a wide period of time.

One reason why it is important to consider Britain's historic buildings in relation to their European counterparts is that the sources of the various styles of architecture are in many cases identical, but the architects of each nation have set an individual stamp on their creations, a fact which makes architecture a national as well as an international art.

Thus there are four great periods in the history of European architecture. The first, which may be termed classical, was derived from Greece and spread outward from Rome between the first century B.C. and the fourth century A.D., and extended to the farthest confines of the Roman Empire. It is to this period that the remains of Roman architecture in Britain belong, for Britain was one of the farthest-flung provinces of Rome in the first four centuries A.D.

The dark age which succeeded this period in Britain has its parallel in most European countries. The second great style of architecture, the Romanesque, spread outwards from Rome with the spread of Christianity and this form, which is represented in Britain by the Saxon and the Norman, is the style inspired by the early Christian Church.

Gothic architecture, the third great style in Britain, also has its European counterparts, though in very modified form. Finally, the Renaissance inspired the fourth major period of building, represented in Britain by the work of Inigo Jones, Sir Christopher Wren and by the later Georgian exponents of this revived classical style.

So we see that this rough and ready division of the architectural heritage into four parts reveals that three of them spread more or less directly from Italy to the whole of Europe, including Great Britain. There is, as we should expect to find, a sequence of styles in other European countries analogous to the sequence so clearly observed in Britain.

This, then, is the best method of study for the student at whatever stage of learning. To explore and note, to widen the experience and thereby develop the æsthetic faculty, to start from a minimum amount of book learning and proceed to increase knowledge through experience. In this way he will build up his own fund of criticism and observation in the light of which more advanced work on architecture will take on a new and deeper significance.

Every student needs tools. The serious student of architecture needs them just as much as any other learner, only his tools are rather less exactly defined than those needed for some other subjects. We have already said that field work should precede the study of more advanced books on architecture. Nevertheless, books of another kind are valuable aids to study at every stage. Reliable guide books are really necessary tools if field work is to have its full educational value. A series such as the long-established Methuen's *Little Guides* is perfectly adequate, is kept fairly constantly up to date, and has enhanced its value through successive revisions. For the student the purpose of these books is to tell him what to look for, not to furnish him with ready-made criticism.

Many of the larger and more important buildings in Britain, such as the cathedrals, are described in detail in more or less official guides published locally. Some of these local guides are admirable; all contain what is for the student the most important of all things, a really detailed plan. As an adjunct to such local and county guides the student will require books which give the background history and the main types of building he will be viewing, such as cathedrals, castles, abbeys, manor-houses and so on. In this connexion it is important that the books chosen should contain a comprehensive selection of photographs, because for the student who has not advanced very far, a single annotated photograph will convey far more than several pages of text. The Batsford series is particularly good in this respect and there are volumes on castles, abbeys, cathedrals, parish churches, villages, inns, old towns etc. All of these are excellent in their own way, though it must be remembered that the size of the book and the amount of text which it contains does not permit of anything but a superficial treatment of the subject.

For the beginner who does not wish to purchase a number of volumes devoted to the various types of ancient buildings there are two volumes published by Odhams Press which contain a great deal of sound information in summary form about churches, abbeys, cathedrals and old towns. These are *Romantic Britain* and *The Countryside and How to Enjoy It*.

Another book valuable for field study is a short outline of the historical styles of architecture to amplify the information given in the chapters in this volume. Here again, it is important to select one that is well illustrated. One that combines a sound factual statement with fair criticism and excellent illustrations of the various styles and their development is *The Story of Architecture in England*, by W. H. Godfrey.

Books are only one kind of tool essential to the student. The other, and perhaps the more important, is the means of making his own record of architecture. A pocket note-book and a larger book rather like the old-fashioned scrap book will be sufficient for a beginning. The former will be used to make notes on the spot, the latter to incorporate these notes in some connected account of the buildings visited.

Just as our advice to the student is to buy highly illustrated books, so it is essential to illustrate one's own "day book." This everyone can do, either with his own work or with that of others. It is untrue to say that a camera is an essential part of the architectural student's equipment (because there are many with a fine appreciation of architecture who have never handled a camera), but it is true that a camera makes the study of architecture much easier and adds further interest to the pursuit of that knowledge. It does not matter whether the photographs the student takes are very good ones so long as they remind him of the places he has visited and recall to his memory the principal features of the buildings he has explored. Ideally the student will take two or more distant views of a large building from different angles and a number of close-ups of interesting details in the external fabric and of the interior. A snapshot camera will suffice for the first two of these, but for interior photographs a camera which allows of a time exposure is necessary.

If the student can sketch, sketches are a practical and adequate alternative to photographs, or may be used to amplify the work of the camera. A sketch is an impression, a photograph an exact record.

If the student has neither the facility for sketching nor for taking photographs, he can illustrate his book by purchasing picture postcards. This is much better than nothing, but many of these commercial photographs, though pictorially good, are not taken from the point of view of the student of architecture, and it is difficult to find just the view required.

In whatever way the student builds up his book, it will ultimately become of far more value to him than anything bought from a bookseller, and he will have the satisfaction of watching his store of knowledge grow. The notes should be partly factual and partly critical. The latter will reveal a development of æsthetic appreciation, which runs parallel with the development of knowledge.

The towns in Britain which have most to offer are first the cathedral cities, secondly the old walled towns, and thirdly the county towns. These three groups between them comprise a much larger number of towns than might be at first supposed, since many modern towns were fortified in medieval days. The cathedral cities which will most repay exploration include London, York, Exeter, Salisbury, Lincoln, Oxford, Gloucester, Worcester, Hereford, Peterborough, Chichester, St. Albans, Canterbury, Winchester, Rochester, Ely, Chester, Norwich, Durham, Bath and Wells. The university town of Cambridge must be linked with these, as one of the principal storehouses of architectural beauty and interest.

A full list of the walled towns is given in *Castles and Walled Towns of England*, by Alfred Harvey. Ludlow, Shrewsbury, Alnwick, Richmond, Colchester, Warwick, Launceston, Wareham, Southampton, Rye, Stamford, Chepstow, and Berwick-on-Tweed are some of the most interesting. A great deal is to be seen in almost all the county towns of southern England and the Midlands, but especially perhaps (apart from those which are also cathedral cities) in Maidstone, Guildford, Oakham, Huntingdon and Lewes.

There are a great number of old towns which do not fit into any of these three categories, places such as Uppingham, Grantham, Windsor, Dorchester (Oxon), Midhurst, Saffron Walden, Tenterden, Tewkesbury (Gloucestershire) and Glastonbury (Somerset).

In Wales there were many walled towns in the south and many ancient towns which have grown up round a castle. From a long list of interesting places one might select Cardiff, Caerphilly, Caerwent, Pembroke, Tenby, St. David's (a cathedral city which is little larger than a village), Cardigan, Harlech, Carnarvon and Conway.

In Scotland, Edinburgh and Aberdeen stand out together with the many towns of the southern uplands, such as Dumfries, Melrose and Peebles. But almost every town in Scotland has its features of interest, from Stonehaven, Montrose and Peterhead on the east coast, to Inverness, Perth and Stirling in the centre. In the west of Scotland there are few towns and these are far between.

In England and Wales the student will quickly come to distinguish between certain kinds of country which show a marked similarity in the materials used for building through the ages, these giving an apparent unity throughout the whole range of architectural styles. As examples, there are the various stone belts of England and, in particular, the one which stretches from the southern extremity of the Cotswold Hills through Gloucestershire, Northamptonshire, Leicestershire and Rutland, where the majority of the great buildings and many of the smaller ones are built of the native limestone. Another distinctive district is that made up by the Welsh Marcher counties, where timber was very plentiful in the Middle Ages and there is the characteristic style of half-timbered building persisting through many centuries.

In some areas, such as Essex and East Anglia, where there is little local stone and timber was not very plentiful during the main building periods, there is added interest from the variety of materials used and it will be noted that brick buildings make their appearance here far earlier than in most other parts of the country.

Then there is the stone belt of north Norfolk, a most attractive district, and many others so numerous that the student can gradually build up a picture of England and give a label, as it were, to every district based on the materials principally used for building purposes. Any one of these areas is admirable for intensive study.

ANSWERS TO TEST YOURSELF

THE degree of success with which you answer the questions will enable you to judge how closely you have followed the text. Since few can grasp all the facts from a single reading, there should be no disappointment if many answers elude you until after two or more readings.

CHAPTER I

1. Although beauty undoubtedly exists as an ideal, no hard and fast standards can be laid down, since there is considerable divergence of opinion as to what constitutes beauty. In addition, individual taste in matters of art is constantly changing from age to age and between one country and another, different types of beauty appealing to different temperaments.

2. Philosophers and even artists, among them Leonardo, have often defined art as the imitation of nature. Yet it is impossible to reproduce nature accurately: two people painting a scene from an identical viewpoint would always produce diverse results. Only the camera can give an impersonal record. Nature is always the starting point of any true work of art. Rubens's exuberant compositions have nothing to do with the everyday world, but they spring from his passion for the human figure and his knowledge of its every attitude. Claude's harmonious, perfectly composed landscapes have not the remotest connexion with actual scenes, but everything in them is based upon the ceaseless observation of nature and of the effects of light. Constable is an example of an artist who seems closer to nature than either Claude or Rubens. Not one of his sketches, however, is a copy of an actual scene. His passion for the Suffolk countryside and his close study of nature were balanced by an unerring sense of composition and colour, a profound understanding of the science of picture-making. We come then to the conclusion that art is a synthesis between nature "seen through a temperament" and design in the fullest meaning of the word.

3. A child's drawing is usually dominated, like much primitive art, by concepts which bear little relation to actual appearances. Features such as the eyes and ears are often made disproportionately large; the eye is drawn in a frontal position though the head itself is in profile. There is concentration on detail without regard for the general form. The drawings of the South African Bushmen on the other hand are strikingly realistic and lifelike; they are based on what the eye observes and are quite uninfluenced by preconceived notions.

4. Both Uccello and Seurat saw more in their art than the mere painting of a picture. Uccello was a keen student of perspective whilst Seurat devoted himself to the study of colours. So much is this the case that the details of their pictures are often subordinated to consideration of the aspects in which they were interested.

5. In his School of Athens, Raphael emphasizes above all else the architectural qualities of his subject, concentrating particularly upon a skilful use of perspective. Human figures are included only to give the impression of space and distance.

CHAPTER II

1. Assyrian art, particularly the reliefs which adorned the rulers' palaces, is characterized by its naturalistic portrayal of scenes from everyday life, carried out in a heavy style with bold-featured figures. Reliefs frequently were carved so that they could be seen equally well from either the front or the side. See the illustration on page 32.

2. Certain Egyptian works reveal careful observation of nature and the ability to reproduce accurately what the eye sees. The painting of wild life in the British Museum fowling scene shown on page 37 is an example. The rigid pose of Egyptian sculptured figures and the usual representation in Egyptian painting of the profile human head with the full-face eye, the frontal torso and profile legs are therefore

371

due not to an inability to portray nature but to adherence to a convention.

3. The colossal scale of much Egyptian architecture and sculpture is due partly to the preoccupation of the people with ideas of immortality and with their faith in the absolute and divine power of their rulers. Size was associated with the awe inspiring and the eternal. At the same time the scale of some of the buildings, colossi and pyramids, was determined by the character of their setting, by the fact that they were intended to be seen from considerable distances across the flat plains and in the brilliant light of Egypt.

CHAPTER III

1. Our knowledge of Cretan art is based on the discoveries of architectural remains—vases and statuettes and frescoes at Knossos. These are all characterized by a feeling for shape and a superb sense of decoration. Subjects taken from sea creatures and plants—for the Cretans were a seafaring people—hunting episodes and bull grappling, a popular Cretan sport, are adapted to the shape of the pots to enhance their plastic value while closely following nature. In vivid frescoes flat, bright colours are used and forms are elongated to give the impression of movement. Great artistry is shown in metalwork, of which the bronze dagger blade shown on page 44 is an example.

2. Early Greek statues, from about 600 to 430 B.C. are characterized by mouths with upturned corners, probably because the sculptors were unable to show clearly the change between cheeks and lips. This is known as the archaic smile.

3. Hellenic art, the art of fifth-century Greece, centred in Athens, is classical and dignified, maintaining a perfect balance between art and nature. It is on the whole grave and static and on the occasions when movement is depicted it is always controlled by the design. Examples include the Parthenon sculptures (page 223), and the Discobolus (page 42). Hellenistic or late Greek art was produced under Greek influence in Alexandria and Asia Minor and centred in the cities of Pergamon, Antioch, Alexandria and Rhodes. The natural

treatment and realistic pose of the subjects, as in the Laocoon group (page 225), and the bronze boxer of Scopas (page 43) is at once apparent. Vigorous movement, as in the Victory of Samothrace (page 40), is also frequently to be found. Nature is often imitated with complete disregard for design and material. The head is no longer formed as in Hellenic art, but frequently has the true-to-life appearance of a portrait.

4. Of the surviving Greek paintings perhaps the Aldobrandini Wedding is the best known, but knowledge of Greek pictorial art is chiefly to be derived from the figure compositions on vases. Later European artists were much influenced by the Greeks' emphasis on the use of space and the grouping of their pictures.

5. The chief contribution of the Romans was in the sphere of architecture. They developed the arch and the vault, which supplanted the post-and-lintel construction of the Greeks, and built great triumphal arches, amphitheatres, bridges, aqueducts and baths. In sculpture they were remarkable portraitists.

CHAPTER IV

1. Very few monuments on a large scale were produced during the Dark Ages, and the practice of the arts survived chiefly in monasteries, where illuminated manuscripts, metalwork and ivory carvings were carried out. During the early part of the period art did indeed continue to flourish at Byzantium, now Istanbul, which had become the capital of the Roman Empire in A.D. 324, the most important contributions being in the spheres of architecture and mosaic. The iconoclastic controversy of the eighth century put an end to the making of large-scale images, and from then onwards small ivories and metalwork were the main products. Greek artists left Byzantium as a result of the image-making prohibition and carried to Italy and other parts of Europe the combination of Greek and oriental elements which characterized their work.

2. In his mosaic of the Empress Theodora from San Vitale at Ravenna, the artist makes no attempt accurately to por-

tray nature. The figures are stiff and carried out in such a way as to impress the spectator. Giotto, on the other hand, is at pains to present a true-to-life study. His fresco at Assisi of St. Francis parting with his possessions, for instance, reveals a close observation of and faithful interpretation of a scene from life.

3. The most important manifestation of the Romanesque period was the development of monumental sculpture which had been practically banished during the Dark Ages. Examples are at Autun, Moissac and Vézelay in France and at Kilpeck in England.

4. Originally used in a derogatory sense in reference to medieval art of the Renaissance which made any departure from classical standards, the term Gothic is now generally applied to the art of the thirteenth and fourteenth centuries. In architecture, the characteristics of this style consist of the use of the pointed arch, flying buttresses, rib- and panel-vaulting with large window-spaces. Sculpture of the period is noted for a more naturalistic representation of life than obtained in the Romanesque styles and the sculpture of the majority of Gothic cathedrals stresses particularly the contrasts between light and shade. Examples of Gothic painting are few, since architectural developments reduced considerably the amount of space available for wall paintings.

CHAPTER V

1. The three most influential masters of the early Renaissance were Donatello, Masaccio and Brunelleschi. Donatello set the pace in true-to-life portraiture vividly expressive of human form and emotions. Masaccio, on the other hand, was foremost in the art of using shadows to emphasize the figures in his paintings. Brunelleschi's chief works were the famous dome of Florence Cathedral and the Pazzi Chapel, Florence.

2. Siena, cut off from the trade routes of Italy by its situation on a high hill, remained isolated and medieval while Florence became the centre of the intellectual activity and enthusiasm for the antique which characterized the Renaissance. The works of the Sienese masters like Duccio, Simone Martini and Sassetta, are linear, rhythmic, tender in feeling, poetic and unreal in colour, with a frequent disregard for perspective, a continued preference for flat gold backgrounds and little interest in volume and mass. The Florentines concerned themselves with the problems of perspective, the rendering of form and the creation of the illusion of natural appearances.

3. The Venetians were the first to attempt, in painting, an interpretation of nature, particularly in landscapes where the background is invariably of equal importance and reveals as much detail, as the rest of the subject.

4. Michelangelo was primarily a sculptor and his painting has a sculpturesque quality in that it is dominated by his interest in the human form and the attempt to realize its three-dimensional character by modelling and drawing. Michelangelo's colour is purely arbitrary and his treatment of background and everything not connected directly with the figures is superficial.

5. Whereas in his treatment of the nude, Titian uses no sharp outlines, relying rather on rich varying tones, in Botticelli's work the human form is frequently deliberately distorted to emphasize its curves and shapes.

6. During the Renaissance, sculpture and engraving were the particular branches of the arts most widely practised in Germany. In the Netherlands, on the other hand, the prosperity of the cloth trade was largely responsible for the elaborate decoration of the cloth halls and public buildings as well as the illuminated manuscripts and stained-glass windows for which Belgium in particular is famous.

CHAPTER VI

1. The Eclectics were a group of painters who combined, in their own works, what they considered to be the best features of great masters who preceded them, using little or no imagination or self-expression.

2. The mark of a baroque building is that it has been conceived as a whole, the relationship of the individual parts being

considered less important than the total effect. The design is made up of curves instead of rectangles; broken pediments are common, as are clustered, and sometimes diagonal, columns. Sculpture and elaborate relief are essential elements of a baroque building. In Salvis' Fontana Trevi, Rome (page 83), the artificial rocks, statuary and the moving water are conceived as making one harmonious whole with the façade, the design being carried up by means of columns and statues to the intricate ornament which crowns the building. The most important exponent of the baroque style, Bernini, was also a sculptor. First practised in Rome, the style spread throughout Europe, finding extravagant expression in Spain in the work of Churriguerra and producing fine church architecture in Germany and Austria. The baroque style in France reflected the personal taste of Louis XVI, as at Versailles, and was heavily magnificent without the dramatic spirit of Spanish and Austrian baroque.

3. Light and shade, technically known as chiaroscuro, had been rendered in painting long before the baroque period. We find a suggestion of it in the work of Masaccio for example, and the sixteenth-century Venetians, Giorgione and Titian had regarded painting as an organization of blended light-and-dark colour masses. But the extremes of chiaroscuro were realized for the first time in the work of baroque painters like Caravaggio, where violent contrasts of light and shade, contrived by artificial illumination, create an effect so naturalistic as to rival that of the camera.

4. El Greco's art was in harmony with the spirit of his age in that the violently emotional religious feeling behind it made it an instrument peculiarly suited to the aims of the Counter-Reformation. His colour is highly personal, but his dynamic contrasts of light and shade, the vigour which characterizes such compositions as the Burial of Count Orgaz (page 86), are typical expressions of the baroque. Rubens, though the complete worldliness of his art removes it so far from that of El Greco, is also essentially a man of his age. The baroque spirit expresses itself in his work in his grandiose subjects, his exuberance and above all in his method of composition.

CHAPTER VII

1. The Reformation resulted in Holland in a new well-to-do middle class who, unaccustomed as they were to classical painting, preferred only pictures of everyday life, landscapes and domestic scenes. In addition, having won their independence from Spanish domination, the people of Holland felt a new pride in their country and lost no opportunity of exhibiting its beauty.

2. The portrait, because it involves someone besides the painter and a possible patron, imposes conditions which do not obtain in other fields of painting. The problem is threefold: to grasp the character of the sitter, to make an æsthetically satisfying picture of the likeness, and, usually, to please the sitter. The fulfilment of the last condition has frequently meant a failure in one of the two more essential points. Gainsborough, compelled by circumstances to paint fashionable portraits and produce flattering likenesses, attempted little more than a superficial portrayal of character. Hogarth, painting an uncommissioned portrait such as the Shrimp Girl (page 108), enjoyed himself with his pigments without showing great concern for reproducing a likeness and painted a lively, impressionistic picture which does not quite fulfil all the conditions a great portrait demands. Rembrandt, perhaps the greatest portrait painter, is always concerned to give a truthful rendering of the sitter's personality with no thought of pleasing. The self portrait provides a unique opportunity for avoiding the necessity to flatter, but Rembrandt is one of the few masters who have had the sincerity to see themselves objectively (page 104).

3. Landscape painting first became an independent art in the seventeenth century. In Holland, such artists as Hobbema and Ruisdael, pandering to the tastes of the Dutch people, devoted much time and energy to painting pictures of the Dutch countryside, thus preparing the way for the great landscape painters of the eighteenth and nineteenth centuries. This influence is noticeable in the work of many later

artists not least Constable, Claude and Gainsborough.

CHAPTER VIII

1. Prior to the nineteenth century the artist had been employed largely by religious societies, the State and the aristocracy. In the nineteenth century, however, this situation was radically changed by the rapid growth of the middle-class population. The increasing popularity of exhibitions and consequent publicity in the Press led to more active and hostile criticism by the public. On the other hand, the demand for exhibition pictures caused painters to seek means of drawing attention to their works.

2. The appearance in the middle of the nineteenth century of the camera had a twofold effect upon painting. In the first place, painters attempted both to imitate the camera in its true-to-life reproduction and also to surpass its achievements. This led to the over-emphasis of colour characterized by the Impressionists, colour photography being as yet unheard of. Later, however, painters forsook this meticulous reproduction of detail and substituted for it an attempt at making their pictures expressive of their own feelings. Whistler, an American, was foremost in England as a champion of "Art for Art's sake."

3. The chief concern of the Impressionists was faithfully to represent nature as they saw it, in terms of light and colour. Their emphasis on colour, which they conveyed by separating the primary and complementary colours on their canvases on the theory of the colours of the spectrum, resulted in some sacrifice of detailed design.

4. Both Seurat and Cézanne, with all their superficial differences, are formal painters. Each is interested in the expression of mass and the relation of forms with the greatest economy of detail. Cézanne emphasizes structure by reducing nature to geometric shapes resembling the cone, the cylinder or the cube, and by using colour, not light and shade, to convey solidity. Seurat creates formal harmonies by a minute observation of the play of light conveyed by tiny round dots of paint

of equal size, arranged with mathematical precision. See page 118.

CHAPTER IX

1. Because of its close connexion with calligraphy—owing to the fact that the same brushes, inks and silks or papers are used for both—Chinese painting depends for its effect on brushwork and tone rather than colour. And just as Chinese calligraphy is an abbreviated pictorial script, so in Chinese painting the subject is always represented with the greatest economy of lines and is based on the selection of but a fragment of natural appearances. In calligraphy the areas of white silk or paper are as important as the script itself, and in Chinese painting empty, shadowless spaces play an integral part. Chinese calligraphy and painting were still further connected by the fact that the greatest painters were poets and philosophers and had all received a literary education.

2. (a) The bright, decorative quality of Japanese colour prints was so striking and was such a revelation to European painters, providing as they did, a cheap means of reproduction, that they had a marked influence on their work. Particularly was this so in the case of the French Impressionists.

(b) Although Negro carvings are not primarily concerned with giving a faithful reproduction of nature, they are striking in their life-like appearance. Influenced by this fact, twentieth-century artists have to some extent forsaken a rigid imitation of nature in favour of concentration on the emotional aspect of their subject.

3. Persian painting is characterized by the Persians' love of open-air scenes— gardens, canals, the blossom of trees and flowers—as well as scenes of life depicting such everyday events as hunting and feasting. The Persians had no knowledge of perspective and never painted shadows. They used only brilliant colours and frequently painted the sky gold to suggest dazzle and sunlight.

CHAPTER X

1. Abstract art is non-representational. It is not a phenomenon restricted to our

own age, but was an expression of Neolithic, Celtic and Islamic cultures among others. In twentieth-century Europe it developed in the first place from the efforts of the cubists to reduce nature to simple geometric forms and this led to experiments in the sphere of pure form unhampered by association with recognizable objects. Whereas in the past, however, abstract art was confined to decoration, and where geometric shapes occurred in sculpture and pictures they were never without some reference to nature, today sculptures, like those of Barbara Hepworth, and paintings like those of Ben Nicholson, are produced which concern themselves only with the relation of shapes. Among the various forms which abstraction took were Futurism, Constructivism, and Abstraction—Creation, the last named a group of geometric painters and sculptors in Paris in the early 1930s, led by Mondrian and Helion.

2. Possible reasons include:

(a) The debunking of academic art as a result of the invention of the camera, and the consequent abandonment of the aims and standards which had obtained in Europe since Renaissance times. (b) The newly acquired knowledge of oriental and primitive art and the consequent influx of influences formerly hardly known in Europe. (c) The lack of State patronage on any scale and the decline of private patronage. (d) The lack of unifying ideals throughout society, and of the philosophical or religious background which all artists and their public had in common before the nineteenth century.

CHAPTER XI

1. Composition may be defined as the art of organizing and presenting shapes, colours and forms so that they achieve a balanced and rhythmical design. Examples particularly expressive of composition include Bellini's Agony in the Garden (page 168), Uccello's Rout of San Romano (page 30), Angelico's Annunciation (page 20), and the Bushman drawing reproduced on page 146.

2. In his presentation of the Annunciation Duccio depends largely upon the formal design of the main figure, the whole conception being flat and lacking in depth. Fra Angelico, on the other hand, whilst portraying flat silhouettes, uses an architectural setting of columns and arches to convey the impression of space.

3. Both pictures are based on a design of diagonal lines which convey the impression of space and lead the eye away into the distance and background. Accenting this idea Bellini has a winding road leading up a hill into the background.

4. In what is termed the painterly approach the effect is gained by skilful application of paint—by careful variations in the thickness of the pigment and by expressive brush strokes. On the other hand, as its name implies, the linear method carefully outlines every detail of the subject so that it forms a pattern. Typical examples of the former include Velasquez's head of Philip IV (page 156), and, of the latter, Holbein's portrait of Christina of Denmark (page 157).

5. Van Eyck's Arnolfini and His Wife is an oil painting executed with fine brushes and with successive glazes on a wooden panel coated with gesso (fine plaster mixed with glue). Titian's Concert is also an oil, but it is painted on canvas with coarser brushes and the effect is of softness and richness of tone instead of clarity, hardness and lustre.

CHAPTER XII

1. Light is equally important to both painters as a means of organizing composition. With Claude, effects of light create the infinite recessions the tranquillity and allover clarity of his compositions. Rembrandt is interested in light as the opposite of dark, as a means of emphasizing the subtlety and obscurity of shadow.

2. (a) The term encaustic is applied to the process of painting in which the medium consists of a mixture of gumresin and wax, converted into a liquid by the addition of an alkali solution and then heated so that the wax and the resin melted and combined with the colours. (b) In tempera painting the surface is first coated with a mixture of fine plaster and glue; the subject is then painted in dry-powder

pigment mixed with egg. (c) Fresco painting consists of a process in which the pigments are mixed with water and applied to moist plaster with which they combine. Considerable skill on the part of the artist is required, since no alterations to the work can be made.

3. The alla prima method implies a single application of the pigments rather than several in layers. Velasquez was one of the first to paint in this way.

4. Gouache is a body colour paint made from a mixture of pigment and gum arabic; today it is frequently made from water colour and Chinese white.

5. Materials used for painting upon in oils include plaster, metal, wood, paper and canvas, of which wood and canvas are the most commonly employed today. For use on wood the most satisfactory priming is gesso, a substance made from slaked plaster of Paris and glue. For painting on canvas an oil priming, consisting of a mixture of lead and linseed oil, should be used on account of the flexibility of the canvas which causes the painting to crack.

6. For oil painting there are in common use three types of hogs' hair brush, of different shapes, and one of sable, the latter being for applying fine touches. Water-colour brushes are made of both camel hair and sable, those of sable, which keep their shape better than camel-hair brushes, are much to be preferred.

CHAPTER XIII

1. In the woodcut all the lines are black; in the wood engraving the lines are all white or a mixture of black and white. Soft woods, pear, maple, sycamore, cherry or apple are used for woodcuts, and the wood is usually cut lengthwise with the grain. The design is drawn on the wood and the white portions of the picture are cut away, leaving the black parts in relief. In wood engraving, a later development, a hard boxwood is necessary, cut across the grain and smoothly polished. The artist cuts the lines white from a dark ground with an instrument called the graver and the method is one of working white on dark instead of as in the woodcut dark on white.

2. In metal engraving the design is cut into the surface of a metal plate, usually copper, with a sharp-pointed instrument known as the burin or graver. The burin cuts a V-shaped furrow which displaces a thin curl of copper, and if the instrument is sharp there should be no rough edge to the cut line. Among the classic engravers were Dürer, Schöngauer and Mantegna. In etching, as in engraving, a plate of highly polished metal is used. The surface of the plate is thinly covered with hard wax, a mixture of beeswax, asphaltum and pitch. The design is drawn on this waxed surface with a sharp point. The drawing is made quite freely and only sufficient pressure is used to pierce the wax coating and expose the surface of the metal. When the design is completed the plate is put into a porcelain dish containing corrosive, usually nitric acid. The acid eats into the metal wherever it is exposed. When a certain portion of the design is considered to have been sufficiently etched the plate is removed from the acid and the portion is painted out with a quick-drying varnish. This so-called stopping-out process is repeated with other parts of the design until the darkest parts are considered completed. The wax is then removed from the plate with turpentine and the design is found to be etched into the polished surface. Among the many great masters of etching were Rembrandt, Goya, Millet and Whistler.

3. A mezzotint is the result of a process in which no acid is used. The surface of a metal plate is roughened all over by means of an instrument known as a rocker, and when finished has the appearance of the pile of velvet. If inked at this stage the plate would print a full rich, dark tone. On this surface of dark tone the lighter tones are scraped away by means of a sharp steel blade and the design emerges. Sometimes an etched line is used before the mezzotint ground is prepared to give strength to the composition. An example of a mezzotint is on page 209.

CHAPTER XIV

1. When books and magazines began to be printed in large numbers the photographic method of making blocks did not exist and its place was taken by very skilful

engravers such as the Dalziel brothers, who made wood engravings of artists' original drawings. Artists rarely prepared the engravings themselves though they used sometimes to draw the design on the wood.

2. Lithography, of all the graphic processes, offers the artist the most freedom and directness in transcribing his design and reproduces it with great fidelity. It gives full scope to personal expression and style, for the artist works directly on the stone or zinc plates from which the design is to be printed. Great richness of effect can be obtained by strong contrasts of intense black and dazzling white, by infinite gradations of intermediate greys and wide ranges of texture. When colour is used the artist can obtain exactly the effect he intends without the distortion of colour which results from the use of the mechanical screen necessary to other methods of reproduction.

3. In the commercial field today the graphic arts play an important part in such vital uses as book and periodical illustration, designs on wrappers for packages and containers of all kinds as well as for posters and advertisements in the Press.

CHAPTER XV

1. The sculptor either models in clay or a similar substance; this process is called the plastic method; or he carves in stone, wood or other materials; this is known as the glyptic method.

2. Photographic likeness does not produce art; the greatest sculpture does not copy nature, but, above all, is expressive of the material in which the artist works, whether it be clay, bronze, stone or wood. Sculpture is the language of forms and the natural object or creature which inspires the sculptor is but the starting point of his work.

CHAPTER XVI

1. The rigidity of the archaic Greek Apollo is due to the artist's inability to render the forms with greater freedom, while the stiff, conventional pose of Egyptian statues is the result of a conscious attempt of an artist in perfect control of his medium to convey the impression of monumentality and to conform to a tradition in methods of representation.

2. The resemblance between the Greek Charioteer of Delphi and the Gothic kings and queens of Chartres lies in the treatment of the drapery. In both cases the drapery is fluted and reminiscent of the shaft of a column. In the case of the Charioteer this was an archaic device, for the early Greek draped statues such as the Artemis, c. 620 B.C., discovered at Delos, and the Hera of Samos resemble columns or tree trunks. With the Gothic sculptor, the fluted impression was the result of a conscious effort to make the figures look like the columns of which they are part.

3. Roman sculpture is characterized by its realistic, life-like treatment of the subject, and is particularly valuable as an almost photographic record of life and customs of the times.

CHAPTER XVII

1. Waste mould is the method generally employed to make a single cast from a clay model. Let us suppose we are casting from a bas-relief. The clay is sprayed through a diffuser with paraffin to assist the clay to leave the mould. Next a quarter-of-an-inch thick layer of plaster tinted blue is applied to the clay model; when this has set a light clay wash is applied over the rougher parts to assist in the chipping out. The final layer of white plaster may be made to any desired thickness and it should be strengthened with iron rods placed in the plaster during its application. When the mould has set, water is poured into the sides and joins to facilitate removal of the mould from the clay model. Next the inside of the mould is thoroughly washed before being lathered with diluted soft soap until the surface shines. Excess soap is removed and the mould given a slight brush over with olive oil before it is filled with the plaster which is to make the cast. When this plaster has set, the mould is chipped away with a blunt chisel, great care being taken when the layer of blue plaster is reached.

2. The materials of the sculptor are manifold—marble, sandstone, limestone, granite, terra-cotta, wood, ivory and bronze,

to name but a few. The problem in each case is to create three-dimensional plastic harmonies, to preserve a balance between art and nature and never to distort the inherent qualities of the material.

3. In the *cire perdue* process of casting a bronze, a fireproof core is covered with a modelled wax figure which corresponds exactly to the finished work. A mould is then applied connected with the core by metal rods. Molten bronze is then poured in replacing wax, which melts and runs out. When the mould, core and metal rods are removed and the surface has been tooled, the wax object reappears in bronze plate.

4. Terra-cotta, or baked clay, for sculpture is cheaper and simpler to use than stone or bronze. Statues found at Tanagra in the nineteenth century are among the finest examples although Donatello and other Florentine sculptors also produced some fine specimens.

CHAPTER XVIII

1. Taste in architecture has varied enormously from time to time. Standards of criticism have altered particularly during the last three hundred years. Sir Christopher Wren described medieval architectural forms as Gothic, by which he meant barbarous. Yet modern criticism is unanimous in regarding the Gothic period of architecture as one of the greatest in the history of the world. Ruskin talks about the base Renaissance architects of Venice but these selfsame buildings in Venice and elsewhere in Italy are nowadays considered among the finest buildings in the classical style. To the Victorians, the prime object of architecture was decoration. Some of the most decorative buildings which were raised in the Victorian Age and which satisfied contemporary critics are today condemned on the score of being in bad taste and unsuitable in construction for their purpose.

2. The greatest modern inventions in the sphere of architecture are the use of iron and steel in the open and the development of concrete as a common building material. Arising out of the use of these two is the invention of placing steel bars within the lower part of a concrete lintel, making it possible for a lintel to bridge almost any distance without creating an unbearable tension. The net result is that ferro-concrete is as strong as stone in compression and as tough as steel in tension. Among the first notable buildings which used iron in the open were the Crystal Palace and the Eiffel Tower. The use of ferro-concrete has influenced the construction of many of the great buildings of the twentieth century, from power stations to town halls and blocks of flats and offices.

3. The chief quality of ancient Greek temples was that they were intended to be judged as a composition viewed from without. Comparatively little care was given to the construction of the interior, which generally lacked architectural distinction and often contained only the figure of a god, which few worshippers approached closely as the religious ceremonies were carried out before an altar in front of the temple. Although Greek forms were adopted by the Romans and later builders they had to be adapted largely to the purposes of creating buildings the main function of which was to be lived in. All Greek temples are rectangular in plan. Most of the principal ones are constructed throughout of magnificent marble stone from Mount Pentelicus, and the general effect is that of a piece of sculpture. This effect is enhanced by the moulding of the Doric or Ionic columns and by the carving of the pediment and of the entablature.

4. The Renaissance, in architecture, as in all the other arts, brought about a revival of interest in classical forms. This did not necessarily imply the slavish imitation of Greek and Roman models but rather the evolution of an individual style based on those models. The most immediate visible effects were the disappearance of the Gothic features, in particular the pointed arch, and their replacement by a classical round arch which appeared in every feature of the building. At the same time greater use was made of columns of severely classical design as embellishments for doorways and entrances. Many large buildings of the Renaissance period were designed to resemble classical temples from the out-

side. In Italy the work of Palladio and in Britain of Inigo Jones (the Banqueting Hall, Whitehall), and Sir Christopher Wren (St. Paul's Cathedral, pictured on page 353), are characteristic of the full flowering of Renaissance architecture.

5. John Nash may be regarded as the father of town planning in the sense that he was one of the first architects to evolve a plan for a whole district taking account of modern conditions and to have the opportunity of carrying out that plan to its logical conclusion. Nash brought together the Pall Mall and Piccadilly districts of London with the fields north of the Marylebone Road by visualizing Regent's Street and Regent's Park and their surrounding terraces and squares. Previously Inigo Jones had achieved a similar effect on a smaller scale with his plans for Covent Garden and Lincoln's Inn; and the Woods, father and son, had laid out Bath on very much the same lines as it shows today. It must be remembered, however, that the Romans more than fifteen hundred years before had proved themselves great town planners who understood fully the advantages of a symmetrical design, as evidenced in modern Chichester and in the excavations on the site of Silchester, to name only two outstanding examples.

6. (a) Sir Giles Gilbert Scott. (b) Gothic.

CHAPTER XIX

1. *Saxon.* Greenstead - juxta - Ongar, Essex; Bradford-on-Avon, Wiltshire; Earls Barton, Northamptonshire; Worth, Sussex. *Norman.* Chichester Cathedral. *Decorated.* Wells Cathedral (west front). Parts of a very large number of churches are in this style and have window tracery of geometrical and curvilinear designs. But very few churches are predominantly in the Decorated style, partly because this represents a period of enlargement rather than of new foundations. *Perpendicular Gothic.* Thaxted and Saffron Walden, Essex; Lavenham, Suffolk; Northleach and Cirencester, Gloucestershire. *Tudor.* King's College Chapel, Cambridge. *Renaissance.* St. Paul's Cathedral and many of the City churches of London.

2. The principal remains of Roman military architecture in Britain are: Hadrian's Wall, the defensive walls of Roman towns, e.g. at Rochester, Canterbury, Verulamium (St. Albans), York, Chester etc.; a line of castles of fourth-century construction along the south-east coast e.g. Reculver (Regulbium) and Pevensey (Anderida).

3. The most significant difference between these two churches is the essential difference between Norman and late Gothic architecture. The theme of the nave of Chichester Cathedral is the round arch and its sub-divisions, that of Long Melford Church is the pointed arch and the long perpendicular lines of every feature of the building allied with the great height in proportion to the width.

4. The relationship between St. Paul's Cathedral and Durham Cathedral is that both are in a classical form of architecture. In both the style is based on the round arch and the classical column. The difference between them arises from the fact that Durham Cathedral is a superb example of the Romanesque style of the Normans while St. Paul's Cathedral represents the most magnificent essay in the revived classical style of the Renaissance. More than five hundred years separate the building of these two churches.

5. The manor-house may be said to have evolved from the castle in that both represent the dwelling places of the medieval equivalent of modern landed proprietors, but each is adapted to the needs of the times. In the eleventh and twelfth centuries it was essential for the castle to act as a symbol of law and order. In the time of the manor-house of the fifteenth century and later, peace in the land could reasonably be expected. Architecturally, early manor-houses retain the form of the castle and, later castles are castellated or fortified manor-houses. As time went on the fortifications were more and more for show and less and less for use. The fortified gatehouse was one of the last features of the castle to disappear in the manor-house. Finally it was translated into the typical porch of the Elizabethan manor-house, thus giving the architect extra scope for introducing his own ideas.

INDEX

Numbers in italics indicate illustrations

ACKNOWLEDGMENTS

The publishers wish to thank the following for permission to reproduce copyright material : the National Gallery for illustrations appearing on pp. 22, 26–27, 30, 46, 66, 72, 74, 84, 85, 88, 89, 94, 95, 97, 98, 99, 100, 102, 104, 105, 106, 108, 109, 114, 116, 152, 153, 156, 157, 158, 168 and 176; the British Museum for illustrations on pp. 29, 37, 130, 131, 147, 184, 186, 194, 196, 248, 249, 250 and 257; the Victoria and Albert Museum for the illustrations on pp. 29, 54, 60, 103, 117, 132, 133, 134, 162, 170, 180, 183, 231, 232, 240, 247, 251, 252, 256 and 257; the Wallace Collection for paintings on pp. 92 and 97; the Dulwich Art Gallery for the portrait of Cowley on p. 107; the Tate Gallery for illustrations on pp. 101, 110, 124, 126, 127, 128, 140, 141, 142, 164 and 265; the Courtauld Institute of Art for illustrations on pp. 118, 121 and 277; the City Art Gallery, Manchester, for the view of Heath Street, Hampstead, by Ford Maddox Brown, on p. 120, and the photograph of Henry Moore's completed Madonna and Child on p. 268; the Ashmolean Museum, Oxford, for the reproduction of a Cretan dagger, on p. 44; the Louvre for illustrations on pp. 35 and 239; the Lefevre Gallery for the jungle scene by Le Douanier on p. 143; the Warburg Institute for illustrations on pp. 150–151, 234 and 261; Mr. Arthur Gardner for the illustration of the alabaster effigy of Sir Richard and Lady Redman on p. 235; the Berkeley Galleries, London, for the illustration of the Goddess of Mercy on p. 254; the Archives Photographique for the illustrations on pp. 258 and 259; the London Passenger Transport Board for the illustration of Night from St. James's Park Station on p. 264; Mr. Henry Moore for the illustration of his partly completed Madonna and Child in Honiton stone on p. 268; Aerofilms, Ltd., for the aerial views on pp. 271, 350 and 354, and Messrs. Boots Pure Drug Co., Ltd., for the view of the interior of their factory at Beeston, Nottingham, appearing on p. 310.